Speak to Me Words

Speak to Me Words

ESSAYS ON

Contemporary American Indian Poetry

EDITED BY

Dean Rader and Janice Gould

The University of Arizona Press

Tucson

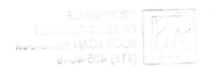

The University of Arizona Press
© 2003 The Arizona Board of Regents
First Printing

♾ This book is printed on acid-free, archival-quality paper.
Manufactured in the United States of America

08 07 06 05 04 03   6 5 4 3 2 1

Library of Congress Cataloging-in-Publication Data

Speak to me words : essays on contemporary American Indian poetry /
edited by Dean Rader and Janice Gould.
p. cm.
Includes index.
ISBN 0-8165-2348-7 (cloth : alk. paper)
ISBN 0-8165-2349-5 (paper : alk. paper)
1. American poetry—Indian authors—History and criticism. 2. American
poetry—20th century—History and criticism. 3. Indians of North
America—Intellectual life. 4. Indians in literature. I. Rader, Dean.
II. Gould, Janice, 1949–
PS153.I52 S64 2003
811'.509897—dc21
2003008354
British Library Cataloguing-in-Publication Data
A catalogue record for this book is available from the British Library.

Contents

Acknowledgments

We have many people to acknowledge. First of all, we thank all of the contributors for their patience, cooperation, and dedication. This book has been a long process, and they have been remarkably supportive. We also want to thank Patti Hartmann, Judith Allen, and Ryan Charles at the University of Arizona Press. They, too, have been helpful and patient. A special note of thanks goes out to our excellent copy editor, John Mulvihill. A number of folks at the University of San Francisco were of especial help. Bexie Towle and Mary Abler were indispensable with the manuscript preparation. Kimberly Garrett, Rachel Crawford, Susan Steinberg, and Tracy Seeley provided much needed collegial and institutional support. Erin Schietinger came on in the late stages of the project and was invaluable.

We would also like to thank the following people who read, commented on, or participated in some way in the formation of this book: Malea Powell, Robin Riley Fast, Norma Wilson, Lee Schweininger, Greg Barnhisel, Robert Bednar, Cary Cordova, Jonathan Silverman, LeAnne Howe, Helen Jaskoski, John Purdy, Michael Strysick, Gwen Griffin, and Jane Hafen.

Janice would like to thank Pat Smith, the late Louis Owens, Paula Gunn Allen, and Joy Harjo for their guidance, mentorship, and generosity as teachers and writers. And she wants to thank her sweetheart, Mimi Wheatwind, for reading parts of the manuscript and offering useful insights and commentary. Janice would also like to thank the poets who created the beautiful poetry the others of us read, thought about, and responded to. Finally, she'd like to thank the Creator for our daily lives and this work and the opportunity to connect and to create.

Dean thanks all of those entities (and any others he's forgetting) as well. He'd also like to thank the National Endowment for the Humanities, the Lutheran Academy of Scholars, Princeton University, Harvard

University, Texas Lutheran University, and the University of San Francisco for providing financial and institutional support for this project over the past few years. Lastly, he must thank LeAnne Howe, Kenneth Bordeaux, Sara Chapman, Brian Clements, Chris Haven, and Susan Paik.

And though we say it in the introduction, we're gonna say it again here: we are both very grateful to each other for the opportunity to collaborate on this project together. It's meant a great deal to us both.

> It is so.
> Speak to me words.
> —Luci Tapahonso

Speak to Me Words

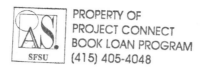
Introduction

Generations and Emanations

Dean Rader and Janice Gould

Failing to recognize the existence of genres is equivalent to claiming that a literary work does not bear any relationship to already existing works. Genres are precisely those relay-points by which the work assumes a relation with the universe of literature.
—Tzvetan Todorov

There is no *genre* of "Indian Literature" because we are all different. There is only literature written by people who are Indian and who, therefore, infuse their work with their own lives the same way you do.
—Wendy Rose

Editors' Note: Because so much of this book arose out of conversation, we wanted our introduction to reflect the climate of interaction and exchange that has marked this project from the very beginning. So instead of one rather homogenized overview, we have chosen, instead of monologue, to introduce *Speak to Me Words* in dialogue.

Dean Rader: I should preface my portion of this introduction with a confession: I am obsessed with genre. It should come as no surprise, then, that this is a book about genre. To be more precise, it is a book about a specific kind of genre—poetry—written by contemporary American Indian writers, many of whom also write prose, plays, literary criticism, and essays. Most importantly, it is a book edited by two people profoundly interested in American Indian literature and the genre of poetry. Given Wendy Rose's above statement on genre and given the fluidity with which Native writers move back and forth between genres, one might question the decision to devote an entire book to a particular genre when, for many Native writers, such distinctions seem irrelevant. However, in the academy, in publishing houses, in bookstores and on bookshelves, in the mind and in the heart, it appears that palpable distinctions among various genres still exist. This book is an exploration of the genre of poetry and of Native literature—in all their complexities.

In my mind, Wendy's comment refers to Indian literature in general, and Wendy herself, whose career has been primarily devoted to poetry, would probably agree that there are some basic differences between fiction, poetry, drama, and the essay. Even among Native writers who engage in all four of these genres, poetry is not the same as prose, which is not the same as drama. For instance, Sherman Alexie's "Owl Dancing with Fred Astaire" is simply not the same text as *Indian Killer*. While Leslie Marmon Silko offers a plurality of genres in *Storyteller*, the poems feel and signify differently than the stories, the photos, and the other texts in the book. And even if Native writers themselves don't always distinguish one genre from another, most Americans do. Publishers certainly do, as many of the poems discussed in this book appear in collections published by small, privately owned presses, which is clearly not the case for many novels written by Native authors. English departments and hiring committees are more than aware of genre, as most of their classes and most of their professors work with fiction. Bookstores remain keenly aware of what is fiction and nonfiction. So do most periodicals. The *New York Times Book Review* and similar publications allot significantly more space to fiction, biography, history, and cultural studies than to poetry or drama. The *Nation* made national news a few years ago when it stopped publishing poetry other than Calvin Trillin's. Without question, students are painfully aware of genre distinctions. Anyone who has taught an American literature survey course to undergraduates or who has taught Shakespeare to tenth-grade males can testify to a general hostility toward poetry. Finally, and most notably, literary scholars remain acutely attuned to genre, as evidenced by the number of books and articles devoted to prose and poetry each year.

Not even Native American studies escapes this bias. None of the best-known critical studies of American Indian literature focus on poetry, and virtually none have anything to do with poetry. Except for Paula Gunn Allen's *The Sacred Hoop*, the most influential book-length critical studies of Native American literature are devoted entirely to fiction. Alan

Velie's *Four American Indian Literary Masters,* Louis Owens's *Other Destinies: Understanding the American Indian Novel,* Jace Weaver's *That the People Might Live,* and Gerald Vizenor's *Narrative Chance: Postmodern Discourse on Native American Indian Literatures* are all dedicated to fiction. Even Arnold Krupat's *The Turn to the Native* implicitly links Native American literature to Native American novels, ultimately defining Native American literature through the novel. One could also list the various monographs on Louise Erdrich, Leslie Marmon Silko, N. Scott Momaday, and James Welch, which, again, highlight novels and short stories while deemphasizing the poetry. In fact, as this collection goes to press in 2002, Robin Riley Fast's *The Heart as a Drum* and Norma Wilson's *The Nature of Native American Poetry* are the only book-length studies of contemporary American Indian poetry in existence, and both were published in the last two years. We find this astonishing. *Speak to Me Words* stands as the first collection of essays devoted solely to recent American Indian poetry, and in so doing, seeks to usher Native poetry into a larger literary and cultural discourse.

The origins of this book go back almost five years. Concerned about the dearth of attention paid to recent poetry by Native writers, I proposed a special session on contemporary American Indian poetry for the 1999 Modern Language Association convention in San Francisco. It was from this special session that *Speak to Me Words* was first spoken into being. In my call for papers, I asked for new approaches to reading recent American Indian poetry. While I expected ample submissions of papers, I was not prepared for the overwhelming number of submissions I received, nor was I anticipating the fact that many of the most respected people working in the field of Native American literary studies would send abstracts. Based on the interest the call for papers generated and the overwhelming success of the panel itself, a book on the subject seemed the logical next step. To this end, I began discussions with the University of Arizona Press with the idea of publishing the first anthology of essays devoted to contemporary American Indian poetry. Patti Hartmann, our helpful editor at Arizona, and I agreed that the book not only needed the input of a Native writer and scholar but demanded a Native/Anglo coeditorship.

Given her reputation as a first-rate poet and an important scholar, Janice Gould seemed an ideal choice. She was contacted first by Arizona, and then I was to give her a call. I remember our first conversation like it was yesterday. I was a bit nervous, knowing very little about Janice except from the poems and essays I'd read. I assumed that we would get along, as I had been assured by many people how wonderful Janice was, but I don't think I was prepared for how well we would get on and how much we would agree about Native poetry, music, and life in general. I also don't think I was prepared for how much she would make me laugh. Soon, it became clear that Janice and I shared (and still share) many of the same concerns about the lack of critical attention being paid to Native American poetry. That Janice and I could work so well together reinforced larger issues of collaboration, such as those of race, class, gender, sexuality, and areas of interest, that have strengthened this field in recent years.

My own aspirations for the book have been basic. I wanted to assemble a book comprising essays as broad, encompassing, and provocative as Native poetry itself. So, as you will notice, *Speak to Me Words* is an assemblage of classic previously published essays (Generations) and new essays (Emanations). I also wanted to achieve a kind of balance—in terms of gender and Native and Anglo contributors, and also in terms of classic and original essays. Additionally, I hoped the book would cover a broad spectrum of approaches, including studies of both established and yet-to-be established poets. Thankfully, because of the impressive scope of the contributors, I feel we have succeeded on all counts.

Janice Gould: I was living alone for the summer on a houseboat on Sauvie Island, rural farmland north of Portland, Oregon, on the Columbia River, when Dean and I first talked about coediting this book. I still remember that long conversation, how nervous I felt awaiting his call. I'd heard good things about Dean from friends who attended academic conferences, but I needed to form my own opinion. Once we started talking by phone, and later corresponding by e-mail, I found it easy to be natural with him, to say what was on my mind.

In our discussion that day, we quickly made each other laugh and were able to reveal to each other some of the hopes and dreams we had for creating an anthology of essays on Native American poetry. We agreed that the critical work on American Indian fiction—that of Gerald Vizenor, Louis Owens, Arnold Krupat, and others—has been a tremendous help in furthering our thinking about the novel, and that other work on oral traditions and Indian autobiography by scholars like Greg Sarris and

Hertha Wong has helped deepen our understanding of literatures produced in what Mary Louise Pratt calls a "contact zone." Yet where were the essays that could help us examine the craft and art of contemporary Native written poetry, its variety and complexity, its themes and concerns? Where were the essays that could help inform us of the political, historical, and literary interactions between and influences on Native and non-Native poetry? Dean and I agreed that there was a growing need for a collective critical work on the genre of American Indian poetry—and that such a genre exists in its own right. Thus, we conceived of our anthology as one that could enrich our understandings of and appreciation for the many Native poets whose beautiful or angry or heartening words, in the last two or three decades, have taught, provoked, inspired, and perhaps even healed us.

DR: Perhaps more than anything else, Janice and I agree on the richness and power of Native poetry, and we believe that there is something unique and restorative about it.

If, as many of the contributors to this collection would argue, there *is* a difference between American Indian poetry and other forms of American Indian discourse, perhaps it is worthwhile to inquire into Native poetry itself. This collection concentrates on work written by Native authors since the 1960s—the putative era of the so-called Native American literary renaissance. Our demarcation of eligible poetry raises further questions, such as the distinction in chronology. For instance, one might argue that little difference exists between a John Ashbery poem of the seventies and a Wallace Stevens poem of the thirties. However, poetry by a Native author appearing in the thirties will probably be significantly different from much of the poetry under discussion in this book. For one thing, the poem from the thirties might not appear in English. It might not be written down. It might be a transcription or a retelling of a chant or song. By and large, most of the poems mentioned in the book were "originally" written in English and are not, usually, specific tribal rituals. Thus, the poetry written about in the following pages rarely conforms to the kind of claims that scholars like Karl Kroeber, Jerome Rothenberg, and John Bierhorst make in their writings about "Native American poetry." On the other hand, some aspects of Native storytelling or the performative power of Native poetic discourse remain utterly relevant for the poets here. When, in *The Way to Rainy Mountain*, N. Scott Momaday claims that the "word has power in and of itself. . . . the word is sacred,"[1] his assertion transcends boundaries of time and place—he could be referring to Black Elk, some ancient Anasazi storyteller, Wovoka, or Sherman Alexie. In fact, he is.

So, what distinguishes poetry from fiction? Or, perhaps a better question to ask is, what distinguishes American Indian poetry from American Indian fiction? In a 1987 article, Joseph Bruchac lists four "shared understandings" of Native American poetry. They are (in abbreviated form)

1. Traditions of respect for the Earth and the Natural world.
2. An awareness of a strong tribal / folk culture which has been transmitted to them either by family or learned through continued personal seeking.
3. Respect for the awesome power of the Word. Power which can quite literally make or destroy, break or heal.
4. The awareness that English, even if they have grown up with it and mastered it, even if they have little or no practical knowledge of their original tribal language, is a different language for them than it is for the average "American" writer.[2]

While all of these criteria are accurate, even insightful, they could just as easily be applied to American Indian prose, drama, and autobiography. Bruchac expands on these four standards by transgressing the boundaries of theme and taking up the issue of form. While offering an explication of a poem by Lance Henson, Bruchac claims that "like a number of other American Indian writers, Henson avoids the use of capitalization in all of his poetry and there is no punctuation. . . . Capitalization and punctuation separate one thing from another by dividing or calling attention to it."[3] While it might seem minor, Bruchac's observation about punctuation and capitalization suggests that the structure of Native poetry reaffirms or underscores a Native worldview. The Native poem's refusal to comply with traditional Western notions of form, the tendency to transform the lyric moment into a dynamic narrative event, and the use of creative typography to emulate spoken diction all suggest that form and content work together. Furthermore, most lyric poems resist linear constraints, allotting poetry the fluidity that Native discourse embodies.

JG: I want to speak a little to the issue of form. In my view, an American Indian poet's treatment of form is not particularly quirky. Though non–

compliance to literary form has characterized a lot of American poetry since the 1960s, we can find examples of poems by Native Americans written in strict form. For example, N. Scott Momaday's poem "Plainview: 1," published in 1974, is a sonnet in heroic couplets:

> There in the hollow of the hills I see,
> Eleven magpies stand away from me.[4]

Poets as diverse as Chrystos, Luci Tapahonso, and I have written sestinas. Native American poets, like poets everywhere, enjoy working, from time to time, with the constraints that various forms impose. The challenge of making speech ring true despite the demands of rhyme, meter, and patterned repetition provides an undeniable pleasure, as long as one feels that the poem has succeeded formally.

Of course, like many other contemporary writers, many if not most American Indian poets write in free verse. Like other poets, Indian poets play with language, allowing the poem to open up, to spatter across a page, much as a lyric by Gary Snyder or Robert Duncan might. Similarly, Indian poets transform lyric moments into longer narrative accounts, much as Tess Gallagher or Robert Hass do in their poems. Then again, a poet like Paula Gunn Allen might take a narrative, shorten it, break it, and interrupt it, perhaps something in the way of poet Brenda Hillman or Adrienne Rich. And while Indian poets, may, at times, reject traditional typography, who writing and publishing today is not aware of E. E. Cummings's mastery of this? Of course, Cummings's inventive and remarkable typographic play was inspiring. The fact that he always managed to make meaning both in how he employed capitalization and punctuation and also in how he dispensed with it reveals the playfulness of poetic work, and that is as appealing to Indian writers as it is to others.

Finally, though Indians are noted for employing or being influenced by oral traditions—of song, humor, and storytelling—these features have been exploited in American poetry by writers as diverse as Langston Hughes, Billy Collins, and Sandra Cisneros. As I see it, Native American poets are part and parcel of the American poetry scene, whether non-Indians know it or not.

Our poetry is influenced by and no doubt influences the poetry being written today by non-Indians. Some of that poetry—whether Native American or otherwise—has centered itself in resistance to literary norms—formally and also thematically. Thus, poetry can be a site for critical thinking as well as for making meaning. The poets I most admire take positions against prejudice, injustice, warmongering, capitalism, our notions of national history, and other things. Many also take positions for the natural world, for humanity, for love, for telling a national story that may go against the grain, against the received story that has glorified capitalism and individualism and their attendant dysfunctions. Thus, rather than being different from this canon of work, American Indian literature—poetry—fits right in.

What is unique about American Indian poetry may be in the particular truth telling it embodies, in the particular kinds of insights Indians bring to this question of who we are or what we are about as a nation. I agree that one function of American Indian poetry has been to "resist cultural erasure," to question the dominant narrative, and to remember our histories clearly as a way to resist both amnesia and nostalgia. We come back to the problem of assimilation, which was the American cure for the so-called Indian problem. One thrust of this cure was to impose English, both spoken and written, on Indian schoolchildren. Literacy was a tool of assimilation and indoctrination: it helped the American government whittle away at Indian identities, frayed the linguistic bonds that provided an intelligible net of communication for the children and their homes, families, and communities. Literacy in English struck a hard blow to Indian languages and to the psychic, emotional, and intellectual ties that children had to their ancestral language communities, to the identities these languages and communities helped provide.

What's interesting and remarkable to me is that while the imposition of English literacy was America's attempt to deal a deathblow to Indian languages, those languages haven't died out completely. In fact, there's an incredible resurgence among the tribes to either keep languages alive or bring them back into daily life in both oral and written forms. And literacy in English has not prevented Indian writers from exploring the possibilities for articulating the truth of their own visions through poetry. These visions come out of an exploration of what it means to be Indian and what it means to come from a cultural and historical past that is unique within American experience.

The fact is none of us can do without form; none of us can do without language. They are conditions of this existence, properties of this spiritual / material realm. For writers, language is the medium and the means for exploration and discovery, a journey that necessarily takes us inside, into our subconscious. At that level, because we are human beings, we shape and render what we find into a form, into a language. Writing, to mean anything, must have an end, a meaning. I would say that for many Indian poets that end is to reclaim and rebuild the identities that the Euro-Americans wanted to annihilate; it is to bring balance back to a place that has been tipped by selfishness, greed, and bigotry, so that we all (human, animal, and nature) can have a chance at fulfilling our destinies and potentials; it is to re-balance ourselves; it is to remind us that, as Harjo says, this is not the first world or the last.

The canon of American literature tells us, in part, that America offers a great promise for justice, liberty, equality, and happiness. This may be true. But the promises made in the world of men, of matter, are always imperfect and can only be made perfect through the spirit. The imperfections of our existence mean that we feel pain, that we suffer, that we make others suffer. We respond to pain and suffering by seeking a healing, a healing that cannot be completed in the human world but must be completed by understanding our ties to the spirit world.

American Indian poetry tries to remind us of this truth about healing because Indian writers are reminded of it when they look back at their own tribe's or another tribe's oral traditions. Poetry often serves to tell us about the places we've been as a people or about the places we wish to be. What we admire about it, or about the poets who make it, are the ways poetry may succinctly distill and render human experience into language. Language is a vehicle of ceremony. But it is not through poetry—or ceremony—that healing takes place. These are only forms and languages that aid in setting the conditions for healing. Healing takes place through the spirit, through love and compassion, which are qualities of the spirit. The American Indian poets I admire most are those whose work seems infused with—informed by—this spirit.

DR: I agree on all counts. The healing aspect of Native poetry demands to be foregrounded, as does the genre's many other artistic, literary, and cultural contributions. Native writers seek the poem because of the poem's ability to fuse disparate elements: present and past, poetry and prose, the lyric "I" and the communal "we." Because of the inherent contingency of poetry, it is the genre that most completely and most thoroughly mirrors Native oral potential and Native worldviews. In other words, Native poetry might just be the best possible genre for expressing

Native American concerns in a way most closely connected to Native ways of being in the world.

Carter Revard makes such an argument in his wonderful essay "Herbs of Healing: American Values in American Indian Literature," which we have reprinted in this volume. Here, Revard offers a comparative reading of various Native and Anglo poems, arguing that noncanonized poems by Native writers carry as much aesthetic and rhetorical weight as canonized American poems by the likes of Wallace Stevens and Robert Frost. Ultimately, Revard suggests that in recent Indian poetry one finds "writers whose work is good for this America." For Revard, American Indian poets offer a particularly useful articulation of what it means to be both American and Native American, and the act of writing and speaking weaves the speaker and reader into the ontology of each other.

Indeed, Revard's essay functions as a good example of what I call "engaged resistance"—the writers Revard explores resist the imperial colonizing thrust of contemporary culture through participation in it. Their inventive use of the lyric transforms both public and private discourses and allows them not only to counter prevailing establishments of identity but also to tell who they are in their own words. They resist cultural erasure by attacking those armaments designed to annihilate their ability to speak themselves into being; yet, through the lyric poem they recoup the performative energies of the oral tradition and engage both Anglo and Native discourses. What, over the last several years, has moved me most about American Indian poetry and the critical inquiries of that poetry are the ways in which Native poetry evokes a holism, a sense of belonging to and being a part of a place and community, while at the same time resisting, with an incomparable force, any action that jeopardizes that sense of belonging.

It is my hope that our book helps construct these dynamic spaces where Native and non-Natives can intersect through poetry that means a great deal to all of us.

JG: That is my hope, too. When Dean and I talked about putting this book together, we felt strongly that critical work needs to focus on poetry produced in the last thirty or thirty-five years, since Momaday's groundbreaking novel *House Made of Dawn*. In the early years of that period, African Americans and others from culturally and ethnically diverse groups made tremendous gains in civil rights, the war in Vietnam was ended, and a strong feminist movement reasserted itself, which helped provide space for the social and political struggles of gays, lesbians, and transgendered people. I was politicized by those events, but also by the literature, which I was hungry for and so began to read.

I remember avidly pouring over anthologies of Native poetry, including *Carriers of the Dream Wheel.* I was looking for a voice, an experience, a take on the world that was anything like mine. I worked at a feminist bookstore in Oakland, so I was always finding these great little chapbooks —stapled editions from Blue Cloud Quarterly, Duck Down Press, I. Reed Books, Strawberry Press, the Greenfield Review, and others. This was in the mid-seventies. By the early eighties, those poets who were becoming established names—Silko, Rose, Vizenor, Harjo, Ortiz, to name a few— were being published in anthologies such as *Voices of the Rainbow* and *The Remembered Earth,* and close on the heels of these books—by the mid-eighties—were the anthologies of Native women poets, Beth Brant's *A Gathering of Spirit* and Rayna Green's *That's What She Said.*

Brant's publication was important because it featured voices by less well known authors, like Chrystos, Vickie Sears, and Winona LaDuke, whose entry into the world of letters sometimes came out of their political and/or social activism. Indeed, some of us saw publication first in leftist, feminist, and/or lesbian/feminist publications whose commitment to multicultural publishing began at least in the late seventies and early eighties.

In the early eighties, Paula Gunn Allen was asked to compile a comprehensive study on Native American literature for the MLA, and in 1983 *Studies in American Indian Literature* came out. In a class I took with Wendy Rose at UC Berkeley, I'd read Simon Ortiz's "Song/Poetry and Language—Perception and Expression," which had been published by *Sun Tracks* in Arizona and which we reprint here. That essay stands against some of the other kinds of academic writing on Native poetry— which mainly sought to link written poetic expression by Indian writers to the oral tradition. Ortiz's essay is a critique of that kind of literary criticism that seeks to dissect a work, break it down until it has no life left.

Allen's book included a few essays on poetry, including a couple by Patricia Clark Smith, who became one of my mentors at the University of New Mexico when I went there to work on my doctoral degree. We are happy to reprint Smith's essay "Ain't Seen You Since: Dissent among

Female Relatives in American Indian Women's Poetry." This essay appeals to me because it humorously takes to task "eagle feather" poetry and because it was directly about women's poetry, their poetic experience. Smith's essay examines the theme of blood relations—specifically the relationship of mothers and daughters—and contrasts Native women's writing about their female relatives with Anglo women's writing. She contends that the Anglo poetry's obsession with alienation is at variance with American Indian poetry's interest in collaboration and connection. Her essay predates Allen's work on Indian women writers that appears in *The Sacred Hoop.*

Another essay we think is important to offer here is Marilou Awiakta's "Daydreaming Primal Space: Cherokee Aesthetics as Habits of Being," a piece formulated out of Gaston Bachelard's concept of inner space. This essay is included in her philosophical book on the wisdom of the Cherokee deity Selu, the Corn-Mother. In "Daydreaming Primal Space," Awiakta hopes to provide readers with an aesthetic that cultivates a new way of seeing: in the round instead of linearly. Such a way to view the world begins, of course, with retraining the actual physical body to see things in a balanced way, "with the right eye . . . the left eye . . . and . . . from the corners of the eyes." To ask ourselves to learn to look around and take things in so quietly and in such a consciously balanced way is a great feat, if accomplished. It is a wonderful wisdom that Awiakta provides.

DR: The rich and often overlooked history of criticism on recent Native poetry proved not only an impetus for this book but also a kind of rallying cry for Janice and me. I think on some level, we wished we could publish a collection of good essays and book chapters that had already been printed —pieces that really shaped how we think about Native poetry. As an example and a tribute, we have woven another previously published essay into the fabric of this collection, an influential essay by Paula Gunn Allen that has been an important essay for me personally. "Answering the Deer: Genocide and Continuance in the Poetry of American Indian Women" links the "tribal present" with the "continuing awareness of imminent genocide" in a way that goes beyond merely the presence of death. I remember reading this essay while in graduate school, not long after I had gotten to know Susan Deer Cloud Clements and her work. I found myself recognizing in Allen's essay things I didn't know I knew.

Allen asks the most provocative of questions: "How does one survive in the face of collective death?" Her answer, "bearing witness," apportions the responsibility of poetry and expression among the writer *and* the reader, the speaker *and* the listener. Thus, continuance demands that poetry happens; it demands both internal and external poetic spaces. Thankfully, Paula's claim in the early eighties that American Indian poetry was "bereft of listeners" has altered dramatically in the last twenty years. Janice and I find this progression hopeful but not enough.

Now, I'd like to speak a bit about the essays we have been fortunate enough to print for the first time. There is no common trajectory to the essays in *Speak to Me Words,* except that each offers a unique reading of important Native American poetry. No particular school of literary criticism finds precedence in these pages, nor does any poet or group of poets attract considerably more attention than others. Authors like Harjo, Hogan, Ortiz, and Allen, who have been writing the longest and who have produced the most work, tend to receive the most coverage, but other writers like Kimberly Blaeser, Carter Revard, Marilyn Dumont, Gregory Scofield, Elizabeth Woody, and Marilou Awiakta have garnered considerable attention from our contributors. In fact, Awiakta makes it into essays by Daniel Justice and Susan Berry Brill de Ramírez. In her piece, Brill de Ramírez takes an approach similar to that of Justice, but she places Awiakta's work in a continuum by reading her alongside the work of Kimberly Blaeser and Marilyn Dumont. According to Brill de Ramírez, these poets call Western literary expectations into question through a combination of Western literary traditions and Native oral tradition. Arguing that their "conversive" approach to literature communicates with listener-readers as both traditions work together, Brill de Ramírez maintains that these poets create a distinctive interactive poetics.

Distinguished critic Elaine Jahner brings us back to California and to still another distinguished voice—that of Paula Gunn Allen. Unlike most critics of Native literature who focus on thematics, Jahner looks at Allen's formal structures, noting that Allen's progression through style is "finally the one that speaks most cogently about Allen as a feminist . . . experimenting with poetic strategies." Jahner finds that Allen's work engenders a poetics that communicates a tribal sense of self, that the individual, and her work, can never be severed from the society of which it is part. For Jahner, form and content are as connected as living and breathing, and a poet's formal concerns are simultaneously political concerns.

In what seems a kind of microcosm for the scope of this book, Silko scholar and longtime *Studies in American Indian Literatures* editor Robert Nelson advances a reading that connects the various generations of Native poets through the birth of Joy Harjo's and Simon Ortiz's daughter, Rainy Dawn. Nelson uses Carter Revard's poem celebrating her birth as a launchpad to sketch the emergence of a new intertribal origin motif. Working through poems by Harjo, Revard, Ortiz, Hogan, and Luci Tapahonso, Nelson confirms pan-Indian tropes of emergence, survival, return, and renewal. I like a lot about Bob's essay, but what I found particularly moving is how he articulates the importance of connection and communication among individual Native writers and entire Native communities. That a single poem by Carter Revard can embody so many components of writing and speaking and living, that one poem can make us reconsider our own connection to people and the earth, is heartening.

Janet McAdams also writes on Carter Revard, though she takes a different approach. Whereas Nelson explores how a Revard text connects people, places, and moments, McAdams focuses on Revard's "amazing paradoxes" and "angled mirrors." Also drawing on Pratt's notion of "contact zones," McAdams gives close readings of three wildly different Revard poems: "Coyote Tells Why He Sings," "What the TV Said," and "Homework at Oxford." According to McAdams, the "deepest meanings are revealed in Revard's poems through challenges to categories that appear both 'obvious' and inevitable." Finally, McAdams argues that the real force of Revard's poems lies in how he irrupts expectation through a kind of doubling.

Eric Gary Anderson turns to the question of genre itself, specifically, the genre of poetry and what characterizes American Indian poetry. The questions Anderson poses in his essay are similar to those in mine (though his may be more compelling) and ultimately suggest that for Native poets, genre may not matter at all. For Anderson, genre behaves like a Eurocentric trap. Instead of obsessing over issues of identity, Anderson uses the poetry of Revard, Hogan, and Woody to explore how Indian poetry both travels and grounds itself. Those who know Eric's book *American Indian Literature and the Southwest: Contexts and Dispositions* will recognize aspects of his approach here.

Perhaps I am happiest to be introducing Janice Gould's excellent essay on maps and American Indian women's poetry. As kind of a map geek, I find Gould's approach fascinating and ingenious. Her claim that "we need maps to help us find our direction, to help describe and explain the kind of spiritual and material terrain that we have walked through before and are walking through even now," gets at the heart of the kind of work Native poetry performs. Thus, Gould's essay is not only an exploration of maps in poetry by Indian women, but it is itself a map—charting the signposts of how Indian women make sense of the world through the cartography of poetry.

JG: Earlier I mentioned Simon Ortiz's essay, "Song, Poetry and Language—Expression and Perception," and I want to come back to it now, as this piece closes our book. This early work on Native American poetry, written by a preeminent poet, offers an almost postmodern approach in its freshness, nonlinearity, and the way it merges the sources of Ortiz's thinking. On one level, the essay functions as a kind of treatise on linguistics; on another, it is a story about and tribute to his father. Ortiz's dad was a woodcarver and thus, like the poet, is a person engaged in doing a craft, making an art. The activity of carving, for his father, is combined with singing. The singing is part and parcel of the craft, an interconnected aspect, because as Ortiz's father sings a song about the Buffalo Dance, the dancer he is carving takes shape out of the solidity and fluid form of the wood he is working with.

Ortiz notes that language—part of the foundation of singing, of making poetry—has much more than just a linguistic function, although it can be seen that way. Language, the words it furnishes, is more than expression. It is a way of perceiving the world. Our perceptions, Ortiz seems to say, are formed through language; without words, full apprehension of the world cannot take place. Language, then, is a sensitive tool for naming how we perceive the world and our relationship to it; it is a way, also, to help us to perceive and know ourselves more intimately. Words function as expression or perception when we feel in our bodies their significance, their meaning, and understand, too, the context that gives them form, whether that context is material or spiritual or both.

Although Ortiz says his essay is a "statement on poetics," it does not take poetry as its primary topic but moves fluidly between the categories of song, poetry, and language, recognizing their inherent similarities and sources. The shape-shifting quality of Ortiz's subject—language's connection to song, poetry, art, and craft—is also a feature of genre, a fact that Dean Rader comes to terms with in his essay "The Epic Lyric: Genre and Contemporary American Indian Poetry." Arguing that "genre functions as a kind of unlikely bridge connecting otherwise opposing cultures and modes of expression," Rader shows how Native writers "fit into various systems of classifications" but have also "transformed them."

Rader makes a persuasive and beautifully articulated case for Native poetry connecting or collapsing the lyric form with the epic, or what Rader calls "epicizing the lyric." Using Michael Bernstein's rubric of epic's formal requirements, Rader shows how contemporary Native poetry typically incorporates these epic features: a narrative of cultural heritage, a voice that bears a diverse and plural sensibility, a sense of addressing the collective whole rather than the individual, and a teaching about the importance of collective survival. At the same time, the lyric's capacity for expressing feeling and its aesthetic is often present in Native poetry: a first-person speaker and the use of compressed, intense, metaphorical language. This merging of the epic and lyric allows the American Indian poem to "link personal concerns with societal demands," turning it from a purely personal and alienated form into one that enacts connection with a larger community. In the process of transformation and relocation, Native American poetry does just what Joy Harjo says it does: it "reinvents the enemy's language."

Reiterating, yet recasting, themes that have been articulated by others in this volume, Cherokee writer Qwo-Li Driskill talks about the political yet healing content of Cree Canadian poet Gregory Scofield's poems. In his essay "Call Me Brother: Two-Spiritness, the Erotic, and Mixedblood Identity as Sites of Sovereignty and Resistance," Driskill looks at the theme of decolonizing the body, heart, and mind through poetry, through language. Because the author of this essay is himself mixedblood, two-spirit, and a poet, he relates profoundly to Scofield's concerns over racism, homophobia, and the other wounding (anti)social behaviors that have taken root in the world. I love this essay for the clarity and urgency of Driskill's remarks, for his defense of Scofield's complex poetics, which investigates the connection between sexuality and sovereignty. If, as Dean has noted, there is a dearth of critical writing about Native American poetry, there is a virtual silence when it comes to considering the erotic in this poetry. The importance of Driskill's work here

The *Origins* is that it rescues a gay and two-spirit consciousness from marginalization. As a source of energy and wisdom, the erotic is a source of true authenticity, creativity, and sovereignty, including self-sovereignty.

Sovereignty and self-sovereignty could also be said to be themes of Cherokee writer Daniel Heath Justice's "Beloved Woman Returns: The Doubleweaving of Homeland and Identity in the Poetry of Marilou Awiakta." This essay takes as its focus the ways in which these two prominent themes—homeland and identity—are evoked in Awiakta's poetry. Homeland and identity are at the heart of issues about sovereignty.

The poems that Justice cites are embedded in a larger work that expresses a Cherokee worldview, one that encompasses a philosophy of peace, respect, and balance. The whole of Awiakta's work—which discusses the meaning and significance of Selu, the Corn-Mother—is a startlingly original piece of writing. Awiakta conceived her book as a Cherokee basket, woven in a specific way to provide strength, utility, and beauty. Justice admirably shows "the wisdom, humor, and patience" of Awiakta's design, revealing her importance as a voice of counsel and encouragement for continuance not only for the Cherokee Nation, but also for all people. Awiakta, says Justice, is one of the Beloved Women who, through her poetry, teaches us to "walk in your soul."

DR: When taken as a whole, a web if you will, these essays not only branch off from one another but also weave back into each other. Thus, rather than serving as individual strands of thought, they blend, forming a kind of intertextual, intracultural web. Of course, the filament holding all of the essays together is the tensile poetry of American Indians. The book, the web, is itself a narrative, a story telling stories of each other and itself.

In *Sensational Designs,* Jane Tompkins attempts to redefine how we read American literary texts by forcing critics to rethink the criteria used to judge literature. She argues that in order to better understand the "cultural work" texts do, we must move away from the elite master texts and begin to see literature "as attempts to redefine the social order" because these marginal texts offer better "examples of the way a culture thinks about itself."[5] While I have problems thinking of Native poems as "marginal" texts, the essays in *Speak to Me Words* exemplify how American Indian poetry redefines our social order and how recent poems by Native writers articulate and preserve how Indian communities think about themselves.

As I said earlier, the origin of this book was some time ago, and that *Speak to Me Words* now has actually arrived in your hands is rather amazing. In many ways, the seed for this book was planted in San Francisco about four years ago, and now it's ready for harvest. Without question, this has been a labor of love for Janice and me, and, perhaps because of that, I can't stop thinking of the final poem in Linda Hogan's *The Book of Medicines*, "The Origins of Corn":

> but you can't stop
> trading gifts
> with the land,
> putting your love in the ground
> so that after the long sleep of seeds
> all things will grow
> and the plants who climb into this world
> will find it green and alive.[6]

In their collection of works by Native authors, Thomas Sanders and Walter Peek claim that "if you would seek to know a people, look to their poetry."[7] Our hope is that these essays turn your gaze to the poetry and, by extension, to the land, the people, and the words from which they are spoken. We hope you find this plant, this gift, green and alive.

Poems as Maps in
American Indian Women's Writing

Janice Gould

We are the Stars which sing.
We sing with our light;
We are the birds of fire.
We fly over the sky
Our light is a voice;
We make a road
For the spirit to pass over.
—Algonquian, "Song of the Stars," quoted in *The Sacred*

The spirit always finds a pathway. . . . If you find a deer trail and
follow that trail, it's going to lead you to medicines and waterholes
and a shelter.
—Wallace Black Elk, quoted in *Selu: Seeking Corn-Mother's Wisdom*

"I wonder if these poems are the path I make," muses Kim Blaeser, as she
considers the path to survival a friend of hers has made through deadly
winter water. "The circular motion of our journeying / is the radius of
sky and sea, deep / territories we name / after ourselves," Anita Endrezze tells her lover, as she explains "the geography of love." "Precious
lamb, take the pencil," Diane Glancy suggests ironically to a creature that
has no use for cartography, "mark your colonial fields, / your revolutionary storage bins and pantry. / Your whole map." "To be accurate and
useful," Marilou Awiakta reminds us, "a Native American story, like a
compass needle, must have its direction points."[1]

The above passages by Native American women poets indicate that
many of us employ the idea of the map or of cartography in our poetry

and other writing. A look at several titles reveals a preoccupation with charts, trails, and mapmaking. We have, for example, "A Map to the Next World" (Joy Harjo), "Indian Cartography" (Deborah Miranda), "Trailing You" (Kim Blaeser), "Mapmaker's Daughter" (Anita Endrezze), "The Relief of America" (Diane Glancy), and "Map" (Linda Hogan). This theme can also be found in works whose titles do not specifically cite maps or ways, but whose subtitles indicate the theme of path or trail. The first subsection of Marilou Awiakta's *Selu: Seeking the Corn-Mother's Wisdom* is titled "Trailhead—Where Path and Stories Begin." My poem "Alphabet," among others I have written, uses the metaphor of a trail and maps out part of a journey. What is this interest in the map about? What do Indian women have to say about maps and cartography that make these metaphors so prevalent? How and why are these metaphors employed?[2]

Native women's literary maps are constructs that symbolically provide direction or describe a known, remembered, imagined, or longed-for terrain. By coming to terms with these inner regions and states of being, we poets offer ways to know ourselves as humans, as Indian people, as people with purpose and heart. Perhaps literary maps are more honest than "real" maps in that their authors claim responsibility for the writing of the "map."[3] And the interest the author has in her composition is clear: she hopes to influence not only how we follow her directions but also what we see when we "read" the world she presents. She is interested in our interpretation of her map and expects us to read her signs and symbols with both our hearts and minds. In this way we may feel as if we have visited, experienced, and traveled an emotional or spiritual landscape that exists both at a remove from and yet is a part of the ordinary landscapes with which we are familiar.

The poem that uses the analogy of mapmaking or cartography thus hopes to tell us about new ways of charting a place or event, or about a new place to be mapped. In the cartographic poem, the focus is on the construction of the "map," the choice of common or unique features of landscape that will help the map become recognizable as a made artifact of memory, imagination, and, ultimately, of knowing.

Why have so many of us chosen to write about maps—or the paths, ways, and trails that are inscribed upon our maps? In the foreword to *Selu*, principal chief of the Cherokee Nation of Oklahoma, Wilma Mankiller, writes,

In the old days the Cherokee people believed that the world existed in a precarious balance and that only right or correct actions kept it from tumbling. Wrong actions were believed to disturb the balance. For hundreds of years . . . our world has been spun out of control, and we have been searching for that balance. . . . Even though we do not ourselves fully understand why, we have returned to searching our own history and teachings for answers to today's problems. Perhaps, like Selu shaking the kernels from her body so that the people can live, we are shaking hundreds of years of acculturation and dehumanization from our minds—also so that our people may live.[4]

Chief Mankiller touches on the basic problem that has plagued our peoples for a very long time. The world is out of balance. This is a phenomenon that has affected us negatively since long before our ancestors first encountered the Europeans. However, colonization under the several foreign powers that came to our shores over the centuries sent us reeling in a state of shock and confusion.[5] We have survived colonization and have continued as Indian peoples; many tribes have reasserted their claims as sovereign nations. Though we are much reduced in power, these facts are a testament to Indian adaptability, ingenuity, perseverance, persistence, and wisdom. Not all Indian individuals or communities are yet healed or thriving, but the potential to find our way back to a sense of wholeness, spiritual coherence, and healthiness still exists. The map or cartographic poem is a tool to help us realize this potential; it offers an imaginative means, based in beautiful, austere, or playful language, to find our way toward balance.

But what are the "right or correct actions" that Chief Mankiller speaks of? What sorts of things should we know and depend on to help us recover our balance? Chief Mankiller echoes other Indian thinkers such as Vine Deloria and Paula Gunn Allen when she suggests that Indians, like other Americans, have become "oriented toward scientific explanations for everything."[6] She remarks that we have lost our ability to "suspend that analytical state of mind and just believe that Selu [Grandmother Corn] can be our mother, that the stars can be our relatives, that the river can be a man, and that the sun can be a woman."[7] Acting in "right" ways must be tied to a system of belief that allows for, willingly embraces, and celebrates the possibility of mystery and the unexplainable.

"Rightness" is also tied to a system of belief that does not put human beings at the center of all existence. "We have never really understood that we are one small part of a very large family that includes the plant world, the animal world and our other living relations," writes Mankiller. Much of the Euro-American world has been particularly narrow-minded and self-serving in this regard, but perhaps Indians, too, have come to think selfishly about our place in creation. Have we forgotten how to listen to, understand, and value nonhuman and even nonanimate lives? Mankiller asks, "How can we possibly keep our world from spinning out of balance if we don't have a fundamental understanding of our relationship to everything around us? We continually fail to see our own insignificance in the totality of things."[8] These acts of mapping help put us in relation to everything around us, both physically and verbally.

Our wise people—our elders—have been warning us and saying the same thing for a very long time. I think Indian women's poetry and other writing offer one way to find our way back to the "right" ways of living, thinking, feeling, imagining, speaking, and praying.[9] Perhaps there is a greater sense of urgency in coming to the reading and writing of poetry than we have experienced before, especially since it is clearer than ever that we live in a world of terrible dangers. These dangers arise out of unmitigated anger, grief, and despair, and these feelings, experienced the world over among those who have suffered poverty and injustice, have at times exploded into intolerance and the desire for revenge, the desire to clean the world of unclean. Now, more than ever, United Statesians should look at the system of greed (and concomitant plunder) for financial, intellectual, and sometimes spiritual wealth and power that has caught us in its grip since the beginning of the U.S. nation and that makes so many dance like fools to its tune.

Sensible people try to create a world that is "made up conceptually or intellectually and emotionally in a well-ordered system of symbols, ceremonials, education, and daily chores," say authors Peggy Beck, Anna Walters, and Nia Francisco in their book *The Sacred*.[10] But in times of great social and political stress, when spiritual traditions have been undermined or are hard to adhere to, living a "reasonable, integrated life" is not easy. Thus, we need maps to help us find our direction, to help describe and explain the kind of spiritual and material terrain that we have walked through before and are walking through even now. Poetic cartography provides a way to imagine and claim those landscapes we know or remember in order to assert what we belong to, what is tied in at the deepest place to our psyches. Poetic cartography is a way for Native poets to know and affirm our integration of identity with place. Map poems furnish a means to see the world of the spirit as it merges with this fleshy planet, this life-giver. With these maps we enter worlds that have been dreamed, imagined, known, felt, grieved over, retrieved, or must still be explored. This mapmaking is important to our concept of sovereignty as Indian nations, and to our self-sovereignty as Indian individuals. Sovereignty is a declaration of a necessary inner dignity, power, and trust, as well as a declaration—however difficult—of unbroken connection to our Mother Earth. The need to make our own maps is a reflection of the need to know and love our Mother, to repair our bond with her, and, through her, with all our Indian family, all our relations.

Forced removals and displacements have marked our history as Indian people. Throughout Indian Country, our numbers diminished due to illness, warfare, and starvation. Still, resistance to white greed for and theft of land and resources did not necessarily die out. Many Native people persist in believing that the land does not belong to us; we belong to the land. That notion, however, is complicated. When Deborah Miranda (Esselen and Chumash) writes in her poem "Indian Cartography" how her father "opens a map of California—," the dash represents a pause before the poet reconnoiters the space. That opened chart connects her to the "traces" of "mountain ranges, rivers, [and] county borders" that appear on the map "like family bloodlines."[11] The dash is also the slash that severs Miranda's father, her family, and the poet herself from those lands, places, peoples, and cultures that made up the lives that occupied these spaces for generations.

Another kind of slash in the poem is the longed-for place that was once the Santa Ynez River. Because of the dam that created Lake Cachuma, the actual river is a dry bed. The Indians who depended on the river for subsistence, the poem reports, were paid by the government to "move away." "*I don't know where they went,*" says the poet's father (Miranda's italics). Similarly, the salmon that renewed themselves yearly in the river after their long sojourn in the sea have also died or disappeared.

In her book *The Sacred Hoop,* Laguna critic Paula Gunn Allen speaks of the "pervasive sense of sorrow and anger" in American Indian women's poetry, feelings shaped by our awareness of genocide or near genocide. "We are the dead and the witnesses to death of hundreds of thousands of our people, of the water, the air, the animals and forests and grassy lands that sustained them and us not so very long ago," she writes.[12] Miranda's poem is perhaps more of a lament than a poem of anger, but anger must certainly fuel the understanding that the only way her father can access his memory and knowledge of the land is through "dreams" and "the solace of a six-pack." One is a traditional way of opening to the spirit world, the other a means of opening that, when taken to the extreme, blurs, distorts, and destroys our ability to connect to anything unencumbered by despair.

At the end of Miranda's poem, her father "swims out" in the dream river. There he

> floats on his face
> with eyes open, looks down into lands not drawn
> on any map. Maybe he sees shadows
> a people who are fluid,
> fluent in dark water, bodies
> long and glinting with sharp-edged jewelry,
> and mouths still opening, closing
> on the stories of our home.[13]

I like the line breaks here and the tropes, the way the word "drawn" can be read as a verb meaning "inscribed" or as a verb in which "not drawn" means "not pulled apart." In the dream, a father can find integrity, a way to belong to a land that is still there, even if that land is drowned, is no longer located on any map. "[O]n any map," the poet writes of her father, "maybe he sees shadows." "Shadows" represent the fish people, the salmon, but also those Indians whose voices of likely protest were drowned out. "Shadows" are also the ghosts of the dead, the shades—of both the returning fish and the humans—who linger and hang around a place they cannot leave.

Angelika Bammer, in her discussion of the psychological theories of Freud and Derrida on the uncanny, explains how displacement works. These theories tell us that "what is displaced—dispersed, deferred, repressed, pushed aside—is, significantly, still there. *Dis*placed but not *re*-placed, it remains a source of trouble, the shifting ground of signification that makes meanings tremble."[14] Miranda's poem attempts to register poetically the shock waves of displacement and disappointment through her father's memories and dreams. The map she opens reveals a home that is no longer there, a people who have been scattered across the lower part of California and elsewhere. Miranda's poem can be placed in that genre of American Indian writing that is concerned with the difficulty of returning home.

But perhaps the story of displacement is nevertheless a story of recovery, for, as I mentioned above, the land that was "replaced" by a lake "is significantly, still there," though unavailable, no longer present. What is present is the poet's ability to remember the stories, even those imagined in her father's dreams. "Indian cartography" is a Native woman's way of drawing a map that claims and reclaims desired space and the space of desire, her father's desire for connection to land, to family, to a people, to home. By carrying this charge of desire in the words of a poem, the poet creates a presence for what is no longer available to her family and many of her people; she thus establishes a balance against anguish, loss, and despair.

A sense of bereavement and despair similarly pervades Linda Hogan's mysterious poem "Map."[15] Beginning with the words, "This is the world / so vast and lonely / without end," Hogan (Chickasaw) personifies the world; it is a domain capable of breadth and terrible feeling. The earth as "world" is immense and immensely lonely. Perhaps the loneliness comes from our human inability to see the world as "Mother Earth," a living, breathing, and knowing creation. Instead, reduced to artifact—a map—the earth is abstracted into the "world," a charted realm that can be named after the men who claim her.

This claiming seems to lead to other disasters, a list that begins with "hunger" and "fear" brought by men "from other lands." The pairing of hunger and fear is the fuel of the poem, and not surprisingly the men's fear of the forest is echoed in their fear of fire, of the wolves that howl among the trees at night, and of the icy cold. The trees can do little but "h[o]ld each other up" against the intruding or invading men, but the wolves and even the ice set up a cry of alarm. This may also be the call that initiates a healing, since ice's refusal to be silent allows it to cry "its broken self / back to warmth." Nonetheless, as if to diminish their fear, the men name the beings who are around them:

ice, wolf, forest of sticks,
as if words would make it something
they could hold in gloved hands,
open, plot a way
and follow.[16]

By turning the world they encounter into a map named with perceived dangers, the men seek to dominate nature, to carve it into "plots"— bounded space, but also narratives of their own creation, "something / they could . . . follow." Hogan suggests these narratives, the dominant discourse, are essentially about loneliness and vastness. As such, they are the opposite of intimate speech and intimate knowing; they create an improper relationship with the earth.

However, Hogan's poem does not end on this note of despair. The first four lines of the second stanza provide an embellished refrain of the first stanza:

> This is the map of the forsaken world.
> This is the world without end
> where forests have been cut away from their trees.
> These are the lines wolf could not pass over.

At first it would seem that this deeper insight into the ways that men forsake the world is the direction the poem will follow. After all, maps show men where to cut "forests away from their trees"; they inscribe "the lines wolf could not pass over" without fear of being trapped, maimed, shot, and killed. But in the next line, Hogan turns the poem's focus to science, the very thing that grants cartography its power in the Western mind to name and to own.

> This is what I know from science:
> that a grain of dust dwells at the center
> of every flake of snow,
> that ice can have its way with land,
> that wolves live inside a circle
> of their own beginning.[17]

Science provides the poet with another way of knowing the "facts" it discovers. As if the "grain of dust" encased in ice at the center of a snowflake is called back to the land, the ice itself has "its way with land." It carves and shapes it, breaks it down as the ice melts and breaks. Land and water reciprocate with one another, exchange energies.

Ultimately, though, it is not science that furnishes the poet with her deepest knowledge. It is "blood." In her essay "Deify the Wolf," published a couple of years after "Map," Hogan discusses a trip she made to northern Minnesota to encounter, with a group of other humans, the timber wolves, many of which were being trapped and killed. Hogan writes,

> Anyone who has heard the howl of wolves breaking through a north-
> ern night will tell you that a part of them still remembers the lan-
> guage of that old song. It stirs the body, taking us down from our
> world of logic, down to the deeper lost regions of ourselves into a
> memory so ancient we have lost the name for it. . . . I can't say why I
> am here, but I have followed a map in the blood, an instinct I don't
> know.[18]

That "instinct," a powerful reminder of connection with what is wild, with what expresses anguish, allows the poet to unearth this truth in her poem:

> This is what I know from blood:
> the first language is not our own.
> There are names each thing has for itself,
> and beneath us the other order already moves.
> It is burning.
> It is dreaming.
> It is waking up.[19]

Against our words for everything, the names we have imposed, the "other order" has named itself in an older and truer language. Hogan's map has led us into this understanding. Beneath the map imposed by science is a map in the blood that takes us back to a more original knowing—that we are not a separate creation. Like the "other order," we may first have to burn away that which encumbers us. Once free, perhaps we can dream—find our way into spiritual vision that teaches us a more profound sense of our place in the order of things. If we understand that dream, perhaps we too will awaken to what it means to be a human creature in this natural world.

Having said this, I feel a "contrary" reading is possible, and that far from joining the "other order" we will always remain outside it, uncomfortably aware and bereft of having once known the language of the other animals, the water, earth, and trees. What Hogan's map may also tell us is that we are irrevocably disconnected or at best holding onto this primal knowledge by a thin strand of memory in the blood. The "contrary" reading suggests that the "other order" may be righteously angry—

"burning"—and that its vision and subsequent awakening will be our human undoing. But a human undoing may be what the lonely world needs as a way of balancing and healing itself and its beloved creatures. Hearing itself speak may be a necessary step in the world's self-healing, which, ultimately, may teach us how to heal (and hear) as well. If we could truly attend to that "first language," perhaps it would teach us how to overcome our hunger and fear in healthy ways. We could balance our terror of the unknown against the warmth and intimacy of our own first knowledge.

Joy Harjo (Muscogee), in the title poem to her newest collection, *A Map to the Next World,* also reminds us of the deeper first knowings that humans seem to have forgotten, or at least are often in danger of forgetting. This theme of memory versus forgetfulness is common in Harjo's poetry, and it is interesting to see how she weaves it through new poems and narratives. The image of the map, too, is not new to Harjo's work. In "We Must Call a Meeting," for example, from her volume *In Mad Love and War,* the poet is "caught in the cross fire of signals" from competing worlds. She finds that she must "draw maps of stars" as a way to renew her spirit. By doing this, perhaps, she helps her "ancestors" to come "perch on [her] shoulders" where, presumably, they offer counsel and advice.[20] In another poem, "The Field of Miracles" in *The Woman Who Fell from the Sky,* Harjo avers that the explorer Columbus and his crew "sailed off the end of the world, though it has been recorded otherwise." She writes, "What they found I will leave to another poem, though it is part of every story, the deepest loam, the veins of the red leaf I kept, a map to the field of miracles."[21] Maps, then, provide tools for navigating one's way across unknown waters, lands, celestial realms, and mystic regions of dreams or nightmares or other possibilities. Maps are records of voyages that have taken place beyond the known world, in strange seas and among the stars, whose presence is a reassurance that we are loved, that we forgetful humans are not forgotten.

A guiding idea Harjo uses in "A Map to the Next World" is the concept, possibly Aztecan in origin, of successive worlds. Among some indigenous peoples of this hemisphere is the prophecy of the ending of an old world and its transformation into a new one. Some Native people claim that the past two thousand years or more could be called the "fourth world," meaning the fourth generation of realms of human and other existence. As worlds begin to collapse or prove unlivable places, people seek a way out of them. So-called emergence stories explain the migrations of people from a lower world to one above, a realm that offers promise of better ways of living together. In Pueblo stories from the southwest United States, various Indian people, with the help of animals, birds, and deities, climb a pole of bamboo or a tall tree and emerge into the fourth world where they take up their new existence.

As Harjo writes her poem, she recognizes that we are in "the last days of the fourth world," and she decides to draw a map "for those who would climb through the hole in the sky." (The poem is dedicated to one of her granddaughters, Desiray Kierra Chee, who may have special navigational abilities.) The map progresses with the usual things a map needs —a legend, warnings, interpretations—but because the map is an imaginative, metaphorical, or spiritual construct, it turns out to be an extraordinary artifact that "can't be read by ordinary light." Suddenly it is a vehicle that "must carry fire to the next tribal town" so that the spirit of the climbers can be renewed. The renewal of spirit puts us in touch with what we have forgotten, that the land is a "gift," and we are a part of the land, both "in it" and "of it."

Harjo's map offers words of advice as well as warning. The poet points to those things that can distract us and thus impede our progress toward the next world: "supermarkets and malls, the altars of money," all of which serve as a "detour from grace," a state of harmony and balance. The map describes "fog . . . flowers of rage . . . monsters . . . born of nuclear anger . . . [and] [t]rees of ashes." These frightening images loom so large that "the map appears to disappear." This loss of a way to go— the loss of grace—is accompanied by sorrow and regret: "We no longer know the names of the birds here, how to speak to them by their personal names. / Once we knew everything in this lush promise."[22]

"A Map to the Next World" takes a turn here, from the catalog of disasters that follow human forgetfulness toward a record of human being and becoming. The spirit enters the flesh and takes on "this immense journey, for love, for rain," as the poet says in her poem "Rainy Dawn" from *In Mad Love and War.* The interesting thing about this aspect of the map is that it's "imperfect." That's part of the human condition, our imperfect knowing. Despite that, we're not without direction. Even as a fetus we can read the map, which "can be interpreted through the wall of the intestine—a spiral on the road of knowledge." We are made up uniquely out of maps of encoded genetic and spiritual material.

It's by being human—alive, mortal, connected to what has come before and what will come after—that we find our way to the next world, the fifth world, which may be a higher realm of existence. That mystic journey is known through the body, through our own births and deaths both physical and metaphysical. The poet promises that as we pass "through the membrane of death," we'll smell the cooking fires of our relatives who are preparing a feast for us, because "[t]hey have never left us; we abandoned them for science."[23] The circle of connection remains unbroken in this poet's vision; the maps we construct and follow ultimately lead us home.

Is the fifth world, the next world, the one where our relatives live—eating, talking, gambling, singing? Is death a stage through which we pass in order to travel on to that farther world? I don't know. But it seems the fifth world is the place where our loved ones await us, and because there is no "guidebook," once we enter that world, we have to navigate by memory of our "mother's voice" and "renew the song she is singing."

As the traveler enters the fifth world, she may see "the tracks of the monster slayers where they entered the cities of artificial light and killed what was killing us." Another important aspect of the poem is that time can spiral back; the monster slayers have made their appearance again, doing the tasks appointed to them but in a new way, meeting novel conditions. We see the "timelessness" of Harjo's narrative. Like a story from the oral tradition, Harjo's tale records events that have already occurred and yet are occurring in this and other worlds.[24]

In the old stories of emergence, though it was difficult and took a long time, people "climb[ed] from the destruction" that had visited them in the form of all kinds of negativity: jealousy, lust, greed. Similarly, Harjo's poem records that possibility, for part of our human condition is to seek a better way to live, to die, to know, and to feel—a way of balance, harmony, and creativity. These cannot be accomplished without work, without prayer, without healing. Thus, Harjo warns us that we have to "[r]emember the hole of our shame marking the act of abandoning our tribal grounds."[25] The shame may come upon us just as we meet the beautiful and sacred white deer that has come to greet us. Harjo's comment about this is, "We were never perfect." We have to forgive our imperfections and heal the hole in our hearts that is left there by shame. By doing this, perhaps, we may find that "the journey we make together is perfect on this earth who was once a star and made the same mistakes as humans."[26]

Maybe realizing that we could make mistakes again is the reason Harjo tells us at the end of her poem that we must make our own maps. For in considering the journey through the hole in the sky, she has described an inner reality that may or may not be one we can claim. No map can really tell us all we need to know, and a map made of language—as all maps are—must necessarily be an imperfect rendering despite the poet's attempts to mark the way. To heal, to find balance, wholeness, a place in the universe, is a journey we make alone, even if we are surrounded by those who love us. The most curious thing about this process of finding the way, writes Harjo, is "there is no beginning or end."[27] Whatever our journey is, our spirits, broken or intact, faltering or on the way toward healing, are always already on the path, perhaps only more or less conscious about it as we learn, grow, and age.

Situating American Indian Poetry

Place, Community, and the Question of Genre

Eric Gary Anderson

To what extent does genre matter to American Indian writers and writings? Since American Indian literature took shape and form as a "legitimate" subject of Western academic and literary critical inquiry in the early 1970s, anthologies of Native writing and critical texts about Native literature have often, though not always, practiced a sort of formal segregation, separating the fiction from the poetry, the drama from the nonfiction, and the transcribed oral stories from pretty much all other Western genres except ethnological commentary.[1] For nearly thirty years now, matters of textual identity—particularly those having to do with the status of the oral in relation to the written and of the "traditional" in relation to the "contemporary"—have attracted more critical attention than other, less easily classified and packaged identities, such as those formed, illuminated, and challenged when African American and Native American writers and writings interact.[2] But, to nudge my opening question a little further, can American Indian literature be properly and best read, taught, critiqued, and understood by way of non-Native categories such as genre? If yes, does Western literary criticism provide the proper categories? the ways and means of so categorizing? And, nearer to the particular topic of this essay, does genre matter as much to American Indian writers and writings as it appears to do to many of their critics, particularly the non-Native critics? Are there ways in which genre is useful when studying Native literatures, as well as ways in which it is not?

In recent years, increasing numbers of American Indian critics have been entering these discussions and articulating the importance of a Native-centered criticism that asserts and in some instances reestablishes connections to Native community as defined, revised, and sustained by, among many other things, the stories Native people speak and write.[3] For these Native critics, as well as for many other Native writers who work in various other Western-defined forms, the question or issue of genre does not loom large. Genres, after all, are forms of identity imported from outside Native cultures and at times imposed on them; by implication, genre identities come to be associated with other suspect methods of determining Native identity, such as those that set out to calculate Indianness on the basis of blood percentiles. In other words, when Native writers talk about who they are as Indians and what they do as Indian writers, they do not wholeheartedly accept, let alone dwell on, Euro-American distinctions between the classes and forms of literary compositions. As Jace Weaver (Cherokee) observes, "the majority of Indians live their lives as if such definitions were largely irrelevant, living out their own Indianness without a great deal of worry about such contestations over identity."[4] "American Indian writers," Weaver argues, "help Native readers imagine and reimagine themselves as Indian from the inside rather than as defined by the dominant society."[5]

Genre, then, may very well exemplify what Weaver, referring to the related concept of the canon, calls a "Eurocentric trap"—a means of measuring and evaluating all things Indian by Euro-American standards, leading, "albeit perhaps by inadvertence and with honorable intentions, to a denial of Native personhood and damage to Native subjectivity."[6] With Weaver's critique and the words of various other Native writers centering my arguments, I want to urge a shift away from Western questions of formal identity—*What* is Indian poetry? What shapes and forms does this poetry take?—and to encourage more attention to a different series of questions having to do with some of the various ways Native literature both grounds itself and travels—*Where* is this work of literature? Where does it come from (i.e., what culture or cultures and which physical places, not which literary-historical provenance)? Where is it going? Where do Native writings express and enact this mobility, this traveling sense of groundedness? To begin to answer these questions, I work not only with Weaver's critical writing but also with the mixed-genre work of Carter Revard (Osage), the poetry of Linda Hogan (Chickasaw), and the poetry and prose of Elizabeth Woody (Yakama, Warm Springs, Wasco, and Navajo) to suggest why American Indian writers repeatedly qualify, question, dismiss, leapfrog over, or revise Western notions and practices of literary genre, as well as how they locate themselves as Native writers. For instance, Revard's *Family Matters, Tribal Affairs* seamlessly mixes autobiography, literary criticism, satire, travelogue, various forms of poetry, and much more. Revard certainly respects these and other genres, as when he translates Old English riddles and offers a few "New English" riddles of his own, "adapting WAS [white Anglo-Saxon] poetics for American Indian themes and purposes."[7] And yet he at times gently, at times more wickedly reinvents and recontextualizes the genres he deploys. In writing, for example, "What the Eagle Fan Says," a riddle about the Eagle Fan he carries when Gourd Dancing, he productively guides readers toward and into places not governed by the expectations of genre so much as they are animated by the surprises and certainties of what Revard elsewhere in *Family Matters* calls "a community of words on Indian ground; good neighbors without fences."[8]

Revard is far from alone among Native writers in his reworkings and deflections of genres and their implications. In fact, one of the earliest "contemporary" Native texts, Kiowa writer N. Scott Momaday's influential *The Way to Rainy Mountain*, mixes and combines poetry, illustrations by Momaday's father, Al, and a multilayered prose that evokes mythic, historical, and personal realities. As Kenneth Roemer explains, Momaday's book does not "fit neatly into generic categories. The varieties of visual, poetic, and prose forms . . . should . . . encourage students [and others] to question standard definitions of *authorship, literature*, and *text*" as well as received processes of "personal identity formation" (Roemer's emphasis).[9] Across the nearly thirty-year span between Momaday's book and Revard's, for example, various other Native writers have encouraged such questionings, publishing poetry with, rather than apart from, prose, in texts that downplay and challenge received Western notions of generic form and function. Laguna Pueblo writer, photographer, and theorist Leslie Marmon Silko combines and blurs genres in *Storyteller*, as does Navajo writer Luci Tapahanso in *Blue Horses Rush In*, a text Dean Rader praises for its "multi-genred design and intertextuality."[10] "At times," Rader writes, "poetry sounds like prose, prose like poetry, fiction like autobiography, and autobiography like a dream. So seamless is her shift from lyric poet to minimalist fiction writer, one begins to wonder what lure genre holds for Tapahanso."[11] As in two other, very different bodies of work—the cross-cultural nonfiction of Greg Sarris (Coast Miwok and Pomo) with its mixings of literary criticism and theory, anthropology, pedagogy, and storytelling, and the complex cross-tribal fiction-writing collaborations of Louise Erdrich (Turtle Mountain Chippewa) and Michael Dorris (Modoc)—Native writers clearly, regularly, and purposefully breach generic and other boundaries. (Is *Love Medicine* a novel or a short-story cycle? or both? Is Sarris's "Reading Louise Erdrich: *Love Medicine* as Home Medicine"[12] more "critical" or more "creative" in its methods and purposes? or a balance of both?) The lure of genre, I want to suggest, is mild at best for most Native writers, as Sarris indicates when he writes that he would like to "broaden what we (academics) mean by academic discourse or to collapse the rather arbitrary dichotomy between academic and nonacademic, nonpersonal and personal discourse." He offers the essays in *Keeping Slug Woman Alive* as examples of such work.[13]

Why, then, do many Euro-American and some Native American critics of Native writers and writings continue to assume that genre carries sufficient explanatory weight and usefulness, continue to afford genre more primacy than most Native poets, fiction writers, autobiographers, and others themselves do?[14] Most of the book-length studies and anthologies of Native literature call attention to these genre-focused approaches in their titles or subtitles, as in Arnold Krupat's *For Those Who Come After: A Study of Native American Autobiography*, David Brumble's *American Indian Autobiography*, and Hertha Wong's *Sending My Heart Back across the Years: Tradition and Innovation in Native American Autobiography*, as well as in the studies—by Robert Nelson, James Ruppert, Louis Owens (Choctaw and Cherokee), Catherine Rainwater, and others —of what Owens in the subtitle to *Other Destinies* calls "the American Indian novel." For Owens, in fact, the Western lens of genre helps him go about the tricky task of demarcating the "field" of Native literature: "it seems there is indeed such a thing as Native American literature, and I would argue that it is found most clearly in novels written by Native Americans about the Native American experience."[15] And, along with two recent book-length studies of American Indian poetry, Robin Riley Fast's *The Heart as a Drum: Continuance and Resistance in American Indian Poetry* and Norma Wilson's *The Nature of Native American Poetry*, there have been several anthologies devoted solely to poetry, as well as Abenaki poet Joseph Bruchac's *Survival This Way: Interviews with American Indian Poets*. (The interview appears to have taken hold as a genre in its own right.) My purpose here is not to critique these studies

and collections, many of which have been foundational and indispensable, so much as to call attention to a dominant strain in the criticism and
to suggest healthy alternatives to work that, in taking genre as an organiz-
ing principle, forcefully links Native textual and cultural identities to
Western literary categories.

Such alternatives can be found, for example, in the work of Jace
Weaver, who calls attention to worldview, a concept admittedly difficult
to generalize: "Although the rich diversity of Native cultures in the
Americas makes it impossible to speak in a general, universalizing way
about 'things Indian,' many believe that one can speak broadly of a
worldview common to the indigenous peoples of the hemisphere."[16] The
worldview Weaver refers to (and demonstrates in the above quotation's
assertion of a working relationship between the one and the many) "includes a shared sense of story, the orature that first served to define and
shape tribal realities. The play of language becomes a common bond."[17]
This supple bond solidifies powerfully in and through "Nature, an understanding of which was [and is] essential to Native survival, [which] is
viewed and characterized in kinship terms. More than simply a sense of
place, though it is often that as well, this view of 'creation as kin' imbues
the work of Native writers, in different ways, with a potent sense of
interrelatedness."[18] These intertwined notions and practices of kinship,
community, and cultural continuity across physical, species, and tribal
boundaries are complex, especially in that the world Weaver describes is a
world in motion, a world in which crossings (as distinct from forced
assimilations) are respected and valued. It is not surprising, then, that
many Native writers see genre as an unevenly useful label at best. Admittedly, these writers identify and discuss themselves as poets or novelists
or critics, and at least to some extent abide by genre-based Western
conventions of book publishing and marketing. But, as Weaver's discussion of worldview suggests and demonstrates, Native writers themselves
often downplay genre identities in favor of other ways of working, other
ways of reaffirming their places as Indians and as Indian writers in "a
community of words on Indian ground."

For example, as I suggest above in my discussion of Native texts that
combine poetry and prose, many American Indian poets do not write
poetry exclusively. In fact, many—perhaps almost all—Native poets, including Erdrich, Momaday, Revard, Hogan, Woody, Kimberly Blaeser
(Anishinaabe), Leslie Marmon Silko (Laguna Pueblo), Simon Ortiz

(Acoma Pueblo), James Welch (Blackfeet and Gros Ventre), Paula Gunn Allen (Laguna Pueblo), Jim Barnes (Choctaw), Roberta Hill (Oneida), Gordon Henry, Jr. (White Earth Chippewa), Adrian Louis (Paiute), Marilou Awiakta (Cherokee), Elizabeth Cook-Lynn (Crow Creek Sioux), and Sherman Alexie (Spokane and Coeur d'Alene), also write prose fiction and/or nonfiction. Some of this prose can be described as "poetic" or "lyrical," and some of the poetry—Muscogee Creek poet Joy Harjo's, for example—resembles and merges with prose. But to locate Native poetry on the much larger map of contemporary Native writing and storytelling, one must also look inside short stories, novels, autobiographies, literary criticism, and films. And one must take into account the fluency with which Indian poets move between poetry and still other forms of expression; Harjo and Ray Young Bear (Mesquakie) are also accomplished musicians, Silko and Woody are skilled photographers, and Momaday, Wendy Rose (Hopi and Miwok), and Silko are also well known as painters. Daniel David Moses (Delaware) is also a playwright; Barnes, Maurice Kenny (Seneca and Mohawk), Duane Niatum (Klallam), Harjo, Gloria Bird (Spokane), Cook-Lynn, and others have made names for themselves as editors; Sherman Alexie has found success as a screenwriter. And, as I have already been suggesting, this cross-genre fluency marks one of the ways in which the very idea of "genre" itself is not particularly helpful as a keyword for understanding American Indian writing. That is, neither the common ground between these writers nor their differences are a matter of genre, first and foremost. Paradoxically, their very engagement with genres typically doubles as, or produces, a strategic disengagement with genres. To understand the poetry of these Native writers, then, one must also be able to move outside and around and through received Western definitions of what poetry is and how it is best approached.

The concept of genre, after all, is a way of not only categorizing written texts by type—their form, their history, the uses practitioners have made of that form and history—but also evaluating the "literary" quality and "cultural" worth of the texts in question. Genre sets one type of literary text apart from another, and it also divides "literary" texts from "nonliterary" texts and "successful" ("memorable," "universal") texts from "failures." And while non-Native writings do not always strictly adhere to the dictates of a single genre or a single notion of literary canon, non-Native writers (and critics, publishers, bookstores) typically manage genre hierarchically, privileging certain genres over others and certain examples of each genre over others: poetry is typically considered more "literary" than science fiction; sonnets are formally distinct from epigrams; sonnets are a "higher" form of expression than epigrams; Shakespeare's sonnets are better than Wyatt's or Surrey's and more likely to appear on the shelves of your local bookstore. Sonnets are also valued, as are various other types of poems, for their accenting of the individual voices of the poetic speaker and the poet. In contrast, as Joy Harjo asserts of *Reinventing the Enemy's Language,* an anthology of Native women's writing that she coedited, "We wanted the anthology to be a collective voice from the women of the continual indigenous presence here," and "We decided that the work should be arranged by theme, rather than by false political boundaries (or any other arbitrary category). This was important."[19] The anthology "includes poetry, fiction, personal narrative, prayer, and testimonials," and it does not compartmentalize contemporary Native women's writing by literary form.[20] Neither does it hold up any one individual voice or piece of writing as more important than the collective voice, the community.

In other words, genre *divides;* it encourages divisions of texts into categories and asserts that these categorical separations are in fact reliable as well as worthwhile. Native writers and editors, however, are often more interested in *adding* and *multiplying,* connecting and centering. They often speak, in interviews, to the common ground between fiction writing and poetry writing: "I feel that I'm always writing from the same world in the poems and the novels," James Welch tells Joseph Bruchac in *Survival This Way.*[21] And when it comes to technique, he says to Laura Coltelli, "I learned from poetry a sense of economy of language, the sense of keeping the poem moving, keeping it jumping, don't dwell too much on transitions, that kind of thing; and so I think in a sense I've brought that kind of poetic technique to my [fiction] writing . . . [which is] chronological, but yet I think it has a more poetic technique in the sense that I hope that my writing doesn't have too many wasted motions."[22] Similarly, Wendy Rose tells Coltelli that "it feels the same way inside—to do a painting as to write a poem."[23] Elizabeth Cook-Lynn explains that poetry and short stories "rise from the same thing. . . . I've written a lot of poetry that is directly related to a story I've written. The poem may say something different, but it is certainly connected to the story."[24] Poetry enters easily into prose, prose often flows in ways that can be recognized as poetic, verbal and visual arts powerfully complement each other, and all is energized and sustained by a worldview in which stories and storytelling and community are paramount and participatory. And even though Native poetry and prose participate, in some ways, in the same worlds—the same language, the same markets, the same literary-critical circuits—as Euro-American writing, I am arguing that the *places* of American Indian poetry also differ in significant ways from the *placings* of Euro-American poetry.

In Bruchac's interview with her, Harjo makes the further observation that categories in general can cause problems when it comes to identities: "I've talked with James Welch and other writers about being categorized as Indian writers. We're writers, artists. We're human beings and ultimately, when it's all together, there won't be these categories. There won't be these categories of male/female and ultimately we will be accepted for what we are and not divided."[25] And, as Simon Ortiz has remarked, these issues tie in with the divisions Euro-American culture encourages between "art" and "life": "art [is] a part of life and not separated. The act of living is art. But poetry isn't seen like that in United States society. Poetry is suspect and is only for weird and strange people like Bohemians, Hippies, lost souls, and Indians."[26] In a culture in which poetry in general is marginalized already, American Indian poetry is in effect twice marginalized, and quite possibly three times if the Native poet is a woman. Wendy Rose has remarked that "there is no *genre* of 'Indian literature' . . . because we are all different";[27] my point is that the workings of the terms *poetry* and *genre* risk classifying, generalizing, eliding, and otherwise doing violence to both the differences Rose refers to and the communal, intertribal worldviews discussed by Weaver.

It will be evident by now that in this essay I want not so much to invent a new approach to Native literatures as to invite intensified attention to ways of reading that are already available in the writings and the spoken words of various Native writers. I have been contending that classifications by genre say more, to Euro-American readers, about what the text is now and how the text falls into established Euro-American cultural vectors; however, these genre identities don't say enough about where the text is going, and they don't adequately recognize that a responsibility to genre is not at all the same thing as a responsibility to one's people. In other words, the concept of genre serves neither Native texts nor Native readers as well as it appears to serve non-Natives. As Jace Weaver argues, "Only when we relate Native literatures to, and situate them in, Native history and the changes in Native cultures can we begin to understand them. . . . Criticism not focused on and rooted in Native community only serves the myths of conquest and dominance that seek to subdue and conquer, render tame, our stories." Genre in this sense acts mainly as an interloper.[28]

Of course, as Weaver and many other Indian writers acknowledge, such boundaries are not automatically easy for Indians to negotiate; Roberta Hill, for example, says that "I must believe in the power of [the English] language to capture my experience, yet I know that my vision will always push against the limitations of that language."[29] Harjo reminds us that "to write is often still suspect in our tribal communities, and understandably so. It is through writing in the colonizers' languages that our lands have been stolen, children taken away. We have often been betrayed by those who first learned to write and to speak the language of the occupier of our lands."[30] And Native critics such as Weaver and Owens have also written powerfully about the limitations and traps of the English language and Euro-American arbitrations of culture (the canon, literacy and the "literary," etc.). To sum up: I am suggesting that genre, a tool used to divide texts into formal classifications for critical and economic purposes, is significantly less important a measure of American Indian literature than community. Weaver, for example, claims that Native writers "reflect and shape Native identity and community in a reciprocal relationship with their communities."[31] And as Simon Ortiz says, Native writers take on the responsibility that these working relationships entail: "Personally, I don't know if I ever 'decided' to be a writer and poet, but I know I have felt it was important to participate in the act of helping to carry on the expression of a way of life that I believed in."[32] Writing is first and foremost a way of giving back to a particular Native community and to larger, cross-tribal communities; writing helps keep the stories, the people, the communities together and going.

For example, in the preface to *Luminaries of the Humble*, Elizabeth Woody writes about the importance of being "responsible for the movement words participated in"—her "personal" or "individual" journeying is inseparable from this communal, participatory world—as well as for the "petroglyphs on rock in the Columbia River Gorge" that also participate, as she acknowledges when she honors them as an important "part of [her] literary heritage."[33] Community, formed and sustained not by humans only, is crucial to Woody's sense of who she is as a writer (and a visual and material artist, and of course as a person). She writes that "my concern in this volume is to give voice to those who are not often heard from, like the salmon, forest trees, our little relatives that nourish us, the edible roots, berries, deer. All that may die from our neglect."[34] Her writings connect and reconnect her to the movements of words and worlds that have existed for a very long time, live now, and move luminously into the future. As Ortiz emphasizes,

> Speaking for the sake of the land and the people means speaking for the inextricable relationship and interconnection between them. Land and people are interdependent. In fact, they are one and the same essential matter of Existence. They cannot be separated and delineated into singular entities. If anything is most vital, essential, and absolutely important in Native cultural philosophy, it is this concept of interdependence: the fact that without land there is no life, and without a responsible social and cultural outlook by humans, no life-sustaining land is possible.[35]

For both Ortiz and Woody, the act of writing is a vital part of a collaborative effort to take responsibility for the land and for the people.

Writing, too, is included in "this concept of interdependence"; it is not an act of separation, and it is not a means of singularizing. Words and stories, human and nonhuman people, all participate in the movements Woody speaks of, and, as I've already begun to suggest, these uncompromisingly powerful involvements not only characterize Elizabeth Woody's and Simon Ortiz's poems but also differentiate American Indian poetry in general from Euro-American poetry in general. And these differences have directly to do with the ways cultures describe and explain the poems they produce: the concept of genre as defined and practiced by Western poets and critics applies much less comfortably to American Indian poems because American Indian poets proceed by a significantly different network of intellectual and cultural assumptions. How pervasive, in Euro-American cultures, is the commitment to a participatory, community-focused sense of writing? How often, in the United States, is poetry written, read, performed, and heard as a vital way of reconnecting people and places and helping communities survive? The workshop model of instruction notwithstanding, how interdependent is poetry? How often is it read at all?

In shifting the terms of the discussion from "What?" to "Where?"

from genre-centered criticism to Native- and place-centered ways of thinking, I do not intend to trivialize the Western notions, but rather to place them properly in relation to American Indian notions. And I want to shift these questions of *where* away from their more familiar Western focal point on exterior landscapes. Elaine Jahner writes that reading Chickasaw poet, novelist, essayist, and autobiographer Linda Hogan's work "involves listening to the life that is within all form, including geological form, so that the text that form itself is can tell the story within which the ethnohistorical specifics of any one person's experiences are a subtext."[36] Hogan's writing is inseparable from this vital and fluent awareness of diverse and articulate forms, some in the process of being formed, all participating in what Jahner calls "the global telling that sustains all our memories of loss by linking them to the physicist's knowledge that cosmic matter is transformed, not lost, as our universe evolves."[37] These forms, like the places they often comprehend, are actively present and strongly interrelated in part because they have been remembered and can still be at least partially articulated.

For example, in "Crossings," a poem from her 1993 collection *The Book of Medicines*, Hogan remembers emergence:

> Sometimes the longing in me
> comes from when I remember
> the terrain of crossed beginnings
> when whales lived on land
> and we stepped out of water
> to enter our lives in air.[38]

Here, the "I" reconnects with a complex "we," and the lightly cloaked evolutionary theory brushes against Native memories of emergence, so that these stories, so often partitioned into highly separate and specialized discourses—genres—come into productive contact. And in "Map," a poem from the same volume, Hogan evokes a sense of forms pulsing and emerging from within forms:

> There are names each thing has for itself,
> and beneath us the other order already moves.
> It is burning.
> It is dreaming.
> It is waking up.[39]

The names things have and keep for themselves are important, *and* there is an "other order," perhaps not yet named and perhaps stretching the names and identities of "each thing." To burn, to dream, to wake up: are these actions also identities? names? She calls to mind, in a third poem from *The Book of Medicines*, "Naming the Animals," a place

> before the speaking,
> before any Adam's forgotten dream,
> and there are no edges to the names,
> no beginning, no end.

In this space,

> From somewhere I can't speak or tell,
> my stolen powers
> hold out their hands
> and sing me through.[40]

Before words and without stories, names and selves still hold power; but what is the nature of this power, and how has naming come to affix identity rather than to participate in its fluid motions and processes?

Hogan's poems often tell the stories of crossings, passages, and various other travels both originary and contemporary. Like both books and medicines—and like names—her words and poems themselves are exchanges that, Hogan convinces us, are of the utmost importance both because they can heal and because they record and enact these processes of emergence and reconnection. As such, identifying the particular literary genres Hogan uses does not go far enough, does not open up many of the routes the poems invite us to travel, and does not enable us to imagine and even, perhaps, to participate in, this richly layered, cross-culturally interactive world of multiple forms and stories. That is, the forms that Hogan and Jahner have in mind can and do overlap with various Western genres, but Western genres do not exclusively name, explain, and otherwise situate this world of diverse yet interconnected forms and places-in-motion. In fact, vital and highly charged as this world is, it bears little resemblance to romanticized, genre-driven Euro-American manifestations of tamed and/or framed nature (or "landscape"). In or around these "landscapes," human beings are cast primarily as observers and/or masters, thereby *dis*connecting them from the richly participatory sense of human and nonhuman persons' relationships with the earth, relationships that come from somewhere and remain both grounded and in motion as they connect with the people and the world and vividly remember "the terrain of crossed beginnings."

Woody signals her participation in these worlds-in-motion when she writes, in the preface to *Luminaries of the Humble,* that she "would bring the stories into new places." She explains further that another of her volumes of poetry, *Hand into Stone,* speaks to and represents her "passionate involvement with collecting personal story and journey," emphasizing again that her identity is centered in and on place *and* that place is mobile, fluid, and flexible.[41] Journeys are stories and stories are journeys. Compare what Simon Ortiz says in an interview with Joseph Bruchac: "You're always on a journey. Especially in this age. Indian people are much more mobile. I think Indian people were always mobile. Not that they weren't settled, nor that they didn't live in one place and call it home, but that they didn't always just stay there all the time. . . . The journey was important."[42] Similarly, when Oneida poet Roberta Hill writes, in "Breaking Through," of "the source of signs, / origin of all roots and wanderings," she gets at the complex relationships between story and journey and identity; the roots, to borrow James Clifford's paradigm, inform and are informed by the routes.[43] That is, Hill, Ortiz, Hogan, and Woody's senses of themselves—as poets and also as members of communities that define and know themselves as Indian—are both solidly grounded in particular places and highly fluid in the act and art of journeying. In these ways, both writers pretty directly say that they would like to be understood less as poets working in particular poetic genres than as American Indians using writing to make available—to their own people, to Indians of different nations, and to non-Native readers— connections between the ways they see and ways their readers might see, connections between where they come from, where they have been, where they are, and where they are going. In the very act of providing a preface to her collection, Woody prepares her readers to travel: to reaffirm, or to unlearn, what they already know.

A body of work such as Woody's poetry (and prose) is intensely interesting for many reasons: its storytelling; its tremendous incantatory power and urge to define; its startlingly original yet always community-centered voice; its combinations of mobility and groundedness; its relative deemphasis in a "canon" of American Indian poetry that is itself relatively deemphasized both within and outside the "field" of Native American literature. Additionally, Woody's volumes *Luminaries of the*

Humble and *Seven Hands, Seven Hearts* begin with prose pieces. She has also published a prose essay in *Speaking for the Generations*, edited by Simon Ortiz, so that all in all her identity as a poet is, like many other Native poets' identities, closely connected to her identity as a prose writer. The categories are permeable and, again, less important than other considerations. In the introduction to *Seven Hands, Seven Hearts*, for example, Woody emphasizes the centrality of stories and storytelling:

> It is through my own story and the stories of my family and my circle of people that I become whole. I learned this as a child. . . . We fed ourselves with these stories that explored how to live and that told of the past. The skill of telling and listening was "handed down," a legacy from a very ancient art form of imparting and storing knowledge and wisdom. It requires patience to listen to hours of "testimony." And one must learn to listen without judgment, overruling, interjection, or suppression.[44]

Woody explains that "these stories shape how I think, especially how I think of the land"; by implication, they also shape how she writes. In and through them, "I learned the meaning of being a granddaughter, a daughter, a niece, a sister, a cousin. I learned how to respect others and how to act with courage, humility, generosity, and compassion. Although this is simple to say in English and is overused in daily language, it is complex to be an independent being, responsible to the nuances and dynamics of ancestral community."[45] It is complex to be both one and many, both ancestral and contemporary. It is complex, too, to learn how to listen, and it is important to remember how intimately Woody's poetry, written to be listened to, is connected to her experiences as a listener.

In addition to preparing those readers who need preparation, Woody's prose introductions to her volumes of poetry demonstrate that her poems signify most powerfully as stories that describe, encourage, and strengthen connections between people and places, downplaying and otherwise marginalizing formal and technical concerns familiar to Western genre theory in favor of Native-centered ways of seeing and being. Craft in her view is inseparable from tradition, from relations, from nourishment, and craft speaks to her weaving as well as to her writing: "I've learned from Margaret [Jim-Pennah, her weaving teacher] that to make things with the earth is a way of nourishing ourselves. We acknowledge our roots in the earth. We must remember our source of nourishment or we will starve."[46] What I am teasing out is in part a way of reading that

Woody herself provides and that is not quite the same thing as what we might call a "thematic" reading of her poems, that is to say, a reading that prefers "meanings" and "issues" to such technical matters as lineation and versification. Again, Woody provides guidance by linking poetry to other arts and to her particular "cultural worldview":

> In my poems I like to think of the words coming to me already "scored" by the voice inside that I had previously thought of as internal monologue. . . . We possess a pattern that shapes our physical nature. In a practical sense, some people, in our cultural worldview, have special inner methods of expanding the connection between the internal and external. It is natural.[47]

Another way of saying this, perhaps, is that the extraordinary originality of her voice is inseparable from the extraordinary interrelatedness of that voice to a specific Native community. These connections between the individual and the community are related to the similarly important connections between interiors and exteriors that come across in the title of the first section of *Luminaries of the Humble*, "Interiors of Landscape." In asserting her knowledge that the spaces between interior and exterior, self and earth, are permeable boundaries, Woody also reasserts the importance of links between personal identity, home places, writing, and the continuity of the people: "Unconsciously, we do bear ideas that emerge as solutions or designs for our continued success as a people."[48] Art, then, is not a matter of Western literary genre so much as it is a matter of relationships within and to "the life span [that] is a string of patterns, as when I make beadwork, poetry, story or art—simplifications of complex life-patterns arranged into a comprehensible shape."[49]

Here is one such "simplification," the first poem from "Interiors of Landscape":

Version of Moon

Light flows westward, optic rays of great nerve,
throws one wave of beam and sight.
One brow of shoreline lunarly undulates white foam.

Birds touch their webs here to sand.
Dark commas flash on horizon.
Leaping whales in shimmering dress.
Rolling sand fizzles.

Promise, comes the sunrise,
pushing into the luster of stars,
crystal and opaque.

The inmost nature of songbirds is daylight.
Ride serenely, the lull of moon,
the deepest waters,
the oceanic marble,
moon bit sculpture.[50]

In this essay, I have suggested that it may be time to begin redirecting the "What?" questions that are often asked of Native writings, downplaying Western-based matters of formal classification in favor of approaches that begin with "Where?" questions and emphasize and encourage flexibility, mobility, and fluidity. That is, I have advocated shifting from "What?" to "Where?" in large part because "Where?" brings even non-Native readers that much closer to the particular places Native poetry comes from as well as the ways it both travels and maintains a "cultural worldview," a centered but flexible sense of home places. To give some sense of how such approaches might actually take shape as a reading of a particular poem, I want now to offer some responses to "Version of Moon." (I have elected not to respond by telling a story, but of course such a response could be perfectly appropriate, if the story is well chosen and well told.) In addition to revealing the startling modesty of Woody's assertion that her writing offers "simplifications of complex life-patterns," this poem exemplifies her awareness that a "version" does not stand alone. That is, a "version" is characterized not by what isolates or differentiates it from other versions so much as by what connects it to others. A "version of moon" might refer to a phase of the moon as well as to a particular poem or story about the moon, but the implication here is that this poem is located in relation to other poems, other versions (but not, significantly, Western versions casting the moon as, for example, Diana), just as one phase of the moon is known in relation to others. "Where?" is also interesting here because it suggests what we *don't* know: the place or places Woody evokes are not located specifically by name, and for that matter they aren't "placed" historically, by date. That is, their significance does not depend on their location in linear history or Western cartography. Place can be both specific and mysterious.

And, to develop a point made above, "Interiors of Landscape" are not set apart from exteriors: "The inmost nature of the songbirds is daylight," and the light itself cannot be separated from the optic rays that perceive that light. But in figuring insight in such a strikingly original way, Woody does not correspondingly assume that that insight is unique to her, or that the most important component of insight is captured in its first syllable. That is, the place of the poet is less important than the places of the poem and of the culture the poem emerges from and honors. And in fact, "Version of Moon" is striking in part because it presents and considers insight in such an *un*individual way *and* in such an original way. Even though the poem has so much to say about the work of the eye, the speaker never directly makes the Romantic connection between the eye and the "I" and in fact never uses the first-person pronoun. Instead, Woody gives images such as "one brow of shoreline," which is not best explained as an example of personification, a "humanizing" of nonhuman things, because the speaker's point is precisely the opposite: the shoreline is a person, like the birds, whales, stars, moons, waters, and poet who, the poem asserts, are all connected, all part of the place the poem describes. As the first poem in the "Interiors of Landscape" section, "Version of Moon" occupies a crucial location in the volume, in part because it carries on the work, begun in Woody's prose preface, of guiding readers toward—or reaffirming—a sense of the connectedness of interiors and exteriors. In this way, Woody moves us away from another set of Western perceptual categories; in the process, she speaks to and exemplifies what Jace Weaver (and many others) call worldview: a shared sense of story and Native community, described in ways that are neither automatically accessible nor impossibly out of reach.

In a poem from "The People," the second section of *Luminaries of the Humble,* Woody addresses related issues of naming and placing. Here, any preconceived distinctions between the people and the poem are blurred as she suggests what happens when "Anonymous" shifts its usual position and becomes the title of a poem rather than the "name" of its writer:

Anonymous

On exhibit, the leg bones melt
from impressions projected in the stare
of strangers.
In unbearable oblivion,
the dry humdrum and line

from each person carries with it the absence of identity,
to the next step of identifying.
There is a crumble of spirit.
Weak in the fluorescent light,
bone on white paper.
Paper in white gown.
Paper alien, go somewhere else,
not here.
We have a finger problem.
It points with accusation.[51]

Again, rather than asking "What?"—a question the poem itself powerfully critiques and warns against—I want to consider "Where?" "Anonymous" is frightening as a statement about the ways depatriation and
museumization displace and remove identity as well as a commentary on
the spaces, public and private, that rehearse and display these removals,
denials, and other absences of identity. The dangers and disruptions of
questions, denials, and blurrings of identity are evident in the title alone:
who and/or what is "Anonymous"? Perhaps more to the point, who isn't?
Names, exhibits, alien stares, "bone on white paper"—all of these speak
to "the absence of identity" as well as to the relentless "next step of
identifying." All of these speak, in other words, to issues and circumstances very much under discussion throughout this essay. The "finger
problem" this speaker experiences resembles in some ways the fingers
that point, sometimes with accusation and sometimes with terms of classification and sometimes with both, at the Native writings that are at
times themselves put on exhibit, museumized. The analogy might seem
overstated, but again, my argument all along has been that the very act of
classifying Native writing categorically and hierarchically risks "the absence of identity" and therefore is not so different, ultimately, from the
exhibitions and accusations Woody accuses. The speaker of the poem
suggests as much when she links the place of exhibited bone and the place
of written poem: "bone on white paper." "Anonymous," she asserts, is
often not a matter of self-determination. But to the extent that "*We* have
a finger problem," there is still space for hope. And to the extent that a
different "we" has poems, such as Woody's, that name and place this
problem, confronting in the process the state of being both present and
absent, both named and unnamed, both accused and accusing, the pres-

sures of "unbearable oblivion" and unbearably illuminated knowledge give voice to a pattern, shape to a story, and, by extension, place to the people.

"Anonymous," then, joins with all the various other Native texts and statements I've brought together to develop my argument in favor of downplaying genre when hearing and reading American Indian poetry. These various yet interrelated Native writers have also spoken, throughout this essay, about the implications of such an argument. In closing, I want to return to some of these implications and to introduce a few more comments about place, in the hope of further clarifying where this essay itself goes and where it might be placed. I have suggested throughout that Native writers, when they attend to Western notions of poetry at all, often dislodge or deemphasize these notions (by merging, for example, poetry and ceremony and prayer and prose). Put another way, I have argued that Native writers do not necessarily "subvert" Western modes so much as they refuse the assumption that underlies this version of subversion, the assumption that subversion moves in only one direction, that Western forms and modes predominate and serve as the means of measuring all other forms and modes and cultures. As Joy Harjo asks in the introduction to *Reinventing the Enemy's Language,* "How do we know what a good poem is, a good story? By whose definition, the community's or the university's? How much have we been manipulated by our educations?"[52] Harjo asserts, in partial response to her questions, that "the literature of the aboriginal people of North America defines America," which is to say that American Indian literature can very well comprehend American literature; it need not at all be the case that American literature is the larger category and the body of work that "opens" itself up to ethnic literatures, a paradigm that only serves to perpetuate dated notions of Western cultural dominance and multiethnic marginality.[53] Rather than seeing Indian literature as subversive (or for that matter as derivative) of Euro-American literature, it might very well be truer and more productive to accept what Laguna Pueblo novelist and poet Leslie Marmon Silko's Navajo-Mexican character Betonie says in *Ceremony:* "We invented white people."[54] From Betonie's perspective, as from the perspectives expressed in many of the Native writings and spoken words discussed in this essay, invention begins responsibility, but responsibility also supercedes this particular invention: Europeans and Euro-Americans enter worlds already fully and richly alive and in motion. And these worlds never have, and do not currently, circulate around Western constructions such as the concept of literary genre.

In other words, I am arguing that good answers to Harjo's question—"How do we know what a good poem is, a good story?"—can be found in the stories and poems themselves, both because Native stories and poems can stand apart from Euro-American texts and because they do not stand in a lonely place without the healthy support of the communities they emerge from and help to define. This center holds, even though (and, at times, because) the places of American Indian poetry are many and complex and capable of change. These places include the reservation, the academy, the American Indian novel, the Native literary anthologies (which are, after all, versions of communities), and the city, as well as travels less clearly or predominantly "contemporary," less measurable historically or cartographically. The routes, not simply mapped and traveled at Euro-American behests, intertwine with the roots. Often, too, the places of American Indian poetry involve crossings and blurrings of generic and other boundaries. But the very notion of "boundary" is tricky, in part because it is tempting to overemphasize the metaphor, in part because Euro-Americans and American Indians often acknowledge—and breach—different boundaries, and in part because, in Indian stories themselves, boundary crossing is such a seamless and, as Woody and other Native writers assert, such a natural experience even when it occurs within the realm of what Euro-American critics are trained to regard as "artifice." The point is not so much the act of crossing or the sheer presence of permeable boundaries but rather the gifts and stories and knowledge that result from crossings and the good stories told about them.

When Dean Rader invited me to contribute to this collection, I began by thinking back over the Euro-American catchphrases associated with poetry, ranging from "emotion recollected in tranquility" to "tradition and the individual talent" to "no ideas but in things," and I realized that none works all that well as a handy description of American Indian poetry. I suppose we could entertain notions of "tradition and the tribal talent" or "connect" (without the admonitory and diminishing "only"). But cross-cultural fusions of this sort, however playful, serve mainly to reinvent the trap of measuring American Indian poetry using non-Indian yardsticks. Again, this is not to say that there is no overlap whatsoever between Native and non-Native writers. Native writers hit the poetry-reading and book-signing circuits, teach at colleges and universities, publish books—written in English—with many of the same publishers as non-Native poets, and face the same mainstream cultural aversions to poetry that any other American poet faces. Conversely and similarly, various Indian poets, including James Welch, Roberta Hill, and Ray Young Bear, have been strongly influenced by non-Native poet and teacher Richard Hugo, while Leslie Marmon Silko continues to speak with powerful emotion about her strong friendship with non-Native poet James Wright. Most Native poets freely acknowledge and honor the connections they perceive between their work and the writings of non-Native colleagues and predecessors.

However, as I've argued throughout this essay, American Indian poetry is *situated* differently, both when it enters into a predominantly non-Native literary canon, more often than not as an ethnic suburb rather than a central and defining force, and when it stands, tribally and intertribally, outside that same canon. Better to remember that Native poets in general are, as Elizabeth Cook-Lynn has said of Sioux poets, self-appointed,[55] and that, as I would add, Native poetry is also to an important extent self-determined, which is to say that it defines and situates itself according to cultural traditions and standards quite distinct from those of non-Native America. That is, Native poetry *situates itself,* very much within the poet's particular Native culture(s) *and* very much within a variety of intertribal places, precisely because it does not come from out of nowhere. It is very skillful at situating itself, and in doing so it works to remove or downplay any cross-cultural forces that threaten to dilute or negate its Indianness. Even the imprimatur of the individual author—the claiming of authorship itself, an act so important to so many writers—is, like the workings of genre as I have described them in this essay, often less important to Native writers than the Native-centered communities that they honor and work to sustain. Elizabeth Woody explains:

> Writing is a way to recall people's generously given motion and strength that can enter other lives and minds by its own momentum. My uncle, Lewis Pitt, recently told me, "A truly great fisherman does not say he is a powerful fisherman because he caught a lot of fish. He says he was able to catch so many because he was sensitive enough to be in the right place and it was provided for him. We do not really

own anything, and have to be grateful that we have these ways, by nature, to instruct us." I feel that this is the process that works best for me as a poet.[56]

That, too, is a process that works very well for all of us as we listen to Elizabeth Woody, Linda Hogan, Simon Ortiz, Carter Revard, and all the other diverse and interrelated voices that inhabit and continue to form not the categories but the places of American Indian poetry and American Indian literature.

Daydreaming Primal Space

Cherokee Aesthetics as Habits of Being

Marilou Awiakta

I

A Cherokee elder told me, "Look at everything three times: Once with the right eye. Once with the left eye. And once from the corners of the eyes to see the spirit [essence] of what you're looking at."

Viewed from the "corners of the eyes," the mountain forest is the round, deep space—immediately immense, intimate, resonant—that the French philosopher Gaston Bachelard calls "the friend of being." It is also the first space in Appalachia that humans inhabited and called home. For centuries, these American Indians sang and danced and lived poetry as a habit of being. They considered themselves co-creators with the All-Mystery, the Creator, whose wisdom spoke through Mother Earth and the universe. In harmony with this voice, men and women spun a web of life so deftly that no limb bent, no flower crumpled beneath its weight. They made each strand strong and elastic, like the spider's, which has almost the tensile strength of fused quartz, drawn out silken fine. The web was an extension of the forest—a sturdy, secure dwelling open to the flow of wind and light and vision. Round living in round space. It gave the people a twinkle in the eye.

When Europeans arrived, they found many such webs among the mountains. The Cherokee had spun the largest, stretching almost the length and breadth of southern Appalachia. Some of the newcomers liked living in the round. Either they brought this holistic ability with them, or they learned it from the Indians or from Mother Earth herself. They looked at everything three times, with a twinkle. For a while everyone lived in harmony.

Other European settlers believed in the perception of the right and left eyes only. Philosophically, their point of view contained the seed of a dichotomy that would bear deadly fruit: God is God; nature is "the other." They feared the wilderness, the "savages" who lived there, and the amorphous power of the intuitive both represented. Out of fear and acquisitiveness they responded. "This new land needs to be squared up," they said. "Squared, boxed, labeled—*brought under control.* These 'primitive' webs are in the way. We'll tear them down and stamp out the spinners." And they did. Or so it seemed.

But the forest knows better.

That's why we're going there by way of a daydream.

II

Even in a daydream, no wise person enters the primal forest without looking at it three times. Having taken its measure from the corners of the eyes, we must use the right and the left eye to take clear bearings: our point of departure, the lay of the trail from beginning to end, the experiences we should anticipate.

We are going from contemporary space to primal space, from life on the square to life in the round, and from the line to the curve of time. There are corresponding differences in language and in the movement of thought, which this essay reflects. The language is intimate, for in the primal mind there is *no psychic distance* between the singer and the song; listeners share the web of context and experience. Also, instead of following the conventional Western linear progression (A, B, C, etc.) and reasoning from the outside in, the essay begins with the center, Part I, and moves in a widening spiral to the conclusion, developing the thought from the inside out. This is the traditional American Indian mode that originated in primal space, where everything is connected.

Experientially, it is probably a familiar mode. Imagine you and I are hiking the Appalachian Trail, beginning at Newfound Gap in the Great Smoky Mountains National Park. The deeper into the forest we go, the less we look at our watches. A vast, varied maze of evergreens and hardwoods leads our gaze from mountain to mountain, each more deeply steeped in blue haze, until the last faint curve becomes a wave between sight and feeling. We relax into the flow of wind in branches, of streams rushing over smooth boulders. Our thoughts web out. Peace webs in. Time is seamless—a slant of sunlight on treetops.

The longer we stay in primal space, the more jarring it is to return to what many American Indians call "the other world"—a world not of poetry but of lists:

SQUARED . . . . THE OTHER WORLD

TIME SQUARED to the clock. LIFE SQUARED to television / credit card / truck / car / train / jet—to cubicles piled in high rude rectangles. FILL IN THE SQUARE: name / address / telephone / sex / age / race / occupation. STAY IN THE LINES. KEEP TO TIME SLOTS: work / play / eat / sleep / love. Box 'em, label 'em, stack 'em up. COMPETE! Claw to the top of the pyramid. COMPUTE! COMPUTE! COMPUTE! ("No, you can't have your veteran's benefits. The computer shows you 'dead.'") GET HERESY UNDER CONTROL. The Creation is clear-cut: God is God; nature is "the other." Choose your side. WOMEN, SQUARE your shoulders, starve your bodies straight. Curves are out. MEN, SQUARE your hearts. Produce! Produce! Feelings don't raise the GNP. The shuttle's SEALS are at RISK . . . ? LAUNCH it! Seven people smeared across the sky translate to the TV monitor, "OBVIOUSLY WE HAVE A MAJOR MALFUNCTION." . . . Obviously.

Via television millions saw *Challenger* and its astronauts explode and scrawl a fiery hieroglyph on the curved wall of space. A warning. *"Humans have lost connection—with ourselves and each other, with nature and the Creator."* We do have a major malfunction. We've felt something seriously amiss for a long time. Now, in the blood of seven—a number sacred to the Cherokee and mystic to many of the world's peoples—we have clear warning. To survive, we must set ourselves right and reconnect.

One way to heal the deep slashes that sever us from relationship and hope is to go back to our home ground—our primal space—and find within it the deepest human root. In Appalachia, as elsewhere in America, that root is American Indians. They were the first to call the mountains home, as most Appalachians of every ethnic background continue to do. Perhaps if we study how indigenous people spun their original web, we can adapt their skill to our own time.

But how can we reach our primal space and the people who "sang and danced and lived poetry as a habit of being"?

We cannot see them with the right and left eyes, which only perceive facts and knowledge. We have to *experience* poetic habits of being from the corners of our eyes. To do that we use the phenomenology of the French philosopher, Gaston Bachelard, which reveals the imaginative movement of inner space. In *The Poetics of Space* he says, "All really inhabited space bears the essence of the notion of home."[1] Through thoughts and daydreams, we bring all our past dwellings with us to our present abode—especially the "original shell" (home) where we were born. This original shell is also "the topography of our intimate being," our soul. Remembering the shell, "we learn to abide within ourselves."[2]

A cross-country trucker from Knoxville put this same idea more plainly: "Wherever I go, I got my mountains inside of me. They keep me steady. Headin' back to East Tennessee, I keep pushin' 'til I get 'em in sight again. When I see that first blue line rise up, I know I'm home."

We're on our way to primal space in Appalachia, to the "spinners" and their web. But we can't get there through Bachelard's paradigm of the house as "the original shell." Although he looks at it from the corners of his eyes, the cast of his gaze—the perception governed by culture—is of the West. It is irreconcilable with the traditional worldview of American Indians and therefore with the model of the web.

For Bachelard, a given is the dichotomy between humanity and nature, between culture and the powerful forces of the universe. Their relationship is adversarial. In the dynamic between human and universe, "the house helps us to say: I will be an inhabitant of the world in spite of the world."[3] This dichotomy is the antithesis of the American Indian belief in the sacred tie to Mother Earth and to the universe as revelations of the wisdom of the Creator, who stands behind. Severance of the tie is basic to Western thought. It ranges God and man together; nature and all identified with it—including indigenous peoples and women—are "the other."

With this cardinal separation as a base, it is logical that Bachelard derives his idea of the house as a "tool for the analysis of the human soul" from the psychological paradigm of Carl Jung, in which the house is detached from nature and compartmentalized. The attic is the intellect—the rational mind—which polarizes with the cellar, the realm of the irrational and intuitive, where "the walls have the entire earth behind them" and we are afraid. The cellar is the unconscious. It cannot be civilized. To be used, it must be rationalized, dominated, "*brought under control.*"[4] In a word, "squared." The other rooms of the house stack up, and we inhabit them one at a time. The mode of the house cannot be applied to the web—an extension of the forest, where the dweller feels the vibration of any one strand as a vibration of the whole.

Furthermore, in the web, the balance of gender replicates the balance of Nature's dynamics and is crucial to communal harmony. "Men and women spun. . . ." The power of change and transitoriness (male) must stay in balance with the power of continuance (female). Otherwise, there is discord and death for the people. From this point of view, Bachelard's "oneiric" house is a bird with one wing, which claims to be two-winged. Although Bachelard says he is studying the "houses of man"—that is, of "humanity"—and the experience of inhabiting, all of the dwellers are male. The wing of their experience is powerful and true. But where is the balancing wing of continuance? No woman speaks of her experience—not even in the cellar, much less in the attic. There is no bedroom and no kitchen in Bachelard's house (extraordinary omissions for a Frenchman) and no nursery—no comfortable space for the fecund and regenerative.

Only in a later chapter, quoting Michelet's meditation on birds making a nest, does Bachelard come close to female experience and gender balance:

> Michelet suggests a house built by and for the body, taking form from the inside, like a shell, in an intimacy that works physically. . . . "On the inside," he continues, "the instrument that prescribes a circular form for the nest is nothing else but the body of the bird. It is by constantly turning round and round and pressing back the walls on every side that it succeeds in forming this circle. The female . . . hollows out the house, while the male brings back from the outside all kinds of materials, sturdy twigs and other bits . . . The house is the bird's very person."[5]

Even with so pregnant an opportunity as this, Bachelard does not apply nature's principle of gender balance to humans. Indeed, he cannot. The psychic distance is too great, for the sacred tie that would transfer it has been severed for centuries.

It would seem then that although the process of phenomenology—the daydreaming of images—is wonderfully applicable to primal space and the web, its paradigm is not. However, Bachelard finally dreams his way out of the squared house and into an immense cosmic dwelling, which "is a potential of every dream of houses. Winds radiate from its center and gulls fly from its windows. A house that is as dynamic as this allows the poet to inhabit the universe. Or, to put it differently, the universe comes to inhabit his house." This house expands or contracts as Bachelard desires. It is "infinitely extensible"—a "sort of airy structure that moves about on the breath of time." Unwilling to be enclosed, the space we love "deploys and appears to move elsewhere without difficulty; into other times and on different planes of dream and memory."[6]

Gaston Bachelard is dreaming the web!

Gradually he makes his way toward it, gathering images from nature that have the quality of roundness, like Michelet's bird nest. "When we examine a nest," he says, "we place ourselves at the origin of confidence in the world. . . . Our [manmade] house, apprehended in its dream potentiality, becomes a nest in the world, and we shall live there in complete confidence if, in our dreams, we really participate in the sense of security of our first home."[7] The shell, with its "protective spiral," engenders similar confidence and evokes the intimate connection of body and soul. Bachelard dreams on through "the curve that warms"—the curve that is also "habitable space harmoniously constituted"[8]—until he comes at last to the primal forest of his ancestors. Here he meditates on "intimate immensity" and "roundness," implicitly yearning for wholeness, for cosmic connection.

Sharing his feeling and transposing his forest to our own in Appalachia, we ponder the mountains and imagine "an airy structure that moves about on the breath of time," a dwelling that is "open to wind and light and vision." Alas, the webs are torn down, the spinners stamped out.

But the forest smiles. Deep in her nooks and crevices she feels the spinners and the harmony of their web. We will dream our way to them.

III

Daydream at midnight: We're back on the Appalachian Trail, somewhere in North Carolina—looking for a Cherokee web and "poetry as a habit of being." By the pressure of our toes against our shoes, we feel the trail descending. Flashlights give us narrow glimpses of a rut here, a rock there. It's like a Cades Cove woman said, "You don't know what dark is 'til you seen night come down on the mountain."

As the trail swings into the open along a ridge, we stop. From the corners of our eyes we see the essence of the mountains. By day, clothed in trees and blue veils, they are so beautiful it's tempting to relax in their embrace and forget they are also what we see jetting against the moonlit sky—mass and mystery, immovable. Only a fool thinks of "conquering the mountains." Mountains nurture the reverent. For the irreverent, the consequences are inevitable—and often fatal. If you're born and raised in Appalachia, this wisdom comes with your mother's milk. Mountains teach you to face the realities of life, to "abide in your own soul"—and survive.

Carefully, we feel our way through the folds of darkness. Since our right and left eyes are virtually useless, other senses become our eyes. The roll of a pebble, the breath of dew-cooled pines, a startled flutter in a nearby bush magnify the vast silence of the forest. Wind and stream are the murmuring current of time, taking us back to where poetry is sung and danced and lived. . . . In the distance a fire flickers—not running wild, but contained, like a candle. The spinners.

Coming closer, we encounter the first strands that define their web: a whiff of wood smoke, the brisk "SSH . . . ssh, SSH . . . ssh" of shell-shakers and a chant/song that dips . . . lifts . . . dips . . . lifts. It's as if, in the still of the night, Mother Earth is making music from her heart. The music draws us on, even shapes our courtesy. Extinguishing flashlights, we approach the large clearing slowly, for it is ceremonial ground, conse-crated ground. Around the perimeter of the web, people are moving among the trees. We stop, wait for someone to acknowledge us.

Waiting is part of the poetics of primal space—a silence that allows the gathering of thought, the savoring of meaning. Alternating activity with rest is nature's way. It engenders endurance and reduces possibility of conflict, giving time for stasis to evolve. Even so, the night is chill and to stand in the dark, outside of community looking in, is lonely. The people, the trees, even round Brother Moon seems to be quietly looking us over. Only the steady heartbeat of the web reassures us:

"SSH . . . ssh . . . SSH . . . ssh. Dip . . . lift . . . dip . . . lift. . . ."

A woman comes to greet us. Her bearing is confident, kind—immov-able. We are respectful. She is the Ghigau, the Beloved Woman, chief of the Women's Council and a principal leader of the nation. Unhurried, she works the conversation around to the key question, addressed to me because of my black hair and high cheek bones. "Who is your mother?" (Meaning of what clan. She would have asked a man the same question.) I answer as my ancestor would have, "My mother is of the Deer Clan from the Overhill (Cherokee) at Tenasi."

With this filament of information in hand, the Beloved Woman begins connecting us to the web. In the forest, as in every town in the nation, the community revolves around seven mother clans. Like protective shells, they ensure the continuance of kin and care in the midst of change. They also keep the peace among the town, for it is forbidden to fight with relatives. Seven arbors, one for each clan, ring the ceremonial ground. In the woods behind them, families have cleared the underbrush and made camp; their small, embered fires are like red stars scattered in the dark.

As the Beloved Woman weaves a path among them, people in the shadows speak or wave to her but courteously avoid looking at us directly. We sense they're taking our measure from the corners of their eyes, intuiting cues for responses. And we do the same. Even by glance, aggression and dominance have no place here.

"*SSH . . . ssh . . . ssh. Dip . . . lift . . . dip . . . lift. . . .*"

The harmony vibrates every strand of the web, as natural and pervasive as air. Breathing the rhythm, we know we should slowly follow the poetic habits of being to their source. Otherwise, we will be disrespectful, unfit—and unwelcome—in the dance. The primary habit is connecting.

As the Beloved Woman settles us into the Deer Clan, people goodnaturedly move over a little—give us greetings, a place by the fire and food from a communal spread nearby—roasted beef, corn, boiled squash and peas, bean bread and spring water, which we dip from a bucket. We take up threads of conversation as they're offered—"Where do you come from? How was your journey?"

Looking at these amenities twice only, we might mistake them for mere courtesies. But the spinners live *poetically*, always moving in harmony with the spirit beyond the tangible. We see the courtesies as they do: the greetings are the first silken strands attaching us to the web. The place by the fire signifies acceptance into the circle. The food and words are tokens of care for us to spin into response. We are entering the ceremony of connecting that originates in the dance. Following its measured pace, we accept what is offered with appreciation—eat slowly, talk with intervals of silence to allow thought to gather and be expressed.

Like an artist's brush, the firelight strokes the spinners only enough to suggest the full life beyond what we see:

— the planes of cheek in the faces close to us and zestful twinkles in the eyes;

— the ebony swing of a woman's hair as she bends over her baby, the smile between two elders who glimpse a young couple edging toward deeper shadows;

— a warrior's arm guiding a toddler away from the fire;

— and slightly apart from the group, the silhouettes of the Beloved Woman and a man walking together, intent in conversation.

"Is that her husband?" I ask the woman beside me.

"No. A chief. The council meets tomorrow."

Societal balances are different here than where we come from, but they generate a peaceful, easy feeling. Gradually we meet other friends and relatives of the clan (and by extension of ours)—a leisurely flow of men, women and children who mingle freely with the adults, not boisterous but *busy*. Conversation and laughter are abundant yet muted. Everyone understands the parameter of behavior at the ceremonial grounds. People gather here to celebrate the oneness of life, to recenter their spirits in the All-Mystery. Although the grounds are inclusive of human needs, there can be no alcohol, no rowdiness, nothing to disturb the harmonies of regeneration and renewal. Do these harmonies translate to twinkles in the eyes? We think so.

They also translate into energy. The dance has been going on for two nights already. When some of the women move, a faint *"ssh . . . ssh"* comes from shells covered by their long skirts. Every clan has its team of shell-shakers and male singers, its poetic expression of continuance and change. The leading of the dance alternates among the seven clans, leaving other people free to participate or rest as they have energy and inclination.

"When do you sleep?" we ask.

"When we are tired."

"And when do you get up?"

"When we are rested."

They are amused by our questions as people in the square world would be by someone asking, "What is a clock?" In the web, as in the universe, everything cycles, circles, assumes a round shape, connects to everything else. Our dwelling is an "airy structure," a cosmic house "open to wind and light and vision." The owl glides freely here. The cricket chirps in counterpoint with the dance. The raccoon ambles impudently at will. The spinners address them with familial respect as Grand-mother, Grandfather, Sister, or Brother. We are among all our relations, which include the standing people—the vast, staunch company of trees who have seen generations of walking people come and go. Resting con-fidently against the bosom of Mother Earth, we gaze along the moun-tains' curve into the dome of the sky, where even the tiniest star has a worthy place—as we do at home in the web.

We inhabit all its parts simultaneously. There is no attic here, no cellar, nothing to keep us from orienting to our whole space and whole being. Instead of cubic rooms, the web has spheres, which—like the auras of a circular rainbow—are distinct and diffuse at the same time. In the outer aura are the campsites, where embering dots signify the presence of perhaps three hundred people. If two hundred more should arrive, the web is "infinitely extensible." Or if that many should depart, it simply contracts. Wind extends the psychic space of our dwelling, bringing scents of deep forest, of distant streams and pollens. From the communal cooking area come aromas of whole beefs roasting on the spit. We know that someone prepares for the morrow—just as looking up at Brother Moon keeping watch over us, we know his sister, the sun, is moving toward the east. Our relatives are dependable—they give us a purring feeling.

In the next aura, people flow continually—visiting, doing errands, or just enjoying themselves while they wait to dance. As comfortable in the night as in the day, the spinners look at everything three times and move easily from the intellect to the intuitive and back again—a habit that many from the "other world" find "primitive and irrational." But in the round world it seems the natural way—in fact, the only sensible way—to move.

The circle of arbors marks the beginning of the web's spiritual cen-ter, the aura where meditative energy concentrates. At sundown on the first day of the dance, the spinners had begun the ceremony of con-nection with special prayers, songs and dances to evoke harmony with Mother Earth, the universe and the All-Mystery. Then they made a great cone-shaped fire of seven sacred woods—to burn continuously until the final day. The ceremonial dance began, a dance so ancient that no one knows its time of origin, a living poem passed from generation to genera-tion. The dancing lasts until dawn.

During the day, although the people move freely in the outer part of the aura, they hold its flaming center in constant reverence. Its sacred meaning is visible at all times from every strand of the web. Because there is no psychic distance between the source, its image and those who express it, the fire is not symbolic in the Western sense. It is analogous to the atom's photon, which is made of the same material as the star. The fire, like the sun, shares the essence of the All-Mystery, Creator, just as the individual shares the spirit of the people. The fire embodies the light of all. To understand its meaning, however, we must experience it in the dance.

We sit among the Deer Clan but withdraw into our inner space . . . into a silence that allows the fire's image to deepen . . .

"SSH . . . ssh . . . SSH . . . ssh. Dip . . . lift . . . dip . . . lift. . . ."

There is ancient magic in the sound. Tuning our ears to the song, we hear predominantly the tonalities of *a*. They seem to resonate from the core of time to a place inside us we feel but cannot name.

Bachelard's voice, soft and discreet, enlarges our thought:

> It is impossible to think the vowel sound *ah* without a tautening of the vocal chords. . . . The letter *a*, which is the main body of the word *vast*, stands aloof in its delicacy. . . . This delicate little Aeolian harp that nature has set at the entrance to our breathing is really a sixth sense, which followed and surpassed the others. It quivers at the mere movement of metaphor; it permits human thought to sing. . . . I begin to think that the vowel *a* is the vowel of immensity. It is a sound area that starts with a sigh and extends beyond all limits.[9]

Through their powerful intuitive skills, the ancient spinners understood the vowel *a* and its effect on the sixth sense. They also knew that dance touches the sixth sense in a similar way, making an "Aeolian harp" of the whole body. In combination, the song dips and lifts the people into immensity while the dance holds them secure. This balance repeats in the dance pattern itself, which alternates man / woman / man / woman.

Looking through the web to the great cone-shaped fire and the figures circling round it, we juxtapose on them the image of Michelet's bird, turning round and round, shaping her nest from the inside out. And we understand the cardinal poetic of primal space: The All-Mystery—the source of all light and energy—animates the breast of Mother Earth and turns her round and round, shaping the spinners, their web and their ways to "curve and hold the curve." Man / woman / man / woman. The power of change and transitoriness balanced with the power of continuance—strong shining wings that keep all life aloft. This is the Great Law, the Poem ensouled in the universe. The people sing it, dance it, live it.

Now when we look at the Deer Clan sketched in firelight, we realize the fuller implications of their habits of being:

The Beloved Woman talks with the chief, reflecting the wisdom of both genders active in government.

The warrior *and* the woman nurture the children, who are spread among us like seeds in the forest. Sometimes the woman is a warrior also.

The old couple rejoices in the life cycle of the young, in the assurance that the people will continue.

We ourselves are included in the web through a social interpretation of the Poem. Regeneration and renewal is the theme of primal space. The plane of our cheeks feels stronger. Twinkles well in our eyes.

We are hopeful that the square world we come from can regain its round shape. As we speak to the Deer Clan of problems there, an old man across the fire listens, eyes half-closed. With his forefinger he touches his head and heart, then makes a slashing gesture between them. Nods of agreement around the circle. "Head-severed-from-heart"—disconnection—has long been a source of conflict with European settlers of the two-eyes-only type. Many spinners believe that this unbalanced condition will cause the whites to destroy the Indian webs and, in the end, to foul their own nest.

Although these thoughts are not articulated, the Beloved Woman feels their movement. "There are also whites who *do* keep head and heart connected," she says. "We can learn from their good ways and they can learn from ours. Maybe we can find the balance between . . ." Her years of work in this endeavor give weight to her words and a tone of irony as she adds, " . . . if not in seven years, then in seven hundred."

Her allusion to the medicine man's prognosis—that a cure will work "in seven days, and if not in seven days, in seven years"—is well understood. There is wisdom in it. And stoic humor.

It is time to dance.

People begin to stand up, stretch their legs. It is the Deer Clan's turn to lead. One of the shell-shakers shows me the cuffs that cover her legs from below the knee to the ankle—row after row of turtle shells, with a scattering of pebbles in each.

"How much do the cuffs weigh?" I ask.

"About forty pounds. It takes years of practice to be a shell-shaker."

And, I think, years to build up the stamina. Holding the rhythm of continuance is not a task for the frail.

Neither is singing. The dance is brisk, the songs vigorous and long. It takes the breath of male athletes to sustain them simultaneously. Some of the singers pass near us. They are strong-legged and supple. It is said that they can run for days with only a modicum of rest, and their skill as warriors is well known. Yet tonight they turn their energies to ceremonies celebrating life, which (apparently unknown to the Hollywood of our time) is what most tribal dances are about.

Along with many other members of the clan, we follow the shakers and singers as they cross the web toward their arbor. The closer we come to the center, the more people gather quietly together. In the aura of the arbors, they move very little, and in the circle ringing the dancers they are almost immobile, absorbed in the rhythm. Around the tall fire almost a hundred people jog counter-clockwise in unison—woman/man/woman/man... round and round... adults on the inside, children on the perimeter... round and round... quick, trotting steps... arms bent at the elbow... faces contemplative... round and round....

Vibrations from stomping feet pass through Mother Earth to our own, making us feel part of the dance already; and though we are silent, our throats contract with the *a* sounds of the song:

"*SSHH*... *shh*... *SSH*... *ssh*... *Dip*... *lift*... *dip*... *lift*...."

The music spirals up, soaring and gliding on perfectly balanced wings. When the shell-shakers cease, the dance ends and the song trails off on a haunting note, like a cry of the loon.

Slowly everyone leaves the dance ground. We wait at the edge... watching flames... following smoke as it drifts toward low-hanging stars.

Deer Clan singers file in silently and circle close to the fire. Leaving a space between each pair of them for another person, they begin a slow, rhythmic pace, calling out on every fourth beat, "ahYO... ahYO... ahYO... ahYO...." Smoothly, the shell-shakers join them, "*SSH*... *ssh*... *SSH*... *ssh*." As we spiral in with other people, the tempo slowly increases, then holds steady. We settle into a rhythm that has endured for hundreds of years... round and round.... The chant lifts and dips in myriad tones of *a* and *o*, synchronizing perfectly with the shells. So intricate is the balance that we cease to analyze and give ourselves up to music... to warm energy rising within, melting away fatigue and cares

. . . round and round. . . . Shell curves to song and song curves to shell . . . the whole moving, moving . . . memories come and dreams far beyond our knowing . . . membranes dissolve between flesh and leaf and sky, releasing all the atoms' tiny stars. . . . They stream round and round . . . into the All-Mystery, a radiant cup that holds our spirits in perfect stillness and perfect peace. . . .

IV

Round, deep space
immense
intimate
resonant
the friend of being,
our first home
in Appalachia.

If we really experience its sense of security in our dreams, we can live in our present home with confidence. Whatever our ethnic origins, we have in common our primal space and ancestors who knew how to live in harmony with it. This heritage is the ground of our hope. It holds us steady as we face the realities of our time, a time "squared" almost beyond endurance.

In Appalachia, as elsewhere in the world, the effects of humanity's "major malfunction" are evident. Through lack of reverence for the web of life, humans have upset the balance of nature on a global scale. Poison is invading the ozone layer, the forests, the waters, the food chain—perhaps even the very heart of Mother Earth. *Challenger's* fiery hieroglyph merges with warnings from scientists, theologians, artists and others who "feel it in their bones": we are reaching the point of no return. We must stop the rending of our web and begin to reweave it.

The pattern of survival is in the poetics of primal space. Balance, harmony, inclusiveness, cooperation—life regenerating within a parameter of order. The pattern repeats the deepest heart of Mother Nature, where the atom—with its predictable perimeter—freely makes its rounds to create new life. Continuance in the midst of change, cardinal dynamics that sustain the universe.

The Cherokee have used these poetics for survival. In 1838, after the Trail of Tears, the Nation's web was in shreds. Surveying the damage, the elders said, "In the seventh generation, the Cherokee will rise again." With the wisdom of the spider, the people ingested what was left of their web and began to spin. It was seven generations later, in 1984, that the Cherokee Eastern and Western Councils reunited at the Red Clay Historic Park near Cleveland, Tennessee—on the very ground where the last council before the Removal was held. For three days I lived in the web that the Cherokee wove on the knolled mountain meadow in the same pattern they had used in 1837.

Recently I discussed the reunion of the Cherokee with Wilma Mankiller, principal chief of the Cherokee Nation of Oklahoma. She is a poet-chief, in the classic American Indian tradition. Traditionally reared, she is also a shell-shaker for her clan at the ceremonial grounds, where many Cherokee come regularly to sing and dance and live poetry as you, the reader, and I experienced it in our midnight dream. I asked Chief Mankiller, "In essence, do you think the Cherokee survived because they kept dancing?" "Unquestionably," she answered. "We've held the center. We've maintained connection."

Survival. It *is* possible. A hopeful twinkle glimmers in our eyes as we Appalachians contemplate primal space—our first home, our friend of being. The question is: Do we have the courage to *be* a friend in return? For the sake of renewed relationships, will we unstack the boxes, take off the labels, and open ourselves to the flow of light and air and vision? It will mean giving up the idea of dominance for the concept of harmony with "all our relations." It will mean balancing the power of change and transitoriness with the power of continuance, in every dimension of our society. Most of all, it will mean that we heal the sacred and severed tie between humanity and nature as the expression of the All-Mystery—the Poem, the Great Law ensouled in the universe, which teaches us to live in the round. Looking three times at what lies before us, I chant: *Out of ashes / peace will rise / if the people are resolute / our courage is our memory.*

Beloved Woman Returns

The Doubleweaving of Homeland and Identity in the

Poetry of Marilou Awiakta

Daniel Heath Justice

To take shape
a journey must have
fixed bearings,
as a basket has ribs
and a book its themes.

Cherokee women have long been respected, within their own communities and by others, for their weaving skills, particularly in the art of basketry. Their baskets, intricately woven together from honeysuckle, cane, white oak, and hickory, painted with rich but modest dyes, have been utilized at various times in Cherokee history for a variety of functions: fishing, carrying and storing foods and medicinal plants, playing games, and bearing the memories of the culture within their deceptively strong weave.[1] Many of the traditional arts of the People have been co-opted by non-Native technologies, but the basketry of Cherokee women is one skill that maintains the ancient weight of tradition, even through its inevitable transformations across the years. If anything, the skill becomes stronger, the meaning more powerful, as Cherokee women pass the knowledge to their daughters (and, sometimes, their sons) in a world of increasing technological complexity and ethnoenvironmental oppression.

This knowledge continues in often surprising ways, and the skill of basketweaving sometimes changes in physical form while remaining true to the heart of the craft. One such transformation is through contemporary Cherokee poetry, particularly the work of Marilou Awiakta, a woman whose Cherokee/Appalachian heritage has provided a rich legacy from which to draw on in her struggle against the oppression of Native peoples, ecocide, and global intolerance and separation. Cherokee traditions —stories, philosophies, perspectives—and the physical landmass of Appalachia come together in Awiakta's poetry, and is made manifest in the craft and form of her primary and most encompassing work, *Selu: Seeking the Corn-Mother's Wisdom:*

> How can a book have the form of a basket? . . . A round, doublewoven basket in the Oklahoma Cherokee style is this book's natural form, arising from the thoughts themselves. As I worked with the poems, essays and stories, I saw they shared a common base—the sacred law of taking and giving back with respect, of maintaining balance. From there they wove around four themes, gradually assuming a double-sided pattern—one outer, one inner—distinct, yet interconnected in a whole. The outer side became my path to Selu, the inner one was the Corn-Mother herself. The basket image conveys the principle of composition quickly. Reading will be easy if you keep the weaving mode in mind: Over . . . under . . . over . . . under. A round basket never runs "straight on."[2]

This interweaving of tradition, personal experience, contemporary (1993) politics and social reality, and poetry come together in Awiakta's own intricate narrative basketweaving. This essay will focus on two of the numerous themes that run through all Awiakta's work—homeland and identity—and the ways in which they are evoked in her poetry.

The very concept of *homeland* evokes images of connection, legacy, continuity. It is a reminder of our tangible relationship to the world around us, as well as a reminder of our interdependence on that world and its mysteries for physical and spiritual sustenance, and for identity. Yet another evocation that often accompanies the idea of homeland is possession. The land of one's own birth is rarely at issue; rather, it is the land of one's *people's* birth, possessed of a sacred and ideological essence that transcends distances of space and time, and carries through in the dreams and collective memories of a community.

For Awiakta, the ancestral homeland of the Cherokees, particularly that of her native Tennessee (named for the Cherokee town of Tenasi), is central to her discussions of everything from appropriation, racism, and isolation to nuclear energy. That land—the 135,000 acres of rocky hill country in the southeast, now known as parts of Alabama, Georgia, North and South Carolina, Virginia and West Virginia, Kentucky, as well as Tennessee itself—is the world in which for thousands of years (or longer) the Cherokees lived, loved, and built a vast and complex civilization, holding fast to the land and the culture even in the face of disease and colonial intrusion. Even the brutal fall and winter of 1838–39, in which the bulk of the Nation was forcibly removed by the U.S. government and gold-hungry Georgians from this homeland on the bloody death march that would come to be known as the Trail of Tears, did not erase the Cherokee presence from the area. About a thousand of the perhaps twenty thousand Cherokees scattered across the region managed to elude capture and hide in the hills. Though starvation, disease, and the ever-present threat of murder followed them, these Cherokees, like their removed kin, survived and continued on. As Awiakta and others can well attest, there are still Cherokees in the southeast.

The physical landforms in the region, named and unnamed, reflect Awiakta's Cherokee/Appalachian worldview, as in the poem "Selu and Kanati: Marriage":

Two peaks
alone . . . apart . . .
yet join at the heart
where trees rise green
from rain-soaked loam
and laurel's tangled skeins
bear fragile blooms
and wind, a honing, ceaseless
sigh, blends with mirth
of streams defying heights
to wend their way unquenched.
Two peaks
they stand against the sky
spanned by a jagged arm of rock
locked in an embrace
elements cannot destroy
or time erase.[3]

Selu and Kanati—the Corn-Mother and her husband, the Lucky Hunter —are the first woman and man of the Cherokees. The mountains Awiakta writes of are the Chimney Tops, "famous twin peaks in the Great Smoky Mountains National Park. One peak is softly rounded, one is sharp. Their beauty is their balance."[4]

The Cherokee philosophy of balance—defined by former principal chief of the Cherokee Nation Wilma Mankiller as the understanding that "the world existed in a precarious balance and that only right or correct actions kept it from tumbling"[5]—is the basic foundation upon which Awiakta crafts her work. Intimately connected with the concept of balance is that of *respect*—one cannot exist without the other. This respect extends beyond the human community to those of the rest of creation. In her poem "Trail Warning," Awiakta expands on a "small sign by our path that distills a philosophy of all my mountain ancestors":

> Beauty is no threat to the wary
>   who treat the mountain in its way,
>   the copperhead in its way,
>   and the deer in its way,
> knowing that nature is the human heart
> made tangible.[6]

Awiakta's ancestors—Cherokees and Celts, Natives and newcomers —are people of the mountains, people who thought and lived in similar ways and treated the land and one another with dignity and respect: "I listened to the 'deepest hollow of my heart'—my Cherokee/Appalachian taproot."[7] Through that listening and understanding—the Cherokee advice to "walk in your soul," to "think purposefully from the center of your whole being"[8]—Awiakta approaches the world not as a removed observer but as an active and integral participant in the whole. In her poem "Dawn Birth," Awiakta expresses what critic Gretchen Legler calls the Native "reconception of nature not as passive matter, as an object of study, but as an active subject with erotic autonomy":[9]

> Sitting in the mountain's cold dark
> I watch the horizon soften, dilate slowly
> water-pale. Astral veins distend
> flow violet   peach   labia rose
> well to red, as the sun crowns
> in the cleft between earth and sky.
> I breathe deep . . .

. . . am drawn back in the womb of space
where we two suns once
turned side by side
warm . . . close . . .
until pain cut through—
a passing star that pulled me out
alone . . .

. . . I pant, breathe deep again
push with the silent rhythm
that brings forth the crimson face
the lusty cry of light.
I bend into the shine
open my arms
to my sister
my spirit-twin.[10]

The speaker and the rest of the cosmos are not simply sharing a similar experience; instead, they are sharing the *same* birth, an intimate interconnectedness between the personal and the universal. As individual actions affect the balance of creation, so too does a spiritual birth send ripples of procreative power through the world and her peoples. For Awiakta, as with other Native poets, this is not mere symbol or metaphor; these relationships are real and tangible.

Awiakta even acknowledges the spirits rarely considered in discussions of one's habitat—the houses, streets, and structures built by human hands. *All* the world is alive with spirit, and all the world speaks to the wary:

Song of the Swinging Bridge

Mind your step.
I'm alive!
Not steel or concrete—
musky sinew. Sunwarm
yet damp and pliant
in my deepest fiber.
I vibrate to your touch
curve to your shape

undulate, sigh beneath
your weight.
But . . .
Stomp me—I fling you up.
Yank me—I break your stride.
Shake me—I swing you
in an arc of fear.
Mind your step.
Blend your rhythm with mine
so I can bear you safely
through the void.
When you reach solid ground
look back.
I sway gently
remembering . . .[11]

From Little Deer, the Cherokee spirit who gives guidance to honorable hunters but cripples those who kill without conscience, to Selu, the Corn-Mother who, when treated with honor, provides physical and spiritual sustenance not just to Cherokees but to people all over the world, the twin philosophies of balance and respect bring a healing understanding to one's relationships with the surrounding world. Homeland, then, is as much the expanded global and cosmic communities as it is the mountains of Tennessee.

But Appalachia is where the history of the Cherokee people was formed, and it remains intimately a part of the Cherokee consciousness, even for those removed to what is now Oklahoma, and those who scattered in the Cherokee diaspora after removal. It is the place where the ancestors were buried, where language was formed, where Selu died and was reborn. It is also a place where, today, Cherokees continue to resist the ceaseless attacks of Euro-American ideals of rampant individualism, unchecked profit making, and alienation. It is in this place of conflict—between the ancient communal understandings of Cherokees, Celts, and other tribal peoples and the Puritan obsession for mastery over the "wildness" in the self and the world—that Awiakta is most eloquent, most passionate, and most evocative.

In her introduction to *Spider Woman's Granddaughters*, Laguna/Sioux scholar Paula Gunn Allen writes:

War stories seem to me to capture all the traditional themes of women's narratives: the themes of love and separation, loss, and, most of all, of continuance. Certainly war has been the major motif of Indian life over the past five centuries, so it is perfectly fitting that we write out of our experience as women at war, women who endure during wartime, women who spend each day aware that we live in a war zone.[12]

Awiakta is no stranger to that war zone. She has fought against the violation of Native graves and town sites, most notably the flooding by the Tennessee Valley Authority's Tellico Dam project in 1979 of Chota, the ancient peace-city of the Cherokee Nation and one of its most sacred sites. She has also worked to educate people about treating modern technology—from nuclear energy to computers, cars, and space exploration—with the twin principles of balance and respect. Having grown up at the Oak Ridge nuclear facility in Tennessee, where her father worked for thirty years, Awiakta expresses both a nuanced understanding of nuclear science and a deep reverence for both the creative and devastating potentials of that technology. She is not devoted to a static version of "unchanging" Nature; instead, while acknowledging the inevitability of change and transformation, she reminds the reader and listener that such change must always be accompanied with humility, especially when it is a result of human ambitions. Otherwise, only catastrophe for ourselves and our various kin can result, an event Awiakta explores, only slightly tongue in cheek, in the following excerpt from "Mother Nature Sends a Pink Slip":

To: Homo Sapiens
Re: Termination

My business is producing life.
The bottom line is
you are not cost-effective workers.
Over the millennia, I have repeatedly
clarified my management goals and objectives.
Your failure to comply is well documented.
It stems from your inability to be
a team player:
  • you interact badly with co-workers
  • contaminate the workplace

- sabotage the machinery
- hold up production
- consume profits

In short, you are a disloyal species.

Within the last decade
I have given you three warnings:
- made the workplace too hot for you
- shaken up your home office
- utilized plague to cut back personnel

The final words of the poem are chilling in their honesty:

Your failure to take appropriate action
has locked these warnings into
the Phase-Out Mode, which will result
in termination.   No appeal.[13]

Awiakta has seen in her travels across Indian Country and the world just how inevitable the laws of respect truly are, and she explores them through her work.

But Awiakta does not simply examine Cherokee concerns and issues. Hers is as much a global concern as it is a local one. As she writes: "All around us we see life 'dying back'—in nature, in our families, in society. Homo sapiens are literally killing their own seed and the seeds of other life forms as well. One cause of this suicidal violence is greed. And that greed feeds on the philosophy that Earth is not our Mother, but an 'it' that can be used and consumed. This philosophy even extends to the 'conquest' of outer space."[14] The echoes of numerous poems appear in this passage: "When Earth Becomes an 'It'" examines this particular idea, where humans "use her / consume her strength. / Then the people die";[15] in "Dying Back," Awiakta explores the effects of pollution, both physical and spiritual, on the trees on the mountains and people in the cities, where "The walking people are dying back / as all species do / that kill their own seed";[16] and in both "Memo to NASA" and "Cherokee Woman on the Moon," Awiakta critiques the colonial "conquest" of the moon and the updated philosophy of Manifest Destiny that accompanies such projects.

In her work, and particularly in her examination of environmental and social inequities, Awiakta continually returns to her center, the understanding she brings to the world from her Cherokee Appalachian heritage, and from being a woman of those backgrounds. In doing so, and in speaking as a Native woman of authority, Awiakta evokes the ancient position of respect and high regard held by Cherokee women.

Because of the Cherokee concern with balance, women possessed a strong voice in the affairs of their people. According to Ameropean historian Theda Perdue, they "had their own arena of power, and any threat to its integrity jeopardized cosmic order. So it had been since the beginning of time."[17] One particular arena in which women exercised their authority was among the societies of Beloved and War Women. Wilma Mankiller describes this role as one of both diplomacy and battle skill:

> The women of each of the seven clans elected their own leaders. These leaders convened as the Women's Council, and sometimes raised their voices in judgment to override the authority of the chiefs when the women believed the welfare of the tribe demanded such an action. It was common custom among the ancient Cherokees that any important questions relating to war and peace were left to a vote of the women.
>
> There were brave Cherokee women who followed their husbands and brothers into battle. These female warriors were called War Women or Pretty Women, and they were considered dignitaries of the tribe, many of them being as powerful in council as in battle.
>
> The Cherokees also had a custom of assigning to a certain woman the tasks of declaring whether pardon or punishment should be inflicted on great offenders. This woman also was called the Pretty Woman, but she was sometimes known as Most Honored Woman or Beloved Woman.
>
> It was the belief of the Cherokees that the Great Spirit sent messages through their Beloved Women. So great was her power that she could commute the sentence of a person condemned to death by the council.[18]

The last Beloved Woman of the old way was the Ghigau, Nanyehi, known to Ameropeans of her day (late eighteenth century until 1824) and ours as Nancy Ward, the Beloved Woman of Chota—the same Chota flooded by the Tellico Dam.

In her long lifetime, Nanye'hi worked tirelessly for peace between the Cherokees and the invaders, always with the survival of her people foremost in her thoughts. So, too, does Awiakta craft her writing, always with the survival of the Cherokees, and the rest of creation, before all else. She refuses to shirk the unpleasantness of the duty, as with her writings on the dispossession of Native peoples and the corrosive effects of greed and ambition on the natural world, but she always maintains her focus: "I am a Cherokee/Appalachian poet. To find the 'eye of my work'—the center —I have to come home."[19] As a modern poetic representative of the Beloved Women, Awiakta returns to the center to seek the connections beyond. Often this is done through unflinching exploration of the inevitable heartache and devastation caused by human alienation. But just as often, Awiakta reveals the deep humor that so richly contrasts with the often stark realities of life in Appalachia, as in her short poem "On Being a Female Phoenix":

> Not only do I rise
> from my own ashes,
> I have to carry them out![20]

Humor is another connecting rib in this doublewoven basket, a reminder that humility and balance include the knowledge that joy is as much a part of the world as the creatures and trees that populate it.

In his essay "Characteristics of Contemporary Native American Literature," critic Craig Lesley sets forward six primary themes that run through most writing by Native authors, and which taken together provide foundations for conceptualizing their works: "importance of the land," "search for the center," "relationship to the past," "bitterness toward white culture," "belief in the power of words," and "silence as a part of Indian literature."[21] Each of these themes heavily informs Awiakta's work, except for the fourth—"bitterness toward white culture." While Europeans and their descendants in this country are certainly held accountable for the damage wrought by their philosophies and actions, there is no room for bitterness in a heart seeking balance. Awiakta's poetry seeks healing and reconciliation among all peoples, not revenge for past wrongs. The past *must* be acknowledged, and responsibility *must* be accepted, but forgiveness often comes, even in the old laws of respect, when right actions work to right past transgressions and injustices.

As Cherokee women have done for ages, Awiakta crafts her basket, a weaving of words and dreams, fire and spirit, to serve the people well, to provide for the future and to endure the unknown. And, just as the

Beloved Women of old, Awiakta listens to the spirits around her, and offers her readers, both Native and non-Native, the choice—

> Against the downward pull,
> against the falter
> of your heart and mine,
> I offer you a gift
> a seed to greet the sunrise—
>   Ginitsi Selu
> Corn, Mother of Us All.
>   Her story.[22]

The Corn-Mother of the Cherokees is a gift from the People of the Sacred Fire to the world, and her spirit still resides in the rocky peaks and valleys of ancient Appalachia. Marilou Awiakta abides there too, a Cherokee/Appalachian woman who stands comfortably on the threshold of the twenty-first century, seeking the center in a time of unweaving, at a time of technology without conscience, consumption without reciprocity, and alienation from the world and one another. Through her poetry, through the wisdom, humor, and patience of her ancestors and contemporary kin, Awiakta writes with the knowledge that now is, truly, "a time to reweave."[23]

The Power and Presence of Native Oral Storytelling Traditions in the Poetry of Marilou Awiakta, Kimberly Blaeser, and Marilyn Dumont

Susan Berry Brill de Ramírez

The poetry of many Native women writers brings together oral storytelling strategies from their respective Native traditions with Western poetic conventions. In much of the poetry by writers such as Marilou Awiakta (Appalachian Cherokee), Marilyn Dumont (Canadian Métis), and Kimberly Blaeser (White Earth Anishinaabe), Western literary expectations are very directly called into question. Written language can either take on a discursively positional stance or a conversively relational form. The former emphasizes the respective positions taken and presented by the writer and her (or his) writing, either speaking *to* the reader at varying degrees of separation and distance, or providing connective links through the sort of phenomenological identification between the reader and writer or persona of the poem in which the reader takes on that positionally subjective stance. In contrast to this, a conversively relational form of writing communicates *with* the listener-reader as both work together interactively through an intersubjective relationship that brings the poem-story into being through their linguistically articulated relationship. This is evident in the poetry explored herein. This poetry combines both Western literary and Native oral traditions in their forms, their orientations, and their effects. As Blaeser writes, "My work is filled with the voices of other people. It crosses boundaries of time and space, of ways of knowing, of what it means to be human."[1]

In the work of these women poets, readers are invited as listener-readers to interactively participate in the stories behind the poems much as a listener interactively co-creates the story that a storyteller tells. Such poetry requires much more work on the part of the reader to bring the poem-story into fruition. This is not a reader-response approach in which each reader as part of an interpretive reading community constructs the work in collaboration with fellow readers, but a relationally defined conversive interaction in which the poem-story comes into being through the interrelational storytelling-storylistening event that emphasizes the range of relationships that occur between the storyteller, the storylisteners, and the storycharacters, too. The co-creative nature of storytelling is such that the actual story comes into being through these relationships. The actual words of the story as told by the storyteller are only part of the story, the skeleton (if you will) that needs to be fleshed out through the interpersonal relationships of all involved. This requires a minimalist style of telling and writing that leaves room for the story-listeners and storyreaders to complete the stories through their own participation.

Unfortunately, the seemingly partial condition of many of these poems might lead readers to misconstrue such works as insufficiently developed. In fact, I would argue that such readings, while generally correct, reflect more about the practice of most readers who nowadays expect literary works to be as artificially constructed and self-contained as expository essays and textbooks. Orally informed conversive writing requires more effort on the part of the reader, who must step into the interactive role of a *listener-reader,* but the rewards of such effort are the greater. Conversive writing is both conversational in mode and transformative (with the sense of conversion) in effect. Writing that really embodies the strategies of an oral storytelling is writing that is the most empowering and enduring for its readers. As Craig Womack (Oklahoma Creek and Cherokee) writes, "scholars of Native literature need to break down the oppositional thinking that separates orality and literacy wherein the oral constitutes authentic culture and the written contaminated culture."[2] As is clear in the poetry of these three women writers, the oral and written, far from being in opposition to each other, in fact, come together in powerfully conversive written stories.

While the co-creative empowerment of storytelling has traditionally been at the center of all literatures in their oral underpinnings, it is notably central in the writings of American Indian, Alaskan Native, and Canadian First Nations writers. As Arnold Krupat notes in relation to

Leslie Marmon Silko's writing, the importance of the listeners "is entirely typical for a native storyteller who cannot go forward with a tale without the audience's response."[3] A close look at the poetry of three diverse Native women writers will show how these writers craft their work to provide the relational pathways that assist their readers in becoming interactive listener-readers of their poems. Marilou Awiakta, Kimberly Blaeser, and Marilyn Dumont draw on various conversive literary strategies (written forms from Native oral storytelling traditions) to establish the structural pathways requisite for their listener-readers' entry into the worlds of the poems. Conversive elements present in the work of these writers include line breaks and spacing for emphasis and for the listener-reader's response; a concern for the sonority of the language; a general absence of Western literary metrical forms; repetition of events (not for memory or as reminders, but for emphasis, deeper understanding, and new understandings with and within each iteration and its respective context); repeated linking words, sounds, and phrases; meaningfulness through relationality and a relative absence of semiotic forms of signification; circular, concentric, episodic, and associational structures; an interweaving and juxtaposition of the imaginary and the real, the mythic and the actual, the past and the present; heteroglossic voice shifts for greater inclusivity (especially voice shifts to the second person that enable the reader to enter the storyworld of the poem as a listening-reading participant); conversive intimacy that brings the listener-reader even closer into the poem's storyworld; verbal framing, especially with traditional or formulaic beginnings and endings; traditional, formulaic, or archaic words and phrases; stories and conversations that extend beyond the boundaries of the text; ambiguity and minimalism that require the listener-reader's contribution to complete the stories; and the centering force of the sacred.

We can see the co-creative power of conversive writing in Marilyn Dumont's "The Devil's Language." Dumont is a Canadian Métis writer of Cree descent. Her poem "The Devil's Language" ostensibly critiques the colonialist impositions of the English language upon the indigenous peoples of North America and of British literary standards upon all writers writing in the English language, regardless of their respective cultural and literary ancestries. Accordingly, the poem takes on a decidedly (op)positional stance in its complaint against the colonizing influences of educational institutions—a primary tool of the state for ideological control (what the French critic Louis Althusser refers to as an ISA, or ideological state apparatus). Nevertheless, upon closer examination, "The Devil's Language" opens itself up through the storytelling strategies of Dumont's background, inviting her readers to step into the world of her story/poem to experience the pain and intrusion of imperial impositions of linguistic and literary standards and also to experience the power and magic of transforming those very standards into the new/old way of one Native writer's literary storytelling.

In oral storytelling traditions, stories are told in ways that assist listeners' access to storied worlds. This is accomplished through storytelling strategies that ensure close connective listening for the purposes of mutual enjoyment, learning, and communal, familial, and tribal coming together. At the center of the storytelling is the relationship between the storyteller and the storylisteners, but equally important to successful storytelling are the range of relationships that come into being between the storycharacters, between the storycharacters and the teller and listeners as the teller and listeners actually become part of the story itself, and between each storylistener and all others participating in the storytelling event. Within the realm of story, this reflects the interdependency that Anna Lee Walters (Pawnee and Otoe-Missouria) and Peggy Beck explain is at the center of life itself: "The elders and the oral historians tell us that . . . our survival depend[s] on maintaining the relationships between animals, plants, rivers, feeding grounds, etc. . . . Through this interdependency and awareness of relationships, the universe is balanced."[4] All of the various relationships established during each storytelling or, for literary storytellings, each listening-reading, determine the interpersonal parameters of the stories, but it is the primary relationship between the storyteller and her listeners that establishes the centering affection and trust that, in turn, facilitates these other connections. As Luci Tapahonso explains, "showing stories or being a part of telling stories is very much a way in which affection is shown. If a person is included within the circle, then in a way it sort of implies that everyone within the circle thinks highly of each other. And so it's a way to show affection and to be included within either listening to or sharing of stories."[5]

Even in a poem as potentially confrontational as "The Devil's Language," Dumont relates her story about linguistic and literary colonization in the inclusive way of storytelling that welcomes all willing to make the requisite co-creative effort to hear the story. This is an important story to relate, and Native and non-Native readers alike are welcomed into the poem's storyworld that, at the same time, critiques and embraces the very Anglo-Canadian tradition that diversely disempowered and empowered Dumont and other Canadian First Nations writers. As Dumont writes,

> I have since reconsidered Eliot
> and the Great White way of writing English
> standard that is
> the great white way
> has measured, judged and assessed me   all my life
> by its lily white words
> its picket fence sentences
> and manicured paragraphs
> one wrong sound and you're shelved in the Native Literature
>   section
>
> .   .   .   .
>
> the Great White way could silence us all
> if we let it[6]

As Kimberly Blaeser asks,

> Looked for your books lately in Powell's
> or 57th St. Books?
> Check first in folklore or anthropology[7]

Dumont begins her poem with a presumably discursive stance, asserting her positionality as a Native writer critiquing the hegemonic imperialism of a literary establishment that expects Dumont's writing to fit British literary standards, which she refers to as the "Great White way." As she writes, "one wrong sound and you're shelved in the Native Literature section / resistance writing." It would indeed be easy to classify her work and this poem in particular as "resistance writing"—thereby neatly categorizing her work within pat ethnic definitions and cultural boundaries, but to do so would be to lose sight of much that is going on in Dumont's work. In relation to the work of several Native women writers, Jane Caputi writes, "we must resist reliance upon both traditional forms of oppositional activism as well as Western paradigms, modern or postmodern."[8] Often it is the case that the boundaries of identity politics and postcolonial interpretation actually impede our intimate entry into a poem that very openly and caringly welcomes its listener-readers into the world of the poem and the larger world of the writer-storyteller's experience and knowledge.

Even though Dumont's poem begins with a strongly articulated criticism of British imperialist literary standards that endure even today, Dumont offers her critique within a conversive celebration of that very tradition and language that she critiques. She has not rejected the English language or the literary tradition of England. Instead, in an openly conversive manner, she presents herself as a part of that very tradition, not only offering her own poem and story in English, but, further, interweaving the historicity of one "devil's language" (here referring to the Anglo-Canadian discounting and vilification of the indigenous Cree language) with another (here referring to the extent to which this very linguistic colonization by the King's English has, in fact, manifested itself as "the devil's language"). Beyond past and continuing discursive embattlements between Native and colonizing European and Euro-American languages, both "devil's languages" are brought together in Dumont's retelling of that/her story that relates both the pain and the joy of both languages and traditions that define Dumont and the world of her poem. Dumont interweaves her worlds and words into a literary conversation that redefines, expands, and enriches both traditions by the very presence of her poem and story. In Dumont's poetry, both tongues come together in an empowering voice that clearly and directly articulates larger and broader truths through the lens of Dumont's own story of "The Devil's Language."

Rather than offering a more oppositionally discursive stance that would step outside the tradition and language and argue against them from without, Dumont provides a far more powerful and enduring response to the colonization of language and literature by being in conversation with it and simply telling her own literary story and inviting readers to *listen* to that story and, thereby, become part of that story, too. In this fashion, Dumont decenters the power of the colonial story away from its colonizing center and reorients the story in a way that empowers herself and her listener-readers as participants in her story. Through carefully crafted spacing, giving time and space for her readers and listener-readers to interact with her and her words and her story, and through her occasional voice shifts to a more personal second-person voice, she provides the needed conversive pathways that help her readers

(Native and non-Native alike) to step into the conversive roles of listener-readers and actually become part of the story that is Dumont's story, but also ours now, too. As she writes, "the Great White way could silence *us* all / if *we* let it" (my emphasis). In the final section and stanza of her poem, she brings her listener-readers even more closely and intimately into her world and words by sharing her memories in such a way that the memories conversively become our own memories as well, through the powerfully transformative effect of conversive storytelling in which diverse persons and times and places all come together in story and in fact.

The first part of Dumont's poem, which she divides into three numbered sections, stays within a largely first-person voice, with occasional shifts from the more limiting self-referential first-person singular voice to the more inclusive first-person plural. In this poem, Dumont's telling of her own early experiences with the racist and colonialist education made available to her as a child and adult in Canada does not turn the focus of the larger poem primarily on herself. In contrast to much contemporary writing that presents the experiences, thoughts, and feelings of the authors for their readers' to identify with in a phenomenological manner or relate to otherwise, Dumont and many Native writers offer their personal stories less as an end in themselves and more as a means toward the larger ends of the larger stories being told. Dumont begins her poem with her own experiences to assist her readers' understandings of the colonizing conditions and effects of linguistic and literary imperialism on real persons in the world, and in the initial storytelling of the poem, Dumont's first-person plural references very directly invite the reader into the storyworld of the poem as a means of sharing in the events and experiences.

In addition to these inclusive first-person referents, Dumont includes shifts to a second-person voice intermittently throughout the poem with diverse immediate impacts and effects, but always reinforcing the storytelling intimacy between a storyteller and her listeners. In the first numbered section of the poem, Dumont switches to the second person three times. In the first two instances, the voice shifts offer a protective and necessary distancing between the related events and the specificity of the writer-storyteller's own life. One of the crucial elements of traditional Native North American storytelling traditions is what I discuss elsewhere as "a muted authorial presence that does not privilege the author but rather privileges the story and the relationship between teller-writer and listener-reader."[9] Tapahonso explains in relation to her own writing, "This writing, then, is not 'mine,' but a collection of many voices that range from centuries ago and continue into the future."[10] Albert Yava (Hopi and Tewa) clarifies this practice in relation to his own stories, noting that even though he is the linking thread throughout his stories, that does not mean that the stories are *about* him. "It is hard to put down something with myself as a center of interest—that is, to say I did this or that. It makes me out as important, which isn't the way I see it. We Tewas and Hopis don't think of ourselves that way."[11] Yava's presence in his stories reflects the fact that he can relate those particular stories about specific events because he was there. As Yava further explains, "In our histories and traditions we don't have individual heroes with names to remember. It is the village, the group, the clan that did this or that, not a man or woman."[12] It is not the specific person, character, or personality that is most important; rather it is the story and what each listener is to learn from the story that is of greatest importance. The stories are their own to come into meaningfulness through each listener-reader's engagement with them. The focus of each story is the centering connective link between each teller and listener. Often storytellers will shift the referents in their stories away from themselves even when they are one of the central characters to minimize their presence and to ensure that the focus of the story is on the larger aspects of the story rather than on one character or person. Regardless of the actual intentions involved in this strategy, such voice shifts effectively decenter the author/storyteller as one of the persons involved in the story, not as a central personage. This shift enables the continual recentering of the story around the storyworld co-created through the interactions and relationship between the listener-reader and the other persons involved in the story.

In one of the previously quoted passages from the poem, Dumont relates her own educational experiences as an Indian woman in Euro-Canadian schools: "the great white way / has measured, judged and assessed me." With this early focus ostensibly on Dumont and her own life, her storyteller's unexpected voice shift to the second person very directly reorients her listener-reader back to the actual story by turning the focus on the reader: "assessed me all my life / . . . one wrong sound and *you're* shelved in the Native Literature section" (my emphasis). Through this sudden and powerful voice shift, Dumont places her listener-reader in the very situation that she laments, having one's poetry shelved not in the poetry section of a bookstore, but in the "Native American" section.

Dumont's next voice shift to the second person follows in this pattern with the unexpected shifts and transitions that are common elements in oral storytelling practice. She writes, "the Great White way . . . / . . . had its hand over my mouth since my first day of school / . . . syntactic laws: use the wrong order or / register and you're a dumb Indian."[13] This voice shift is especially interesting in its syntactic ambiguity and complexity. Similarly to the previous example, this shift unexpectedly places the listener-reader within the storyworld of the poem as the individual suffering the painful consequences of the linguistic and literary colonization by "the Great White way." In this case, the listener-reader listens to Dumont as she steps into an explanatory mode, stating the consequences if "[you] use the wrong order or / register."[14] This added explanation helps the reader to identify more closely with the situation Dumont describes, but much more is going on here in this one brief example. By appending this second-person statement punctuated by a colon to an independent clause relating Dumont's childhood experiences, the second-person shift takes on another direction and voice, namely that of "the Great White way" (including teachers, principals, and other children warning the Indian children and, possibly, the white children, too) of the consequences of straying from the proper order and expectations of a colonial educational system: "use the wrong order or / register and you're a dumb Indian." I remember quite vividly the taunts directed to the children at my own grammar school who strayed from the expected and approved order, and the taunts we feared the most were those that came from the other children. In the storyworld of Dumont's poem and in the world of her childhood, I imagine that both Indian and white children would fear the dreaded taunt: "you're a dumb Indian."

Beyond these two voices (the storyteller stepping into the voice of the Great White way directed toward the straying child and the storyteller speaking directly to the listener-reader to explain the consequences for anyone, including the listener-reader, who does not obey the correct order), Dumont's voice shift at this point takes at least one other interesting turn. The imperative tone and syntax of the dependent clause can also be read as the storyteller's imperative order and prescriptive warning to the listener-readers of the poem: "use the wrong order or / register and you're a dumb Indian." Here, the storyteller plays on the listener-readers' familiarity with the pejorative attribution of being "a dumb Indian." Regardless of whether one's concern with being labeled "a dumb Indian" comes from an internalized or externalized racism in not wanting to be labeled an Indian (dumb or otherwise), from one's avoidance of being stigmatized by the stereotypical designation of the "dumb Indian," or simply from one's discomfort in even hearing the pejorative label, the storyteller's warning places Dumont's listener-readers in the uncomfortable position of being recipients of the very same warnings given to generations of Native Canadian and American children. As Dumont comments in another poem, in which she relates an experience at school in which a little white girl asks her publicly if she is an Indian,

> How could I respond? If I said yes, she'd reject me: worse, she might tell the other kids my secret and then they'd laugh and shun me. If I said no, I'd be lying, and when they found out I was lying, they'd shun me.
> I said "No," and walked away.[15]

As Dumont's voice shifts and other conversive literary strategies indicate, the complexities of the oral tradition as manifested in its literary transformations require much more active work on the part of the reader *as* listener-reader. In the second voice shift in "The Devil's Language," an apparently simple change in voice proves to be much more complex than might be the case in terms of grammatical syntax and linguistic structures. The greater ambiguities possible in oral delivery than in the more fixed options on the written page permit far greater complexities of meaning and connections for storylisteners and for the listener-readers of those Native literatures largely informed by the writers'/tellers' respective oral traditions. This is further evidenced in the third shift to a second-person voice in the first long section of "The Devil's Language." Similarly to the previous two voice shifts, this one turns directly to the listener-reader again, reinforcing the relationship between the teller and listener and emphasizing the inextricably crucial co-creative role of the reader as a listening-reading participant *in* the poem. In contrast to the previous shifts with their explanatory and imperative emphases, this voice shift speaks directly to the reader in the interrogative form of two questions: "how many of you speak Cree?" and "is there one?"[16] This simple question proves to be more complex than is first apparent. Dumont repeats this question, giving it added emphasis and specificity. The second question clarifies and strengthens the first: "correct Cree not correct English / grammatically correct Cree / is there one?"

In these two questions, Dumont confronts her reader's linguistic assumptions about the extent to which Cree people who speak their own language are acceptably educated and knowledgeable. The confrontational tone of these questions pushes the reader away while at the same time drawing the listener-reader even more closely into the world of the poem as the recipient of two very direct and pointed questions. These questions end the first section of the poem and are followed by blank spacing down to the bottom of the page. Here Dumont leaves the open space for the listener-reader to consider and respond to the questions. The spacing between the second and third sections is briefer, only one blank line separating the two sections. The much longer spacing between the first and second sections provides the necessary space for the listener-reader's response. I also want to point out that it is very interesting that in Dumont's storyteller voice relating this past and continuing story of linguistic and literary colonization, she frequently steps outside the boundaries of grammatically correct English to speak her story. Between the two grammatically complete questions challenging her listener-readers' capacities to speak Cree, Dumont places two dependent phrases, offered as complete declarative statements: "correct Cree not correct English / grammatically correct Cree." These two sentence fragments demonstrate Dumont's linguistic challenge to "the Great White way of writing English." While such fragments are more the rule in poetry than in prose, Dumont's placement and substance of these fragments is telling. In the co-creative storytelling world of Dumont's poem, these "fragments" are not grammatical fragments in and of themselves. In the poem, they are presented as complete ideas with a clearly conveyed meaning. The storyteller's words are not the whole story, but merely the linguistic structure of the story that comes into being through the storyteller's, storylisteners', and storycharacters' interactions with one another.

The conversive intimacy of oral storytelling traditions is manifested in the caring relationship that exists between the storyteller and the storylistener, and this relationship is at the center of the stories and the storytelling process. Even in the potentially oppositional poem "The Devil's Language," in her role as storyteller Dumont tells us a story about the racist colonization of Native peoples in Canada and those peoples' endurance toward survivance, sharing parts of her own life and experiences to help her listener-readers understand the larger story that has been the story of so many Native peoples and others in Canada and throughout the world. The content of her story could easily distance non-Native readers away from the poem, but Dumont helps us hear this story through her continual awareness of the necessary relationship between herself as storyteller-poet and her readers as listener-readers. This is the sort of relationship that descriptive psychologists Keith E. Davis and Mary K. Roberts describe as one in which "each person's world has a place for the other person in it [and] the worlds are thus shared worlds in which each other's interests and values have a place."[17] These worlds come together through the transforming and convergent power of story.

Dumont ends her poem with the conversive intimacy of a traditional storyteller, inviting us all (her listener-readers) into her (now our) own memories, family, and home: "she fed you bannock and tea / and syllables / . . . and sings you to sleep / in the devil's language."[18] From the initial oppositionality presented in the first section to the conversive intimacy of the ending, Dumont gradually brings her listener-readers into a loving Cree world in which the lullabies of one's childhood are heard and remembered "in the devil's language." The warmth and love and beauty of those songs transform any preconceived notions the listener-reader might have about the Cree language and any presumed inferiority it might have to standard English. As the poem ends, these remembered Cree songs bring us full circle back to the judgment of Native poetry as categorically distinct from other poetry and thereby removed to be shelved in a separate Native section. Rather than permitting us to objectify the Cree lullaby in ethnocentric terms, Dumont leaves us with those songs as part of our now collective and personal memory of childhood intimacies and loving dreams. As Simon J. Ortiz (Acoma) writes, "The stories. The words in the stories. / They go on in some way, leading away / from a start, even away from me, and then / finding their own road, getting lost / at times until they discover the way / there is to go."[19]

This relationship between storyteller and listener is also evident throughout Kimberly M. Blaeser's recent collection of poetry, *Trailing You*. Although the volume is named after one particular poem dedicated to one specific person, the title of the volume is more open ended, providing a direct link between the reader and Blaeser. By choosing to name the volume *Trailing You*, Blaeser offers her poems to her listener-readers with the assurance that in return for our engagements with her poems, she will respond in turn. As she assures us, she is following us and watching us—"trailing us." Following in the traditions of oral storytelling, Blaeser, like Dumont, provides the necessary trails or pathways for her readers to become conversive listener-readers, actually stepping into the worlds and words of her poems, even beginning with the chosen title of the book.

One of the very first pathways Blaeser offers her listener-readers into the storyworlds of her volume takes a visual form. The page that faces the title page includes thirteen photographs from Blaeser's collection of family photos. Much as in Leslie Marmon Silko's volume *Storyteller,* in which photos from Silko's own world are interspersed with her stories and poems, the fact that Blaeser begins her volume with these very personal photos emphasizes the originating importance of the world out of which her poems are created. As she says, "My work is filled with the voices of other people."[20] Her book both provides a means for Blaeser to re-member into her life those who are part of her world ("Like many Indian people, I write partly to remember, because remembering, we recover; remembering, we survive")[21] and a means for Blaeser's listener-readers to re-member themselves into that world, too. As she further explains, "poetry is connection and these are the connections—the poetry —we all carry in our soul, the poetry that writers try to bring to the surface."[22] It is significant that Blaeser does not identify the photos or the persons in them. They are simply presented as a beginning visual representation of her world—a world that meaningfully informs every subsequent poem in the volume. Blaeser's listener-readers are conversively welcomed into her world, but that welcome is gradual, just as Marilyn Dumont gradually brings her listener-reader into the close intimacy of her own world in "The Devil's Language."

The first sections of Blaeser's book offer depictions from her recent experiences, thoughts, and feelings. Discussions about her family and home back on the White Earth Reservation are somewhat guarded, presented from a safe distance away from the bounds of the reservation. For most of the readers of the volume, who are unlikely to be members of the Chippewa tribe, or residents of White Earth, the initial sections of the volume provide the needed transitional distance for listener-readers to gradually wend their way from their own worlds through the worlds of Blaeser's early poems and finally to the later poems that bring her listener-readers more directly and closely into the world of her family and tribal community: "I wonder if these poems are the path I make and I wonder / how far it is / to shore."[23]

The middle section of the book is also titled "Trailing You." By this point, Blaeser begins to bring her listener-readers even more closely into her world, as the poems become less textually poetic and more conversively storied. This pivotal section provides the needed "trail" that continues to bring the listener-readers to White Earth, the arrival finally occurring in the last section, titled "Sewing Memories." As Blaeser writes in the title poem of this section, "One of the best things about the threads of this sewing / is that they keep pulling in more / more people, more years, more colors of events."[24] This interweaving brings together not only the remembered people of her past and present, but all of us, too.

"Sewing Memories: This Poem I've Wanted to Write" is the longest piece in the volume, being divided into two long sections. Here Blaeser interweaves many of the various threads of the volume and her life into one poem that she tells us she's been wanting to write. The poem is ostensibly about her memories centering around the ever-present activity for women in her community, namely sewing. When I first read this poem, I had a hard time with it. I didn't want to make the conversive effort necessary to open myself up to this piece. Other poems were easier for me to connect with, and I wanted to write about them, but this poem and section of the book kept drawing me in. For several days, I tried to convince myself to write about another poem, until I finally gave in and settled down to work on this poem and its sewing memories of the prom dress that didn't fit in a crucial area, the sleeves sewn upside down, the skirt made from an old pair of pants after a fire destroyed just about everything else, the ridicule in school from not knowing how to use the school's electric sewing machine, a first quilt, a lucky dress, memories upon memories that cut across generations. For Blaeser, sewing is more than a metaphor that brings times and places and people together in remembered stories; it is one of the central activities that brought people and generations together through the co-creative love and artistry that made "that pink and white gingham dress . . . / . . . decorated all across the hem with black cross-stitching / . . . [and] my lucky dress with the covered buttons."[25] Explaining the importance of sewing in her family and community, Blaeser says:

Into all those things we made
  we sewed bits of our bodies
  and bits of our dreams

> we stitched in errors more bold
> than those required in sand paintings
> And what we created seemed truly to be ours[26]

The sacredness of this act of sewing is evident in Blaeser's comparison of it with the sacred sand paintings of the Navajo: both are acts of creation, both ways of telling stories in their respective media, both creations of beauty in the world, much like Blaeser's own poetic creation that brings all three together in her written poetic story. Leslie Marmon Silko explains in a letter to James Wright: "in one sand painting or another all things in Creation are traced out in sand." Continuing, Silko says this is also the case with words: "What I learned for myself was that words can function like the sand."[27] Reading myself into Blaeser's "Sewing Memories" as a listener-reader, I realized that this is also true in sewing and, I would imagine, in any form of human creation. In these three (and other) ways of creating/telling stories, we see and hear persons and places and times and worlds brought together in each telling, thereby creating the new worlds that can come into being only through their telling.

In the telling of "Sewing Memories" that I listened myself into, I found that this poem that Kim Blaeser had been wanting to write was the poem/story that I'd been trying not to hear for much of my life. My mother's rural Appalachian background was a world kept far away from most of us growing up under the East Coast influence of my father's educated Jewish Manhattan family. In contrast to the sewing world of Blaeser's family, in my family, the sewing and creating never really was co-creative in the sense of really bringing us together. There were simply too many racial, ethnic, familial, class, and generational barriers that kept pulling us all apart in spite of my mom's attempts at wholeness. Maybe it was the lack of faith and agnosticism that emptied out some of the past pain. Maybe it was the electroshock, Thorazine/Melleril, and psych wards that sedated my mom from the past generations of loss, pain, and confusions we all suffered without the strength of the sacred. As a small child watching the struggles toward and away from survivance, it just seemed that the old-time efforts (sewing, cooking, growing much of our own fruits and vegetables, etc.) never worked the way they were supposed to. Somehow my mother's sewing became the sign of all that we (especially the women) were supposed to struggle away from . . . in silence and without the stories that would have helped bring our worlds and times together as we really needed. While writing this essay, I asked my sister about our mother's sewing, and she got really angry. Something about some saved baby-sitting money that was spent on fabric for a special dress that my mom never got around to making, even though the money had already been spent and the fabric bought. When she related that story to me, I thought my sister's anger (still strong after forty years) was funny, but now as I re-member the place of sewing in our family, I realize that it offered us the elusive dreams of continuance and faith and strength that always seemed to be just beyond our grasp. As Blaeser writes, "these pieces of time / all multi-colored and mismatched fashion / tell their own stories / of life lived in loss and in longing."[28]

When it was time for me to learn to sew, I resisted, afraid that the learning would pull me back into that world that no one really spoke much about. Television shows like *The Beverly Hillbillies, Green Acres,* and *Hootenanny* reinforced my embarrassment about our silent family roots. And yet those roots never really were silent; they were there in the sewing: "I remember you sewing away your loneliness / days when we were at school / . . . / I remember all the Barbie Doll clothes you made / . . . / I remember the matching outfits you sewed / . . . / Others I remember because there was so much of you in them."[29] When it was time for me to learn how to sew, the old black Singer sewing machine was brought downstairs for me to learn on. I must admit that there was a special beauty to that old machine, and there was something very satisfying about the touch of foot to pedal and hand to cloth. When the old machine was moved to the attic for good, being replaced with a new electric one, the absence of that machine was a reality whose loss was felt but not acknowledged by either my mom or me. Almost as if this one more loss signaled the eventual end we so desperately sought to avoid in our race toward it. After the purchase of the electric sewing machine, my mother's sewing faded into the past like the old black pedal Singer sewing machine that had been banished out of sight. In Blaeser's poem, she writes about those inevitable changes that can be embraced without denying or rejecting that which becomes past.

When we moved into this house
    and I unpacked
    I put on many of those stories of my past
    and remembered you with love

and all our times
of happiness and of sadness
and found them all to have their own beauty

. . . .
. . . . stories
of life lived in loss and in longing
and yet in fulfillment, too[30]

When I began to work on Blaeser's "Sewing Memories," little did I realize the extent to which her stories and memories would invite my own to become interwoven with hers. But then, this is the nature of poetry and storytelling, as we are all brought together in words and in story and in fact. As Greg Sarris (Coast Miwok and Pomo) points out, "the context of orality covers the personal territory of those involved in the exchange."[31] Just as the accomplished storyteller ensures permeable boundaries between the actual storytelling event and all those other events and times and places and persons potentially relevant to the story, Blaeser opens her own memories and stories up to her listener-readers, inviting us all gradually into her worlds and remembrances. But our movement into Blaeser's world is not so linearly one directional. All true storytelling is definitionally circular, associational and thereby episodic, and interactively co-creative. Blaeser offers her episodically interwoven memories to her listener-readers to interweave our own sewing (and other) memories into these remembered stories.

In the fashion of traditional oral storytellers, Blaeser offers her stories to us through her highly crafted poetry in which she uses many of the conversive skills of the expert storyteller, including repetition, ambiguity, minimalism, and the conversive intimacy of the telling that brings all closely together. The minimalism that is one of the trademarks of oral storytelling requires the listener (and here, listener-reader) to complete the sketched-out story to bring it to life. Blaeser's ever-so-brief brush strokes merely allude to so many different sewing memories, each of which might bring to mind very real memories for her listener-readers. When Blaeser writes, "I remember you sewing away your loneliness," with a line break at this point, I, too, remember my own mother "sewing away [her] loneliness." When Blaeser writes, "I remember the matching outfits you sewed," also followed by a line break, I remember those matching Christmas outfits that my mom made.[32] Even though the subsequent lines help to specify Blaeser's own memories, the minimalism, occasional ambiguity, and pauses (line, stanza, and section breaks) open her words and stories further up to her listener-readers. And the powerful repetition of the first-person refrain, "I remember . . . ," additionally invites us all to remember our own sewing memories. As Blaeser explains in her book *Gerald Vizenor: Writing in the Oral Tradition,* "Oral culture thus owes its vitality, at least in part, to the relational contexts of language."[33]

Even though "Sewing Memories" relates past and present experiences from Blaeser's own life, through the conversive storytelling voice of the poem those experiences are offered to her listener-readers as the beginning base for all our stories to be potentially woven together. David Moore explains that "relationality across time and space entirely blurs the boundaries of subject and object, of human and nature, of persons."[34] Reed Way Dasenbrock notes, "Precisely the opposite of the Western tradition of closure and boundaries obtains: stories are valued for their overlap, for the way they lead to new stories in turn."[35] As Blaeser tells us toward the end of her poem, "One of the best things about the threads of this sewing / is that they keep pulling in more / more people, more years, more colors of events / and the stitches can attach all the things of memory."[36] Just as the remembered sewing stories tell of the beauty of clothes created out "of happiness and of sadness," "in loss and in longing," "with love," "and yet in fulfillment, too," so too are Blaeser's poems offered to her readers for our own conversive responses.[37] Is "fulfillment" too strong a word for our receipt of Blaeser's poems? I think not, for her poems, like Dumont's, are stories that elicit in their listener-readers potentially transforming responses. This has certainly been the case for my reading of/listening to "Sewing Memories," much as I tried to resist the welcoming voice in the poem. For those *listener*-readers guided to Blaeser's White Earth over the course of the volume, from the first section "Living History" to the last "Sewing Memories," we are now part of these events and times and worlds; through story, they have become a part of our own worlds. As Sarris explains, "The dialogue that starts in one place opens the text and the readers' stories of their relationships with the text, stories that, in turn, inform other readers' stories."[38] This is the very process that Leslie Marmon Silko (Laguna Pueblo) describes as "the boundless capacity of language which, through storytelling, brings us together, despite great distances between cultures, despite great distances in time."[39]

Throughout *Trailing You*, Blaeser provides the needed conversive pathways to assist our journeys through her words and worlds. The early photos of her family offer an introductory visual sketch that begins her listener-readers' journeys to White Earth, and the poems and stories in "Sewing Memories" provide our final welcoming arrival. Where Blaeser ends her volume, Marilou Awiakta begins, welcoming her listener-readers immediately into her Appalachian Cherokee world. Just as Dumont and Blaeser conversively interweave their worlds and words and listener-readers, Awiakta welcomes her listener-readers into the Appalachian worlds of Cherokee country and the Oak Ridge nuclear facility. Although Awiakta is very critical of Oak Ridge, that is nevertheless part of her ancestry and world, and in the inclusive fashion of oral storytelling traditions, Awiakta interweaves both Cherokee and Oak Ridge worlds with an informed welcome that from a discursively oppositional stance is shocking, but from a conversively relational approach makes complete sense. She even begins her volume with a quotation from the father of atomic energy, Albert Einstein, who writes, "The fairest thing we can experience is the mysterious."[40] And with this quote, Awiakta welcomes her listener-readers into the mysteriously, and often disturbingly, intertwined worlds of atomic energy and Cherokee mountain country. In *Abiding Appalachia: Where Mountain and Atom Meet*, Awiakta interweaves these worlds with a healing energy that moves her listener-readers in life-giving directions and reminds us that her mountains and her people have the enduring survivance of the centuries. As she writes, "My mountains are very old."[41]

To help her readers become listener-readers of her Appalachian story, Awiakta (like Blaeser and Dumont) uses a range of conversive literary strategies. Right from the beginning, Awiakta takes an intimate voice, welcoming us into the worlds of her poems and her own life. As Caputi explains, quoting from Awiakta's volume *Selu*, " 'They' and 'we' are inseparable for, in the traditional wisdom of the Cherokee, 'All of creation is one family. We are all interconnected, sacred.' "[42] This intimacy pervades the volume, beginning with her credo poem, "An Indian Walks in Me." This poem tells us the story of Awiakta's Cherokee ancestry, its telltale signs left "in hair and cheek" and in the ever-present pull of the land. Here and elsewhere, Awiakta uses spacing on the page to invite her listener-readers to respond interactively to her words. She writes:

"These [rustling leaves] speak."
She said the same of sighing wind,

of hawk descending on the hare
and Mother's care to draw
the cover snug around me,
of copperhead coiled on the stone
and blackberries warming in the sun—
"These speak."   I listened . . .[43]

Both in her repetition of the refrain "These speak" and in the blank spacing that follows each of these statements, Awiakta invites her listener-readers to listen to and hear the voices of her world. Initially, the assertion of fact and invitation to listen come from her mother, telling Awiakta as a child, "[Listen.] These speak." First, we watch Awiakta as she is taught to listen to the voices of the world around her. Then, Awiakta turns directly to us, reminding us and re-emphasizing in her reiteration that there are voices that we all must listen to: "These speak." In her response, "I listened . . . ," Awiakta and we, too, briefly pause and listen to those voices. Both iterations conclude their respective sentences and are followed by either the spacing of a line break (in the first appearance) or blank spacing in the middle of a line (in the second appearance), thereby serving to further emphasize the passages to her listener-readers and offer the space necessary for us to respond to Awiakta's story and her invitation to join her in listening to the voices.

In the very next poem, "Prayer of the Poet-Hunter," Awiakta draws her listener-readers back in time and into mythic space by means of these same conversive strategies. In this poem, she writes about a mythic ancestor of the Cherokee, the chief of the Deer, Awi Usdi, who speaks to the Cherokee people with his words of guidance: "When I shall hear my grandchildren I shall hold up their heads."[44] Speaking directly to him, Awiakta writes, "Because you have said it, draw near and listen. . . ."[45] These words are followed by an ellipsis and additional blank spacing, which provide the co-creative spatial silence for the listener-reader's response. Here we are invited to join Awi Usdi as we listen to Awiakta's story and a poet-hunter's prayer. In "The Coming of Little Deer: A Myth of the Cherokee," the *small white chief of the Deer* asks, "Have you heard . . . ," followed by an ellipsis and blank spacing for the awaited response.[46] Interweaving the atomic energy industry and ancient Cherokee mountains, Awiakta underscores the importance of our responses, for our responses to her stories and to all of creation that our very survival is dependent upon. As she ends "The Graphite Queen," a poem about the nuclear reactor, "No answer comes. No sign. No sound. Except the wind . . . that lifts our thoughts and spins them into silent hope."[47] But that hope turns to us, asking whether we will begin to tell new stories, which are the same as the old stories, in which life and the sacred and hope and human continuance are returned to their centering place. Remembering back to go forward. As Blaeser notes, quoting a friend of hers, "Sometimes you have to go in the wrong direction / to get where you're heading."[48]

The poetry of Marilou Awiakta, Kimberly M. Blaeser, and Marilyn Dumont demonstrates the conversive (conversative and transformative) strategies of their respective Native oral storytelling traditions—traditions whose stories were and still are presented in the various forms of story, chant, prayer, and song (forms that throughout the ages have always served as the origins of written literatures). As Simon J. Ortiz notes, "contrary to those who say the 'old ways' are dissipating and disappearing, oral tradition narrative is still the main way in which human cultural knowledge is conveyed today."[49] Contemporary creative work by American Indian, Alaskan Native, and Canadian First Nations peoples does not need to be in the forms of oral performance to reflect the power and presence of those oral traditions. Evident in the range of conversive literary strategies present in the poetry of these three Native women writers, Native storytelling traditions endure not only in their more traditional oral forms, but also very powerfully in their new literary forms. As Ortiz writes, "Story has its own power, and the language of story is of that power. We are within it, and we are empowered by it. . . . Simply put, story speaks for us."[50]

Ain't Seen You Since

Dissent among Female Relatives in

American Indian Women's Poetry

Patricia Clark Smith

Until very recently, I think it was relatively easy for a casual reader to tell if a poem was American Indian in origin, whether the poem was traditional or contemporary, and even if the author's name was something sneaky like Johnson instead of Running Wolf.* A reader could almost certainly identify such a poem by its subject matter, and often by its diction and sound as well. A quick flip through most anthologies of American Indian poetry compiled before ten or more years ago will prove the point.[1]

The American Indian poet—usually presumed to be a male, a "brave," unless the song in question happened to deal with corn grinding or child soothing—was most given to speaking of nature or praising the gods or urging them to do something, like bring rain, or simply desiring them to continue in their cycles of existence. The poet might—rather touchingly, considering what we know in retrospect of his romantic destiny to fade away—boast of the prowess of himself and his people in hunting and warfare, of the beauty of his woman, or of his whole way of being. Sometimes he gave voice to sorrow over death or a reluctant lover, but his stance was almost always nobly resigned. He was never crabby or depressed about the vagaries of human life. Even granted that there was and is a genuine American Indian cultural tendency away from what A. Grove Day calls "the soul cry of the impassioned individualist," it does seem especially remarkable, and not at all in accord with the '49ing spirit of his present-day descendants, that the poet's hard times never seemed to arouse in him either wit or satire.[2] If we rely on most of the anthologies and

Bureau of American Ethnology (BAE) collections, we will conclude that the American Indian poet's emotional world is always either joyous or solemn. For all we know from what has come down to us through the work of anthropologists and translators, the Indian did not in any form of literature save oratory—and, later, autobiography—concern himself with contemporary conditions of soldiers and forts, boarding schools and treaties, trading posts and removals.

As far as form is concerned, if we are to believe English translations and "renditions" of the songs, we must assume that American Indian poets of all tribes were inclined to a quaint archaic diction sprinkled with *Lo!*'s and *thou*'s and awkwardly inverted sentence order, as in this Omaha ritual chant for the sick:

Aged one, eçka

He! The small grasses grow about thee, ecka,
Thou sittest as though making of them thy dwelling place, ecka,
He! Verily thou sittest as though covered with the droppings of birds. . . .[3]

Most popular poetry in English was a long time catching up with Wordsworth's plea for "language really used by men," but the unusually archaic poetic language assigned to the American Indian poet in translation seems in keeping with the fading-into-the-twilight quality of the entire culture. Finally, the poems, as they appear in the old collections, are marked by a strongly rhythmical and repetitive character, not because a recorder or editor made a concerted attempt to reproduce the intricacies of a given rhythm, the particular pattern made by a given phrase repeated with slight variations, but because *any* use of rhythm or repetition served to give the effect of primitiveness, for that is what all primitive peoples do with their language—speak simply and carry a big drumstick.

I have been mocking the worst Anglo versions of traditional American Indian poetry, and of course I have exaggerated at the expense of some fine early scholars who did what they could and did some things well and with great sympathy for another culture and an alien language. I apologize to their bones. But certainly those early collectors missed a great deal. Their expectations influenced what they asked to hear, what they chose to record, and especially how they rendered what they heard into English. The astounding thing to me is how many characteristics of the old BAE collections, and how many more marks of the sentimental "renditions" fashioned from them, appear in the sort of American Indian poetry that has until very recently been most widely anthologized. The kind of poetry I am speaking of, often written in workshops at schools like the Institute of American Indian Arts in Sante Fe, is very close in its technique and tone to many nineteenth- and early twentieth-century versions of Plains love songs and Woodlands laments. It is strongly biased toward American Indian themes, and it is conventional, as opposed to traditional; that is, cradleboards and dances and spirits of one stripe or another are rife, but if there is, say, a dance, that dance seems to have little connection with the Gallup ceremonial or the powwows and '49s, or even with a dance occurring in its natural setting and sequence at an active pueblo. The poet appears to have written the work, not after experiencing something firsthand or reaching back into personal or family memory, but rather after being tied down in a dark room with a headset strapped on and forced to listen to tape after tape of the works of Natalie Curtis and Alice Corbin Henderson. A friend calls such works "eagle feather poetry." Perhaps these poems come about because teachers find it difficult not to voice, aloud or silently, expectations of what an "Indian poem"—or a fourth grade poem or a Chicano poem, for that matter—should be about. But I am not sure this is necessarily the cause, any more than I know why my freshmen on the University of New Mexico campus, who are certainly not readers of scholarly journals, often write critical prose that reads like a parody of the dreariest paragraph in *Dissertation Abstracts.* Perhaps all beginning poets find it difficult not to sense the world's expectations of what their poems should be about. In any case, my point is that for the general public not in touch with certain small presses, American Indian poetry has probably meant, if it meant anything, something like this:

> Thus it was I heard the feet beat—
> My ear down,
> On the ground—
> Yea, I put my lips to thee and drank song,
> My mother,
> O, ho![4]

or this Sigmund Rombergian lyric:

> August is laughing across the sky
> Laughing while paddle, canoe and I,

Drift, drift
Where the hills uplift
On either side of the current swift.

. . . .

Dip, dip,
While the waters flip
In foam as over their breast we slip.[5]

or these contemporary poems:

Sun dancers
Whirling, twirling madly—
Feet churning Mother Earth
Until clouds weep.[6]

An eagle wings gracefully
    through the sky.
On the earth I stand
    and watch.
My heart flies with it.[7]

Only during the last ten years or so, largely through the work of a few editors and a few small presses, has poetry appeared that is both genuinely American Indian and genuinely fresh contemporary poetry.[8] This is not to say that American Indians have not written such poetry before now; they have, but their work has seldom seen print. The latest and most inclusive source of good American Indian poetry is Geary Hobson's *The Remembered Earth*, and, as Hobson remarks in his introduction, many recent poems share subjects with the larger culture, and are not exclusively devoted to American Indian themes.[9] Of course, many poems do deal freshly with traditional culture, but a great number concern themselves with contemporary life on and off the reservation; in these works one finds bars and anthropologists, '49s and soybean fields, and, as the title of a book by one poet, nila northSun, suggests, Diet Pepsi and Nacho cheese. Moreover, there are poems on themes important to anyone living in America these last years—Vietnam, outer space—and themes that have always been important to people in all places and circumstances—youth and age, love and death, nature and loneliness.

The American Indian poet, then, is no longer writing inside a box fashioned of birchbark or woven willow. But, as Hobson also suggests, even if a poet shares themes and techniques with other poets, "emphases may differ." I think we have come to a time when it is both possible and compelling to ask whether there is something that might be called a contemporary American Indian "way" of writing poetry—if, despite their undisputed citizenship in the world at large, these American Indian poets do share something. I want to talk about a relatively narrow category— poems by contemporary American Indian women about female relatives— to see what these poets are saying, how they say things, whether these poets, different as they are, have anything special in common, and whether they differ in any marked way from Anglo women poets also writing about mothers and daughters and grandmothers.

II

I do not pretend to be an expert on the emotional landscapes of either Anglo or American Indian women, and one needs to be especially wary of generalizations, given the great differences not only among American Indian tribal cultures but among the wide variety of Anglo groups as well. Instead of starting with pronouncements about the nature of relations between female relatives in any group, I prefer to work with the poetry itself. I want to begin with a brief, nonstatistical survey of an anthology convenient to the purpose—Lyn Lifshin's *Tangled Vines: A Collection of Mother and Daughter Poems.* Save for the works of a few black writers like Lucille Clifton and Nikki Giovanni, Lifshin's selection presents the works of contemporary white American poets and is, to my mind, an excellent representative collection of poetry on the subject of mothers and daughters.

Browsing through these poems, one is of course aware of the diversity of what the poets choose to emphasize about mother-daughter-grandmother-aunt relations, and one also notices the wide variety of tone and technique. But if one happens to have read a good deal of American Indian women's poetry on the same subject, one is also likely to notice certain things these Anglo poems share that are simply not to be found in American Indian women's writing. Most strikingly, a surprising number of the Anglo poems in Lifshin's anthology—a good half—center on a woman seeing a woman relative as an alarming, alien creature. I would like to discuss this characteristic Anglo imagery at length and to ask what American Indian women poets use in place of such imagery.

In the Anglo poetry, the image of the woman relative as alien can range all the way from seeing the other woman as suddenly unfamiliar in some way to seeing her as a monster. The alien creature, be she daughter or mother, is at best disquieting, at worst genuinely life-threatening, in her estrangement. Mothers may see their daughters as usurping, draining, devouring strangers who have somehow invaded their lives; daughters see mothers as ogres out to mold, reshape, and imprison them and thwart their growth. A few passages from these Anglo poems will provide examples of the kind of imagery I am speaking of. Here are mothers on the subject of daughters:

> Her feet
> are bare. I hear her breathe
> where I can't get in. If I
> break through to her, she will
> drive nails into my tongue.[10]

> My daughter has no teeth. Her mouth is wide.
> It utters such dark sounds it cannot be good.[11]

> I think, although I fear to know for certain,
> that she becomes a cat at night.
> Just yesterday, I saw tiger shadows
> on the wall of her room. . . .[12]

And daughters on mothers:

> Like small crazed animals
> We leaped before her
> Knowing there was no escape

> She had to consume us utterly
> Over and over again
> And now at last
> We are her angels
> Burned so crisp
> We crumble when we try to touch[13]

> My mother
> the magician

can make eggs
appear in her hand.
My ovaries
appear in her hand, black as figs and
wrinkled as fingers on wash-day.[14]

she turned her face to stone
her curly hair to snakes

. . . .

trying to escape her children.[15]

I had about as much chance, Mother,
as the carp who thrashed
in your bathtub on Friday,
swimming helplessly back and forth
in small hard pool you made for me. . . .[16]

From wider reading, I feel safe in saying that the profusion of imagery in these examples does not simply reflect a bias on the part of this particular anthologist. In my culture, or at least among the woman poets of my culture, it does seem common for daughter to regard mother, mother to regard daughter, as some sort of stranger—unreachable, unknowable, and threatening to her identity. Whether unknowingly or by intent, whether by her actions or by her mere presence, the mother inspires fear and wonder. Perhaps there is among us an arrested fixation on the stage of our development when, as Nancy Friday puts it in her popular book on mothers and daughters, we realized with amazement and rage that "we could not control Mother, that she was *not* us, that she could go away and leave us," or that she could do things to us that showed us plainly that our desires and hers were not in harmony.[17] In the works of mothers writing about daughters, the moment that takes great hold on our imaginations seems to be the time when a woman perceives that the life she has borne, once part of her own body, is now a separate and quite willful entity. (It may be that this moment makes mothers more uneasy if the child is a daughter; perhaps women *expect* men, and hence a man-child, to be different.)

The image of mother or daughter as *other* is central to a good many Anglo women's poems that are positive in their tone; because such imagery is used does not mean that the poem is not about loving. Often, the climax of a poem is a resolution of the sense of otherness. Daughter or mother finally acknowledges the humanity or mortality of the other woman; accepts her as simply a person rather than as a mythical figure of frightening, unpredictable power; begins to see human connections and resemblances between herself and the other woman; or comes to some adult and freeing perception about the nature of mother-daughter alienation:

> Dear clown, dear savage daughter
> So different from me and yet
> So much like me, I know
>
> . . . .
>
> Sharpening your claws on me first
> Is how you begin to grow.[18]

> I have made hot milk
> & kissed you where you are.
> I have cursed my curses.
> I have cleared the air.
> & now I sit here writing,
> breathing you.[19]

The image of a woman relative as an alien being simply does not appear in American Indian women's poetry. I don't mean to say that dissent between women is absent from that poetry; it is not, although its occurrence is far rarer than in mainstream poetry. But when an American Indian woman poet speaks of separation between female relatives, she does not depict it as a mythologized personal struggle between two individual women. What separates the two is not a quest on the part of one or both for power or ascendancy, nor is it a sense that the antagonist is somehow of another order of being altogether. Instead, American Indian women poets see personal discord between women as a matter of cultural alienation.[20] A female relative—a mother, for example—may seem strange, not because she is a Medusa or a harpy or a killer of her hapless carp-child, but because the daughter literally cannot speak to her, since the mother's language and ways are literally, not just metaphorically, different from the ways of the daughter. Language, custom, and geographical environment, rather than psychological barriers, effect the separation between the generations.

One might raise the possibility that American Indian women are not psychologically sophisticated enough, or poetically honest enough, to deal strongly and directly with conflict between women relatives in their poems. But surely this is not so; we are talking about poets who display great honesty and sophistication in writing about other matters, and it seems unlikely that relationships among women would be the single subject they would all choose to sentimentalize, to sidestep. It seems far more likely that for all the diversity of American Indian tribal backgrounds and circumstances, there is something here that might be called a genuine cultural tendency, a tendency to see conflict between women as not totally a personal matter but, rather, as part of a larger whole, as a sign that one of the pair has lost touch not with just a single individual but with a complex web of relationships and reciprocities. The tendency to see family conflict as inevitable, natural, even healthy and worthy of being encouraged in some measure is a mark of Anglo culture. We may regret certain things; for instance, we may speculate, as Friday does, that a greater sexual honesty between mothers and daughters might ease our estrangement from one another. Nonetheless, we accept separation, rebelliousness, alienation between the generations of women as the not entirely regrettable norm.[21] This is not at all the sense of family one finds in American Indian women's poetry.

Of all American Indian women poets, Marnie Walsh (Dakota) and nila northSun (Shoshone-Chippewa) are probably the sharpest depicters of the breakdown of family. Both write in a tragicomic tone, often in first-person narratives flatly presented in a colloquial reservation English that rings wonderfully true. Their comic sense is both bitter and wise; as Carter Revard remarks, Walsh tells these grim stories of reservation life in Coyote's voice, a Trickster's and survivor's voice.[22] To tell stories of separation and fallings away with such wit and perspective is to survive, to go on, to surmount pain.

When Walsh and northSun speak of the separation between women relatives, they refer to a *cultural* separation, precisely the kind of gap that exists, as northSun puts it in the title of one of her poems, between "the way and the way things are."[23] Walsh's "Bessie Dreaming Bear: Rosebud, So. Dak. 1960" pares the story about mothers and daughters down to its barest bones:

we all went to town one day
went to a store

bought you new shoes
red high heels

ain't seen you since[24]

northSun's stories, too, have to do with separations brought about in large part by the lure of a larger culture that offers plastic shoes and Diet Pepsi. In an entire cycle of poems, she describes with greater leisure than Walsh the gaps and connections between a number of women in a single family.[25] The alienation in these poems happens not all in a moment, after one Saturday morning purchase at Woolco, but over three, perhaps even six, generations. Most poems in the group treat with affection, humor, and poignancy the granddaughter-speaker's maternal grandmother, "gramma." The speaker's parents and siblings, who come into the poems very little, are obviously West Coast urban; we learn that gramma's children have married Anglos and moved away. But, for the speaker, to return to gramma's house on the Paiute-Shoshone reservation is to return to the center of something, if not precisely the center of her own being. There, "the way" at least temporarily envelopes her, even if she is always slightly an outsider at heart; her cousin, not the speaker, can talk Indian and must translate when gramma isn't in the mood to speak English or feels the need to "say indian words / if the english ones embarrassed her / quithup for shit / moobee-ship for snot."[26]

The grandmother's world is touched by the larger culture in that those around her drink Kool-Aid, smoke Salems, and watch Lawrence Welk. But these are small encroachments. This gramma still prefers to "talk Indian." Her ancestors built brush shelters in summer; she moves her bed outside under the shade of the trees during the high heat. Spirits, at least of one sort, are still real for her: the affectionate, attention-demanding ghost of grandpa plagues her at night. The social controls of tribe and family are something she has felt strongly, even if she has not always complied with them; she lives where she does because she had to move away from home after violating a marriage custom by running off with the fiancé of her sister, who, as eldest, was supposed to marry first; she respected her mother-in-law enough to bear twelve children, trying for the male child the mother-in-law had hoped for. And, above all, this gramma tells stories. northSun's poems about her early years in gramma's house abound with circular, reciprocal imagery of shared food, space, talk, activity:

on hot summer days gramma laid
on a bed under one of the trees
she'd visit with my mother in the shade
drinking kool-aid
smoking salems
talking indian
we made mud pies
dozens & dozens of mud pies

.   .   .   .

when evening started to come
so did the mosquitoes &
we all went into the house
grandpa would come home[27]

we would whisper from our beds
"gramma tell us stories"
we all slept in the big living room
my cousin
us 3 kids
& gramma

.   .   .   .

late at night
she'd whisper back from her bed[28]

The night comes when, asked for another story, she whispers that she
has no more stories to tell: "ask your mother / she can tell you more."[29]
But exactly what more the speaker's mother can tell is not clear. She can
"talk Indian," although she has not taught her own children to do so. And
although she has elected only occasionally to visit gramma's bed under
the tree—that radiating center—the mother is clearly closer to "the way"
than her daughter; she is less a dweller in the world of Diet Pepsi and
Nacho cheese. In the title poem of northSun's book, the mother reminds
her speaker-daughter, perhaps wistfully, that when the daughter was a
child she ate with relish foods nourishing and natural, foods that suggest
a rich and earth-connected life, foods that the poet makes seem valuable
in more than a nutritional sense:

my mother says when I was little
i liked it all

crab crayfish ketchup cauliflower
asparagus pumpkin pie rabbit deer
quail pheasants prawns & rice rudding. . . .[30]

This urban-born daughter has, by now, limited her menu to convenience
foods—"it makes / it easy to figure out"—and by implication her life, too,
is limited, less nourishing than it once was, poorer than her gramma's has
been. As she says in another poem, "moving camp too far":

i don't know what it
    was to hunt buffalo
    or do the ghost dance
but

. . .

i can eat buffalo meat
    at the tourist burger stand
i can dance to indian music
    rock-n-roll hey-a-hey-o
i can
    & unfortunately
    i do[31]

The grandmother, for all her warm sense of family, with which
northSun endows her in other poems, is at a loss to understand her pizza-
eating grandchildren; perhaps this is why she feels that she has "no more
stories to tell" and that her daughter, the speaker's mother, can tell more
useful stories. In a cultural sense, the grandchildren she loves have become strangers:

gramma thinks about her grandchildren
they're losing the ways
don't know how to talk indian
don't understand me when
i ask for tobacco
don't know how to skin a rabbit
sad sad
they're losing the ways

but gramma
you told your daughters
marry white men

told them they would have
nicer houses
fancy cars
pretty clothes
could live in the city

gramma your daughters did
they couldn't speak indian anymore
how could we grandchildren learn
there are no rabbits to skin
in the city
we have no gramma there to
teach us the ways

you were still on the reservation
asking somebody anybody
please
get me tobacco[32]

The granddaughter accuses gramma of having begun the process of alienation. For all her warmth and strong identity, she has urged her own daughters down a road from whence there is no turning back, though none of them may have anticipated that.

One interesting thing about this poem is northSun's attitude toward the grandmother's failure as a teacher. Anglo poets often show a marked fear of the older woman who will insist on telling others what to do:

She thinks of my life
as a bed only she
can make right[33]

              you would
pull me from my element

. . . .

scrape away the iridescence
chop me into bits and pieces . . .
to simmer in your special broth.[34]

northSun's poetry, however, expresses regret and longing for missed instruction, for someone to "teach us the ways." The speaker's wry self-examination shows that she knows what she has lost, what it means not to speak Indian, to eat Nacho cheese instead of rabbit. But, with brilliant honesty, she makes it equally plain that she is unable or unwilling—probably both—to return to the old ways, to graft those ways on to herself and play at being old-time Indian. Her strength is that she knows who she is and what has happened to her; she knows that she cannot go back, and she's out to survive. That, in the old stories, is Coyote's strength. No matter how many poses he may strike before others—and in these days one of those poses is surely to pretend to be exactly as one's ancestors have been in the past—at the bottom line he does not fool himself. Neither does northSun. She values "the way," but she also acknowledges, and even celebrates a little, "the way things are."

Self-knowledge, shrewd judgment, and an eye for irony are not the strengths the grandmother herself possesses. Another poem, "what gramma said about her grandpa," suggests the origins of the gulf between gramma and her grandchildren, as the gramma's voice relates without a trace to conscious irony the story of her own white grandpa:

he was white grandpa
his name jim butler
he's good irish man
he was nice talk our
language
big man with moustache
boss of town
tonopah
he found silver mine
we still on reservation they
come tell us 'your grandpa
found mine' so
we move to tonopah
he say 'buy anything you want
don't buy just little things
don't buy just candy
buy something big'
that's what he used to say
4th of july he make
a great long table
put sheet over it
then put all kinds of food on it

he say 'get your plate &
help yourselves'
he fed all the indians
he was good man
but then
he marry white woman
and we go back to reservation[35]

Grandpa Jim Butler remains in gramma's mind a nice man because he, like a number of the Irish who made successful Indian scouts and fighters and traders, possesses certain qualities valued highly by most American Indian cultures. He has the gift of tongues, "can talk our language," and he is generous when it suits him, sharing expansively his table and his possessions. That he is inconstant seems not to register on gramma; perhaps it is just that his leaving the family flat is so much a given of "the way things are" in the world of Indian-white relations that she considers it all too unsurprising for comment. The important thing is that she seems to make no distinction between two very different kinds of giving. One kind is Jim Butler's too easy Celtic generosity, which is a western version of the picnic-sponsoring generosity of Tammany Hall bosses, the generosity of the boss of the town who intends that his gifts will reflect well on himself. The other kind of giving is well described by the Navajo medicine man who said

> I can travel all over the Navajo Reservation and never be without a
> home. Each clan has a history and we are all of one family. When
> I am miles from my hogan, I introduce myself to a stranger, name
> my clan. He asks me to stay with him and eat.[36]

This generosity is an integral part of American Indian cultures, the sharing that takes place because that is what nature does for men and women, what they do for nature, what they do for one another unthinkingly. This generosity is not for show but is a traditional way of living in the world. But gramma seems not to notice the vital difference between these two kinds of giving. She remembers the past plenitude without emotionally recalling the cost, and the result, generations later, is that her own grandchild must remain something of a visitor, however loving a one, in her grandmother's house.

This maternal grandmother has suffered a certain amount of cultural alienation, and yet she and her family make as many connections between the generations as love can accomplish and distance will permit. The maternal grandmother's world remains relatively intact, always there for her urban descendants to enter into as fully as possible. This is not true of the speaker's "other gramma," the paternal grandmother, a cheerful urban alcoholic who is far less recognizable as a relative:

> she staggers down streets
> and maybe somebody think
> there go somebody's gramma
> yeah well i spose she my
> gramma
>
> she old indian wino
> big toothy smile
> like the one my dad wears
> like mine[37]

The genetic connection must be acknowledged, but beyond facial structures there are few links between this gramma and her family. Though originally from a culture where tribal and family history and the reckoning of kinship are vital, she is even uncertain of her grandchildren's names. A visit to her is not a time of sharing food and talk in crowded intimacy, but a time to exchange hurried token greetings in a bleak neutral zone:

> when we go visit gramma we
> don't go to her house
> she only sleep there
> we head straight for bar
> us kids wait in car
> my parents go in
> it's a short visit
> it always is
> she staggers out tries to guess
> who's who[38]

But what makes this poem about the family drunk different from Anglo poems on the same subject—Anne Sexton's poems about her father, for example—is the real nature of the grievance, the source of the alienation:

> gramma's got a world of her own
> just her a few old cronies the

bartender oh yeah and her
husband who wears the beer can
hat . . .[39]

It is not this gramma's drunkenness per se that sets her apart. Other members of the family do not regard her as a monster who degrades and shames them; rather, they regard her with a patient affection. The trouble is that she has chosen not just to abandon her old-time native culture but also to abandon almost completely the web of relationship in favor of the exceedingly private culture of the alcoholic. Exclusivity, as opposed to sharing, marks her "world of her own," and that world, unlike the maternal gramma's, is certainly not accessible for restorative visits. But the mere fact of her alcoholism need not make a difference. In another poem, northSun acknowledges drinking as well as a toothy smile as part of her "heritage"—the title of the poem—and imagines the possibility of a coming-together with this other gramma, of them drinking together. But that cannot take place on gramma's narrow turf. The speaker imagines forging for herself a "way" that is possible for her to live within "the way things are," and invites the wino gramma to join her there:

no gramma i won't be like you
i don't like cheap wine
i won't wear jersey print dresses
& fake pearl earrings
or hang on the edge of the
bar in oakland
not for me gramma
i'll get drunk from tequila
sittin in my trailer
on a montana reservation
wearing blue jeans & buckskin
no gramma i'm not exactly
like you
but come visit
let me be your shugur
and we'll have anuthur[40]

This vision is not comparable to life lived under a shade tree within a close family circle, where even such everyday actions as the drinking of Kool-Aid seem nearly ceremonial because they are shared. But it isn't a bar in Oakland, either. It is an imaginative attempt to envision a way of life that would enable the speaker to maintain some connections with "the way"; it is a vision of the speaker established and at ease in a kind of halfway place where, perhaps, either grandmother might join her.

I have dealt so extensively with northSun because of the tough excellence of her poetry and because, of all contemporary American Indian women, she writes most extensively of the estrangements between women in a family. But other American Indian women also write of the problem of alienated women as a cultural rather than a personal affair. Janet Campbell Hale (Coeur d'Alene) writes of returning to her father's wake where she feels a stranger to the old people, not because of her youth or because the relatives are presented, as in many Anglo poems, as faintly grotesque and morbid living specimens, but because

> I
> Don't speak
> The language
> And so
> I listened
> As if I understood
> What it was all about[41]

Again, Joy Harjo (Creek) in "White Sands" writes of driving to her sister's wedding:

> my sister is getting married
> in a white dress in Tulsa
> the way my mother knew it would be
> with her daughters
>> (a December wedding
>> under a pure sky)
>
> but i am the one
> who lives alone with two children
> in the desert of a place
>> in New Mexico
> and she never saw me in a white gown
>
> when i drive to Oklahoma for the wedding
> i will be dressed in
> the clear blue sky

that burns the silvery white sand
near Alamogordo
and my mother won't see this
my eyes burning
behind my darkened glasses[42]

This time it is perhaps more the mother than the child who has forsaken a traditional way of life for the ideals of Norman Rockwell paintings and *Modern Bride;* because of those adopted values, she is disappointed in her daughter. The speaker herself has moved away from the Creek country of Oklahoma. Much as northSun imagines creating for herself a compromise world, drinking tequila in a reservation trailer, the speaker lives by herself, but in at least one sense she preserves the older ways: her connection with the earth is so close that land becomes garment and body, flesh of her flesh. Harjo holds out not even a fantasy, as northSun does, of making connection with her mother; she just assumes that the mother will not see her daughter with clear eyes. The affirmation of the poem lies not in the possibility of a renewed relationship with the mother, but in the daughter's unbroken and radiant connection with something larger and more important than a single individual.

The difference between the Anglo poet's emphasis on personal, psychological alienation between women and the American Indian poet's emphasis on cultural alienation between them may come about simply because the difference between "the way" and "the way things are" is something most American Indians are troubled by daily. Many of their parents and a great number of their older relatives still speak the old tongues, dwell in the old communities where people still follow, in some measure, the order ways of life, behaving in certain ways toward mothers-in-law, for example, or being wary of contact with bears, even if there is a tv set in the hogan. But the great waves of European immigration, the great changes in language and behavior and belief that marked so clearly the differences between first and second and third generations in this country, lie farther in the past for most white Americans. (Even in that past, most Europeans came voluntarily, and many with the idea that it was desirable for their children to leap gladly into the melting pot. European immigrants had fewer ways to give up and gave them up more easily than did American Indians.)

If the daughters of turn-of-the-century immigrants had had more leisure time in which to write, and if writing poetry about family conflict had then been in vogue, American literature might contain more poems about cultural alienation in the kitchen. Interestingly, the only contemporary Anglo poet I can name offhand who touches on mothers and grandmothers in a way similar to that of American Indian poets is Carolyn Forche, who, in her *Gathering the Tribes,* explores her connections and disconnections with her Eastern European grandmother. Perhaps, too, something of this sense of cultural mother-daughter alienation can be found in the work of Jewish women poets of the first half of the century. But for most of us now, the question of what it means to be Irish or Estonian isn't much of a question any longer, and we have the leisure to focus on personal conflicts, to create for ourselves personal instead of tribal mythologies. Intramural rivalries become most intense when there is no longer any possibility of being a member of a varsity team.

The sense of the family unit as being only a part of a very real and much larger entity, a people, still remains, I think, with American Indian women and emerges in their poetry in the absence of one-on-one battles between women. The phenomenon that marks Anglo women's poetry—the mother or daughter seen as private and personal enemy and the bitter relish with which both often regard such conflicts—is, unlike cradle-boards or Vietnam or Tastee-Freez stands, simply not an American Indian theme; the monster-mother and the usurper-daughter are not American Indian images. But the pain and conflict caused for women by the gap between "the way" and "the way things are" and the attempts women make to build bridges over that ravine are among the most vital stories American Indian women poets have now to tell.

The Epic Lyric

Genre and Contemporary American Indian Poetry

Dean Rader

Contemporary American Indian Poetry and That Shape-shifter, Genre

Like the book in which it appears, this essay is concerned with genre. Of course, it concerns itself with many other issues, but its primary focus remains genre and the limits of genre. Issues of genre are always tricky when discussing contemporary American Indian literature. As John Bierhorst and others argue, for "traditional" Native communities, an effete term like "poetry" simply did not exist.[1] And if there was no such animal as poetry, then certainly something such as "prose poem" or "villanelle" was nowhere to be found in the linguistic bestiary. Perhaps that was for the best; perhaps not. What is important to note is that the verbal performance we now define as poetry was just that, performance. According to Jonathan Culler, "performative utterances . . . are statements which themselves accomplish the acts to which they refer."[2] This notion of the conflation between what texts *say* and what they *become* is a distinctive element in contemporary American Indian poetry, and one that I will attempt to unpack throughout this inquiry as it relates to questions of genre and audience.

At this juncture, the reader may be wondering why, if Native communities and Native writers are impervious to distinctions of genre, I am devoting so much time to a classification that may be a nonissue to the communities on whom I focus.[3] I have the same reservations; however, there are a number of concerns problematizing Bierhorst's discussion of Native languages and terms like *poetry*. First of all, while Native American languages may not contain the word *poetry*, the English language does. What's more, English and creative writing departments along with publishers and professors are well aware of concepts like poetry, prose, and drama and their connotations and denotations in English. Moreover, all of the poets discussed in this book write primarily in English and are aware of traditional Western distinctions of genre. They have made decisions to write in verse as opposed to prose or dramatic dialogue. Many of the writers I will examine attended M.F.A. programs and earned graduate degrees from places like the Iowa Writer's Workshop, Johns Hopkins, Stanford, the University of New Mexico, and the University of Colorado —programs known for their ability to produce writers who excel at writing within the Western tradition of academic artistic verse. So, can Bierhorst's taxonomy apply to these writers? Are these writers "traditional" Natives? Sherman Alexie bristles as such appellations, as do many writers and critics of Native American literature. Thus, one reason to consider matters of genre is because, as Kimberly Blaeser (Anishinabe) asserts, American Indian "literary works themselves are always at least bi-cultural: Though they may come from an oral-based culture, they are written. Though their writer may speak a tribal language, they are usually almost wholly in the language of English. And though they proceed at least partly from an Indian culture, they are most often presented in the established literary and aesthetic forms of the dominant culture."[4]

Genre is a form—perhaps *the* form—of the dominant culture. And while Native writers want to write outside of the box that is America, they find they are limited in terms of what forms are available to them. Can one write from within the system and without the system at the same time? I would argue that many contemporary American Indian writers do just that. For Kimberly Blaeser, Louise Erdrich (Ojibwe), Linda Hogan (Chickasaw), Sherman Alexie (Spokane and Coeur d'Alene), Luci Tapahonso (Navajo), N. Scott Momaday (Kiowa and Cherokee), Elizabeth Woody (Yakama, Warm Springs, Wasco, and Navajo), and Janice Gould (Maidu and Konkow), genre functions as a kind of stealth bridge connecting otherwise opposing cultures and modes of expression.

Linked to questions of genre are questions of audience. Anyone who has read the *New York Times Book Review* or looked at the royalties for a book of poems or taught poetry to surly college males knows that genre is oftentimes the determining factor of whether a certain text gets published, read, taught, written about, and canonized. For the purpose of this essay, I am concerned with the "read" and "written about" portions of the above catalog, as I am intrigued by the fact that until the year 2000 no full-length study of contemporary American Indian poetry existed. Furthermore, I am baffled by the preponderance of studies of American Indian fiction and the relative dearth of studies of American Indian poetry, particularly at a time in which some of the best literary critics in America—Helen Vendler, Marjorie Perloff, Albert Gelpi, Harold Bloom, Geoffrey Hartmann, James Longenbach, Alan Filreis, James Breslin, and Sharon Cameron—are working in the field of poetry and when perhaps the most interesting Native writing is being done in poetry. I have argued elsewhere that Anglo critics shy away from writing about Native poetry because they can't characterize it.[5] It doesn't fit into any category or movement. Additionally, contemporary poetry by most Native American writers rarely resembles typical academic lyric poetry; in fact, at times, recent American Indian poetry feels less like lyric and more like epic. Perhaps this is why there are so many interviews with Native poets and so few essays that engage their work—it's easier to have the other discuss her poetry than to try to inhabit the discourse of the other. Thus, it seems to me that it might be time to advance a theory of reading Native poetry that acknowledges the historical, cultural, linguistic, and tribal components of Native oral and written discourse while simultaneously acknowledging the reality of teaching, studying, and buying contemporary American poetry.

Some Notes on My Theory of the Epic Lyric

Let me say at the outset that I have some reservations about this theory. First of all, I'm no big fan of the name. Granted, *epic lyric* has a kind of rhyming trochaic charm, but the term is too clinical and too grounded in the language of Western literary criticism. Secondly, my fear is that some readers will misread my aims here and assume I'm trying to twist and fold Native poetry into a mold so that it can fit into these non-Native classifications. In reality, the opposite is true. My goal is to demonstrate how these terms do not take Native poetry into account and how poetry by American Indians forces us to rethink long-standing terms that we have taken for granted. Furthermore, I'll argue that Native poetry is forcing us to expand our vocabulary for reading and talking about Native poetics.

Kimberly Blaeser, Craig Womack (Creek and Cherokee), Robert Allen Warrior (Osage), and others have argued for some time that we need an indigenous theory of Native literature, and I think that in regard to fiction by Native writers, we are off to a good start. However, in my mind, while there are a number of good examples of Native criticism of American Indian poetry, no real indigenous *theory* of reading poetry has emerged. While the essay in front of you is not that, it is something else that I think is needed as well—an approach that looks at the two worlds in which contemporary American Indian poetry currently exists. As happy as I would be to see an astute indigenous theory of reading Native American poetry, I would also like to see important critics of American poetry like Helen Vendler, Marjorie Perloff, Charles Altieri, James Longenbach, and Robert Haas publish pieces on Luci Tapahonso, Joy Harjo (Muscogee), and Linda Hogan in *American Literature, Harper's, Modernism/Postmodernism,* the *Yale Review,* and the *New Republic.* Surely, there is a way to read Native poetry that addresses the growing audience for Native poetry and how it fits into both Native American and Anglo-American discourse. Surely, there is a way of reading Native poetry that embraces inclusion as opposed to exclusion.

In her article on Native literature, Blaeser urges readers to eschew binarisms or oppositional approaches that reinforce the Western literary aesthetic. I couldn't agree more. Too often, critics of American Indian texts submit to a palpable Native essentialism, or they offer a reading firmly grounded in New Critical or recent theory-based strategies of the Euro-American academy. Ideally, this essay will draft a method of reading that resists the colonial drive to appropriate and subsume. At its best moments, it intends an approach that acknowledges not only how these writers fit into various systems of classifications but also how they have transformed them. In her introduction to *Reinventing the Enemy's Language,* Joy Harjo argues that "these colonizers' languages, which often usurped our own tribal languages or diminished them, now hand back emblems of our cultures, our own designs. . . . We've transformed these enemy languages."[6] Harjo's astute observations lead me to my most important points. First of all, I think that American Indian poetry explodes traditional notions of genre; thus, it probably cannot be talked about in generic terms unless the generic terms have also been exploded. Secondly, I want to transform the language we use to talk about Native poetic texts. I want to take some steps toward handing back the critical language used to read and explain American Indian poetry. My aim in the remainder of this essay is to sketch a means of reading American Indian poetry that keeps a foot in both cultures, that is as transformative, inclusive, and bicultural as the poems themselves.

Toward a New Genre: The Epic Lyric

For some time now, I have been using what I thought was an innovative term, the "lyric epic," to describe Dante's *Divine Comedy* and Walt Whitman's *"Song of Myself"* to undergraduates. Like most teachers, I try to show how Whitman and Dante fuse the lyric obsession with the self with the larger, more society-based epic project. Imagine my disappointment when I discovered that term had already been coined and happily utilized by James E. Miller, Jr., in his book *Leaves of Grass: America's Lyric-Epic of Self and Democracy*. For Miller, this term is useful because it more accurately describes the *form* of Whitman's poem. According to Miller, *"Song of Myself"* is not really an epic but a lyrical epic because of the generous use and importance of the lyric "I" in the poem. Miller never suggests that Whitman invents a new genre, merely a new form (a claim that is itself highly suspect even in its Eurocentrism). Thus, for Miller, Whitman, despite the innovative thrust of his project, is still working within accepted and easily delineated boundaries set forth by centuries of literary codification. For me, the term "lyric epic" marks its own genre. Lyric does not modify epic as it does for Miller; rather, the two genres mix into one inventive system of articulation. Say what you will about Whitman's complex and utterly contradictory politics, but his poetics endure and work because he is able to fuse the best aspects of the lyric and epic, a facility he probably gets from Native American oral expression. Indeed, as James Nolan argues, important aspects of Whitman's form and his voice arise out of Native sensibilities, particularly the orality of his lines, their incantatory gestures, and his metaphors of inclusion.[7]

That Nolan and others link the collection of diverse presentations with Native American discourse is no surprise. Traditionally, Native Americans succeed like no other culture in uniting divergent strains of just about anything into a collective entity. The same holds true for poetry. In fact, I would argue that what distinguishes Native poetry from mainstream Euro-American poetry is its unique conflation of lyric and epic modes. But, unlike Whitman who lyricizes the epic, recent American Indian poets turn this formula on its head—they epicize the lyric. By this I mean that while the poems technically fall within the lyric genre, most poems function as more than a mere lyric; they carry the weight, the history, and do the cultural work of an epic. It's rather remarkable. Like no other national literature written in English, contemporary American Indian poets take on the role of the bard but in a lyric, rather than epic, form. These poems possess most or all of the major characteristics of the epic—they transmit cultural traditions, they valorize deeds, they form national identities, and they preserve culturally specific linguistic patterns—within the more accessible and acceptable model of the lyric. In so doing, poets such as Tapahonso, Silko, Woody, Hogan, Harjo, and Erdrich create a provocative new genre: the epic lyric.

The epic lyric walks like a lyric and sometimes even quacks like a lyric, but it *feels* like an epic and actually performs more like an epic than a lyric. For instance, is the contemporary American Indian poem public or private? Is it personal or communal? Is the voice of the poem, the speaker, an individual or a community or a tribe or a nation? Of course, the answer is both. All. However, were one to ask these questions of typical Anglo-American poetry, one would come up with very different responses. James Wright's poems are decidedly personal, as are Jorie Graham's. There is no doubt of the singular lyric voice. The same can be said for most Anglo-American poets. What distinguishes the epic lyric from other mainstream American poetry is its inherent hybridization. It grafts traditions and techniques from both Anglo and Native literary traditions into one bolder, stronger, more inclusive, more collaborative genre. In other words, the epic lyric, while grounded in Native discourse and experience, is informed by non-Native discourse—as is Native American literature itself. In fact, the American Indian epic lyric functions as a provocative and pertinent metonym for American Indian life in general. On certain levels, there may be no more powerful metonym of resistance, survival, persistence, beauty, and dialogue.

Because the epic lyric both adheres to Western literary conventions and explodes them, and because its bicultural blueprint enables it to reside in both Anglo and Native spaces, it engenders a unique kind of poetry that demands a theory of reading as unique and inclusive as the genre itself. While I'm not suggesting that this study serves as the definitive articulation of that theory, I would like to offer some strategies that might give some insight into what I see as the most exciting literature being written in America today.

But, before I chart the course of the epic lyric in contemporary

American Indian poetry, it would be useful to clarify the two terms in use and discuss their relationship to both Anglo and Native literary discourse.

Public or Private Discourse:
The Lyric and American Indian Poetry

As we will see in the next section, the epic poem is much easier to demarcate than the lyric. In fact, it would seem that any poetic text that is *not* an epic is a lyric. For some scholars, all American poetic texts, written in English, are lyric poems, even *Song of Myself*. Traditionally, one associates the following characteristics with the lyric: personal, subjective, short, meditative, emotive, private, musical. The origins of Greek and Latin lyrics were songs addressed to a particular person expressing a specific emotion, and over time the lyric poem distinguishes itself from the epic through its interiority. In his *The Idea of Lyric*, W. R. Johnson claims that where "there is, usually, in our hearts and minds, a boundless, depthless indistinction of feelings and thoughts, suddenly, in the lyric story, at its essential, dramatic moment, emotions and thoughts are organized in lyrical discourse and find in metaphors . . . intelligible re-creations, visible patterns for the inner tempests and stillnesses, configurations that are at once ordered and dynamic."[8]

Traditionally, where the epic poem is objective, the lyric is subjective; where the epic is public, the lyric is private; where the epic concentrates on deeds and events, the lyric explores emotions and feelings. And, particularly important for Native American storytelling, the epic is generally narrative or linear, whereas the lyric remains notably nonlinear. Thus, to capture the nonlinearity of much of Native telling, the lyric, ironically, is a more appropriate vehicle than the confining narrativity of the epic.

According to Helen Vendler, while the lyric "may contain the germ of a story"—say, a man's regret that a love affair is ending—it "dwells less on the plot than on the man's feelings."[9] Additionally, in epic poetry, there is often considerable distance between the speaker and the author. This is not always the case for the lyric. Of course, the poetic persona is an important concept; however, in most poetry after 1945 and in almost all American Indian poetry, the distance between the speaker of the poem and the poem's author is very small indeed, perhaps even unidentifiable.

In terms of form, American Indian poetry adheres to lyric expectations; however, oftentimes, the typical poem by Leslie Marmon Silko (La-guna) or Luci Tapahonso or Simon Ortiz (Acoma) doesn't really explore emotions or feelings; rather, it tells a story. Consider Ortiz's Coyote poems. They look and feel like lyrics, but they are clearly at variance with Vendler's assessment of the lyric because the poems foreground story over emotions. The same can be said for many of the poems in Silko's *Story-teller*. But on the other hand, the stories being told are often utterly personal and find articulation in a form closer to song than prose. Indeed, Western lyrics and poems by Native writers share a common history in that both derive from songs and chants; so on some basic structural level, recent poems by Native writers are charged with the energy of the original lyric impulse. At the same time, the lyrics tell stories, they are often wildly public, communal texts, and frequently the author of the poem is merely a vehicle for a kind of expression that does not simply seek a connection between author and audience but literally creates it.

A Poem That Includes History:
The Epic and American Indian Poetry

Out of nowhere, it seems, in the vast vortex of Canto 85, Ezra Pound makes the following statement about American poetry and culture up to the moment that he is composing his cantos:

> No classics,
>   no American history,
>   no centre, no general root,
> No *prezzo giusto* as core.[10]

Pound's suggestion that there are no American texts that rival the great cultural icons of classical "civilization" reveals the depths to which he is either unaware of the vast and complex Native poetic expression or unimpressed by it. Similarly, in his study of the American epic, James E. Miller, Jr., argues that before the 1800s, American culture, like its land, was an abyss: "America needed a new literature to match the new land and the new society, the land, largely empty, the society hardly established."[11] As we all know, culture in the Americas was hardly new, the land hardly empty, and societies had long been established; however, since these cultures and spaces and discourses were inhabited by the "savages," they tend to be left off the cultural and literary map of America, at least until the

1940s. One of the first really important anthologies of American poetry, Oscar Williams's *A Little Treasury of American Poetry: The Chief Poets from Colonial Times to the Present,* published in 1948, acknowledges the importance of American Indian expression to American literary culture. However, in his introduction to the American Indian texts, Williams clearly draws a distinction between "savage and barbaric folk-lore, warrior songs and ballads" and the finely wrought poetry of modern-day American poets. Like Pound and Miller, Williams laments the fact that America has no *Odyssey,* no *Aeneid,* no *Beowulf,* no *Song of Roland* to connect its current language and culture to a glorified epic past. And despite the fact that he includes some translations of oral literature in his anthology, Williams cites the fact that this oral tradition is the only "indigenous epic material" as a "peculiar handicap of American poetry."[12]

Williams's comments are shocking and disappointing but not surprising. Instead of focusing on the disturbing stances of Pound, Miller, Williams, and scores of other American writers and critics, I will instead use as a point of departure Williams's observation that despite the fact that American Indian texts are barbaric and savage, they are, nonetheless, America's "epic material at its foundation." On this count, I would agree with Williams, but what does it mean for a text or a series of texts to be "epic material"? In fact, what is an epic? Perhaps the most famous and most perfunctory definition of the epic issues from Pound himself, who claims that an "epic is a poem containing history." Since Pound's program for Imagism ruled out anything as pesky as history, the injection of a bit of historical data here and there seems to qualify any text for epic status. Because of the limits of space and personal interest, I will not trace the history of the epic in America; rather, with a passing nod to the more programmatic explications of this classic form, I find that I am most persuaded by Michael Bernstein's breakdown of the American epic.[13] In his *The Tale of the Tribe: Ezra Pound and the Modern Verse Epic,* Bernstein offers a subtle, mutable, and thorough theory of genre, through what he calls an "uneasy mixture of *a priori* criteria and *a posteriori* features."[14] According to Bernstein:

a) The epic presents a narrative of its audience's own cultural, historical, or mythic heritage, providing models of exemplary conduct (both good and bad) by which its readers can regulate their lives and adjust shared customs.

b) The dominant voice narrating the poem will, therefore, not bear the trace of a single sensibility; instead, it will function as a spokesman for values generally acknowledged as significant for communal stability and social well-being. Within the fiction of the poem, the dominant locatable source of narration will not be a particular individual (the poet), but rather the voice of the community's heritage "telling itself."

c) Consequently, the proper audience of an epic is not the *individual* in his absolute inwardness but the *citizen* as participant in a collective linguistic and social nexus. Whereas a lyric is addressed to the purely private consciousness of its hearer apart from all considerations of his class, circumstances, or social bonds, the epic speaks primarily to members of a "tribe," to listeners who recognize in the poem, social . . . as well as psychological, ethical, emotional, or aesthetic imperatives.

d) The element of instruction argument . . . is deliberately foregrounded in an epic which offers its audience lessons presumed necessary to their individual and social survival. . . .[15]

Had I not confessed that these criteria marked that of an epic, most readers of this essay would believe that I had sketched four major criteria of Native American discourse. Indeed, the degree to which Bernstein's theory of the epic applies to Native American literature is downright spooky. Native American poetry already contains one key component of all epic literature—a grounding in orality, but I contend that recent American Indian poetry does the cultural work of epic above and beyond its roots in the oral tradition.[16]

One is hard pressed to think of a lyric by John Ashbery, Jorie Graham, Robert Lowell, Anne Sexton, A. R. Ammons, Billy Collins, T. S. Eliot, Charles Olson, or any other important Anglo-American poet that meets one if any of the criteria above. On the other hand, one is equally hard pressed to think of a recent poem by a Native poet that does *not* meet at least one of the criteria enumerated, and often the poem will meet three or four. Because many Native writers see the lyric poem as a means of preserving historical heritage, because they see poetry as the voice of the community "telling itself," because the primary audience of the American Indian poem is the citizen of a collective nexus and the members of a tribe, and because contemporary American Indian poets see the poem as "necessary to their individual and social survival," Native writers have been constructing and are continuing to construct numerous epics in the history of America—through the unlikely vehicle of the lyric.

In the remainder of this essay, I would like to examine how various Native writers use the epic lyric to link private concerns with public demands and in so doing show how they create a kind postcolonial genre that not only reinvents the enemy's language but also reinvents and preserves a uniquely Native American and American poetics.

Inventing a Cartography of Language:
Mapping the Epic Lyric

When I think of the contemporary American Indian poem and the lyric epic, I think of the beginning of Carter Revard's (Osage) "Making a Name":

> The authors of this story are
>   my Ponca folks, Aunt Jewel and
> Uncle Woody. I'm directing the movie
>   made from the story.
>   So come on with us—Here we go now,[17]

What seems like an informal, even chatty opening is, in fact, a complex salutation, invocation, and attribution. Calling traditional authorial authority into question, Revard suggests that, despite his name on the frontispiece of the book, he is not the actual author of the poem contained within its covers. Of course, he *wrote* the poem, but that does not necessarily make him the *author.* The true authors are his uncle and aunt who tell him a story about him and about them. The story, brief as it is, chronicles not only little Carter's burgeoning predilection for profanity but the family's forced migration from Nebraska to Oklahoma, and these lines, the opening lines of a short, first-person lyric, meet all four of Bernstein's criteria for an epic. Perhaps they don't meet them as fully as he would like, and perhaps they require the totality of the poem to drive home their effect, but I am struck by how much is accomplished in such a short space and how frequently similar moments occur in contemporary American Indian poetry. Space and simple good sense prohibit me from offering a detailed map of lyric poems, like this one, that work as epics, but I would like to offer a crude map for a new kind of poem, indigenous to American Indian discourse.

Contemporary American Indian poetry is marked by a provocative fusion of what Walter Ong calls "primary orality" and "secondary orality." According to Ong, the orality of cultures that bear no trace of written language are "primary," whereas cultures in which there exists writing, print, and other media possess a "secondary orality."[18] Traces of language before it became locked in a visual field seep into the poems by modern Native writers, and at moments, we feel the power of performative language, a language that lived only through telling. Not surprisingly, many Native poems are tellings. Revard's "Making a Name" is a classic telling poem. So is Sherman Alexie's "Sonnet: Tattoo Tears." Alexie begins the poem with the following one-line stanza: "No one will believe this story I'm telling, so it must be true."[19] Like Revard's poem, the author tells us the text before us is a telling, but unlike Revard, Alexie's text adheres to a more traditional use of the lyric "I," and its title, "Sonnet," suggests it further falls within a standard genre. But, not surprisingly, Alexie irrupts our expectations, composing his sonnet with fourteen prose stanzas instead of fourteen poetic lines. Each stanza is a mini-telling, a mini-history. Present Native concerns find voice amid the backdrop of historical data; thus, the fourteen stanzas work like fourteen cantos or fourteen chapters of a community telling itself through Alexie's crossed lyric.

Perhaps a culture or a tribe most commonly tells itself by documenting historical moments. In these situations, the voice narrating the story is rarely the alienated or isolated lyric speaker, but a kind of spokesperson for a community's heritage. Likewise, such a poem intends a collective audience who will recognize and respond to the poem's role as nexus and bridge. For instance, Janice Gould's "History Lesson" begins in 1832 and works it way through various historical moments (indentured servitude in 1849; treaties in 1851; the treaty broken in 1852; removal in 1863) until the poem lands, in the present, in 1984, when the author attempts to tell the history of Columbus while confronting a troubling passage about California Indians in a history textbook. Without question, Gould's poem meets Bernstein's first three criteria head on; yet, at the same time, the poem resists the sprawl of the epic project in favor of lyric compression.

Whereas Gould takes us on a tour of important tribal and personal moments, in "Baskets" Deborah Miranda (Esselen and Chumash) takes us on a tour of important tribal artifacts. The woven baskets tell stories themselves; they place a people, an artistic enterprise, and cultural articulation: "Indians evolve like everyone else / . . . We grow into / what comes next."[20] Thus, the poem is a story of how nonliterary texts tell stories—a story of a story, yet related in the nonlinear form of the lyric.

Like Gould's poem, "December" by Wendy Rose (Hopi and Miwok) takes as its point of departure a historical act of violence. In Rose's case, the incident referred to is the massacre at Wounded Knee. She writes:

do you see
it was that way
    we became the stones
    that bruised your feet
    on the prairie
    so that every twisted ankle
    and broken wheel
    would remind you
    of the babies in the snow
    of the blood and wind,[21]

For the poet, the landscape wears its history of bloodshed just as the surviving generations of the massacre wear theirs. We are unsure of the voice(s) narrating the poem, but sense that the speakers are a collective, that they speak from the past, present, and future. On the other hand, the intended audience is clearly Anglo, though perhaps more past than present. The text's intense verticality, its mythopoetic language, its rich imagery, make it feel like a Deep Image lyric of James Wright or W. S. Merwin, the most lyrical of lyric poets. However, in a typical poem by Wright or Merwin, the speaker remains alone, isolated, decidedly separated from the world around him or, for that matter, to history; whereas in Rose's poem, the speakers seem like the years and decades themselves —people become stone, stone becomes years, years become voice. Simon Ortiz's riveting book *From Sand Creek* takes Rose's and Gould's project one step further. His entire collection centers on one horrible day in American history. On November 28, 1864, U.S. troops and other volunteers massacred 105 Cheyenne and Arapaho women and 28 men. Ortiz uses this event to dramatize a culture and history of violence, which becomes a controlling metaphor for his entire collection of poems. In some way, the Sand Creek massacre resonates in each poem of the book, indelibly tying contemporary cultural, political, and social intricacies to one defining instance. Thus, while Gould stitches together diverse patches of history in order to weave together a mosaic of meaning for a singular cultural reality, Ortiz tears off strips from the tapestry of a singular event and ties them to their corollary in the present. Though each poet manipulates historical realities uniquely, both transform the past into the poetic present in way that remains atypical for the modern American lyric, yet each of these poems pulses with the intensity and emotional currency of the lyric.

The epic lyric not only unites historical positioning with personal desire, it also blends traditionally prosaic expression with poetic locution. Perhaps no poet does this better than Luci Tapahonso. On one hand, Tapahonso invokes and poeticizes Navajo prayers and spirituality, and on the other hand, she invokes and poeticizes the mundane rituals of everyday life, like cooking, cleaning, traveling, talking, and listening. By combining the sacred and the secular, Tapahonso paints one of the most comprehensive and nuanced portraits of Navajo life. In the poem "Hills Brothers Coffee" (which is served up in the middle of an essay), the poet and her uncle enjoy the dual ritual pleasures of morning coffee and storytelling, while in "This Is How They Were Placed for Us," Tapahonso, in hypnotizing, incantatory language, evokes the spiritual and historical powers of the holy mountains:

> The San Francisco Peaks taught us to believe in strong families.
> Dook'o'oosłííd binahji' danihidziił.
> The San Francisco Peaks taught us to value our many relatives.
> E'e'aahjígo Dook'o'oosłííd bik'ehgo hózhónígo naashá.[22]

By offering her poem as a gift to both the spirits of the San Francisco Peaks and her readers, Tapahonso reveals the source from which her poems and their magic derive:

> All these were given to us to live by.
> These mountains and the land keep us strong.
> From them, and because of them, we prosper.
>
> With this we speak,
> with this we think,
> with this we sing,
> with this we pray.
>
> This is where our prayers began.[23]

Because Tapahonso's voice rings with authenticity and purpose, we find ourselves utterly drawn into both of her ritualized worlds, feeling unusually connected to each, and we realize we have learned, as the poet has learned, what it means to become part of something larger than ourselves. We have participated in ritual. In an amazing poetic move, Tapahonso shifts us back and forth from historical rumination to ritual participation. Through the transition from English to Navajo, we move from the potentially static language of history to the dynamic interchange of performative language. In the poem "Daané'é Diné," a similar movement transpires. The first half of the poem, a survey of the site, finds expression in verse, while the very lyrical revelation of the dream demands prose.[24] Both Tapahonso and Simon Ortiz use ritual even further to turn the poem itself into ritual and in so doing incorporate the reader into the process. Tapahonso's "The Motion of Songs Rising" and Ortiz's "Earth and Rain, The Plants & Sun," respectively, speak Yeis and Katzinas into being through the poetic process.[25] One has to ask if such performative language is *either* epic or lyric. Both Tapahonso and Ortiz revitalize language and experience through a ritualization of the poetic endeavor and restore the site of the poem to its most ancient energies: the narrativity of the epic and the impulse of the lyric. Ultimately, one concludes that it is both and neither; rather, it is a new genre that, like the poets themselves, conflates public and private histories and desires.

Not surprisingly, Tapahonso is not the only Native poet to fuse lyric's private trajectory with public ritual. In Paula Gunn Allen's "C'koy'u, Old Woman," the speaker addresses the oldest of women, the earth. However, again, the speaker seems to be a community: "old woman there in the earth / outside you we wait" and "old woman there in the sky / we are waiting inside you."[26] This poem, the title poem of the first section in Allen's collection, sets the stage for the entire book by informing readers that in their hands exists a text that doesn't just straddle diverse genres but problematizes them. Similarly, Joy Harjo calls forth the jaguar priest Thantog in "Song for Thantog." Unlike traditional lyric "songs," Harjo's text moves beyond mere panegyricism and into ritual space. In fact, the poem morphs from song into prayer. And while Harjo's use of the lyric "I" lends the poem a lyrical interiority, the poem finally winds up a prayer from and for all humankind. Another Harjo text, "Eagle Poem," works similarly. In this text, written a few years later, Harjo transforms the site of the lyric into the site of a very public prayer.[27] Through the act of reading, we pray along with Harjo for her and our connection with the divine, an act that collapses Bernstein's well-segmented criteria of epic procurement into one expansive speech act.

Despite the generative force of ritual and prayer, perhaps no poetic gesture serves as an engine for the epic lyric more than myth. One of the characteristic qualities of Native poetry is the frequency with which it either captures and preserves or reinvents American Indian mythologies. Through myth and the telling of these sacred stories, contemporary Native poetry truly designs its own genre. No other American poetic form works on both the lyric and epic levels as provocatively and as uniquely as American Indian poetry, and within the world of Native poetry, there is no better interlocutor of the poetic myth than Simon Ortiz. The opening section of *A Good Journey*, entitled "Telling," remains one of the most important moments in contemporary Native writing. The temptation is to refer to this section as a document, but such language is imprecise. These poems, even though they are written down, cannot be considered documents but rather are dynamic texts that happen to be preserved in written codes.

In this section, Ortiz generously supplies the reader(s) with various narratives about Coyote, wolves, Canyon de Chelly, the Kawaikamehtitra (the Laguna), Acoma, Crow, Magpie, chili, and telling itself. What's interesting about Ortiz's poems is the means of telling. He doesn't simply offer a third person account of the myth; he attempts to recreate the actual telling. The first poem in Ortiz's *A Good Journey*, "Telling About Coyote," fluctuates between myth, poem, and symbol so quickly and deftly, the shifts are difficult to detect:

> ". . . you know, Coyote
> is in the origin and all the way
> through . . . he's the cause
> of the trouble, the hard times
> that things have . . ."

> "Yet, he came so close
> to having it easy.
>   But he said,
> "Things are just too easy . . ."
> Of course, he was mainly bragging,
> shooting his mouth.

The existential Man,
Dostoevsky Coyote.[28]

From here, the narrator proceeds to tell a story involving Coyote and gambling; in effect, the speaker of the poem recounts a myth to the faceless reader in the form of a lyric. The quotations puzzle because they appear and disappear unexpectedly, which suggests a conscious effort to distinguish between the speaker of the poem and the teller of the Coyote myth, though both feel like Ortiz. One is tempted to read this not as a poem but as a myth in verse; however, that would be a mistake because Ortiz the poet seems to be keeping tabs or commenting on Ortiz the storyteller. To think of this poem or any of the poems in the collection as merely a myth with fancy line breaks is to oversimplify. Similarly, in "They Come Around, The Wolves—And Coyote and Crow, Too," the narrator of the poem literally becomes both coyote and crow.

At the risk of sounding repetitive, I would merely point out that, yet again, these poems meet all four of Bernstein's criteria for the epic head on, particularly the first two: preserving cultural values and a communal narrative voice. One finds these two gestures best articulated in the poem "And there is always one more story." Ortiz offers this introduction to the poem, which his mother overheard at a Sunday meeting: "The woman was telling about her grandson who was telling the story which was told to him by somebody else. All these voices telling the story, including the voices in the story—yes, it must be an old one."[29] Thus, in the poem, Ortiz not only retells the story of the Quail Women and recreates their dialogue, he imagines how the woman told the story and recreates *that* dialogue as well. What might seem at first cacophonous voices emerges in the end as a mosaic of utterances that, like the book itself, are woven into a single narrative thread.

Whereas Ortiz recreates the mythical moment, Louise Erdrich uses myth to launch a lyric moment. In "Windigo" and "The Strange People," she takes as a point of departure mythical creatures; however, both poems turn from cultural expectations of these creatures toward lyric introspection.[30] Thus, the poems assume a funnel-like structure in that they begin in the public sphere (within the myth) but spiral downward into the private sphere of the self. "Windigo" reimagines the windigo, a flesh-eating demon with a man buried inside and uses these metaphors of devouring to implicitly comment on a kind of monstrous pursuit to devour or eradicate Indian cultures, lifestyles, and myths. In "The Strange People," Erdrich's persona speaks from the perspective of the antelope people, though in the first-person singular. The poem reads like a lyric but swims in the sea of epic cultural reference and myth.[31] Erdrich's desire to fuse lyric and epic gestures is best seen in her Potchikoo poems. In both *Jacklight* and *Baptism of Desire*, Erdrich devotes space for sections of prose. These prose segments, stories of the loveable trickster Potchikoo, further blur the boundaries between prose and poetry, personal and communal narratives, and public and private expression.

For poets such as Harjo and Linda Hogan, the lyric poem provides a provocative space to create new mythic moments. To a certain degree, "Song for Thantog" takes up residence in the realm of myth, but in her collection *The Woman Who Fell from the Sky*, Harjo invents a hybridized prose/poetry format to blend epic and lyric signifiers. In poems like "The Woman Who Fell from the Sky" "A Postcolonial Tale," and "The Flood," Harjo uses scraps of older mythologies to create modern corollaries.[32] Whereas Erdrich riffs on older mythologies, Harjo creates new myths that echo older, more traditional stories but resonate with complex and contemporary thematics.

One of my favorite poems, Linda Hogan's "Crow Law," works through this formula more subtly. Signifying on the various crow myths, and, perhaps, Ortiz's crow poems in *A Good Journey*, Hogan also creates a contemporary myth, one that, like all of the poems mentioned here, does the cultural work of the epic poem, yet moves on the page and in the mouth and in the ears and in the heart like a lyric. My own preference is for the reverse to happen as well, that every time someone reads *Beowulf* or *Odyssey* or *Song of Myself*, that person hears Simon Ortiz or sees Lucy Tapahonso. In the narrative of the western epic, they identify the native lyric.

At first, the poem may seem an overly simple pastoral, but upon closer inspection Hogan's text opens up to multiple possibilities. Similar to Harjo, Hogan creates a new kind of mythology of crow but one that participates in the ancient and sacred motif of renewal and regeneration, motifs that extend beyond cyclical patterns of nature to Native communities themselves. Like crow, Native people create their sacred spaces out of what walks toward them, out of what lives and what dies. The boundaries of crow, moose, and wolf disappear; as for a poet like Erdrich, so do the lines between human and animal, wilderness and civilization—just as the borders between epic and lyric also disappear.

And here is the space in which Native poetry both nests and flies. And here is where terms of classification like *epic*, *lyric*, and even *epic lyric* feel flat, useless, unnecessarily demarcating. For, when it comes right down to it, embedded into the architecture of Native poetry is its own theory for reading. If we think of theory as a set of principles or assumptions used in specific situations to unpack or make sense of a text or idea, then one finds really no better theory for understanding Native poetry than Native poetry. That is, the belief in and the practice of enacting performative language to make things happen are, by default, theoretical stances on how language works in the world. Thus, perhaps the best or at least the most welcoming theory for *experiencing* American Indian poetry is the theory of the poem itself. The reliance on performative language, the connection between poetry and ceremony, and the necessity of speaker / audience interaction form a kind of interpretive web that, in my mind, helps us see the interrelation among language, culture, history, gender, land, and, perhaps most importantly, tribes.

The third mark on Bernstein's epic yardstick claims that the epic "speaks primarily to members of a 'tribe,' to listeners who recognize in the poem, social . . . as well as psychological, ethical, emotional, or aesthetic imperatives." The first-person plural in the last line, the only instance of it in the poem, comes as a surprise. We aren't sure who the *we* is exactly—Indians? All humans? Other animals? This line recalls the plural speakers of Erdrich's poem "Jacklight," in which nameless entities watch, afraid, from the wilderness. In Hogan's text, though, the *we* is not merely watching; it / they are participating.

> It is the oldest war
> where moose become wolf and crow,
> where the road ceases
> to become the old forest
> where crow is calling,
> where we are still afraid.

Crow is calling *them*. They are calling *us*. They are telling us a story of themselves, of their personal experiences in a public realm.

The second mark on Bernstein's yardstick is his claim that the epic is the tribe telling itself, which means that perhaps the most compelling argument for the epic lyric and the bicultural importance of Native poetry requires the critic to step back into the wilderness and let the voice of the tribe—like Crow itself—do its work out in the world:

The temple where crow worships
walks forward in tall, black grass.
Betrayal is crow's way of saying grace
to the wolf
so it can eat
what is left
when blood is on the ground,
until what remains of moose
is crow
walking out
the sacred temple of ribs
in a dance of leaving
the red tracks of scarce and private gods.
It is the oldest war
where moose becomes wolf and crow,
where the road ceases
to become the old forest
where crow is calling,
where we are still afraid.[33]

Answering the Deer

Genocide and Continuance in the

Poetry of American Indian Women

Paula Gunn Allen

In the ancient bardic tradition the bards sang only of love and death. Certainly these twin themes encompass the whole of human experience. Loving, celebrating, and joining are the source of life, but they necessarily occur against a background of potential extinction. Thus, these themes become the spindle and loom of the poets' weavings, for from the interplay of connection and disconnection come our most significant understandings of ourselves, our fellow creatures, and our traditions, our past. The American Indian women who write poetry do so in that ancient tradition, for like the bards we are tribal singers. And because our tribal present is inextricably bound to our continuing awareness of imminent genocide, our approach to the themes of love and death takes on a pervasive sense of sorrow and anger that is not easily reconciled with the equally powerful tradition of celebrating with the past and affirming the future that is the essence of oral tradition.

We are the dead and the witnesses to death of hundreds of thousands of our people, of the water, the air, the animals and forests and grassy lands that sustained them and us not so very long ago.

"Blessed are they who listen when no one is left to speak," Chickasaw poet Linda Hogan writes in her poem "Blessing."[1] The impact of genocide in the minds of American Indian poets and writers cannot be exaggerated. It is a pervasive feature of the consciousness of every American Indian in the United States, and the poets are never unaware of it. Even poems that are meant to be humorous derive much of their humor directly from this awareness. American Indians take the fact of probable extinction for granted in every thought, in every conversation. We have become so accustomed to the immediate likelihood of racial extinction in the centuries since Anglo-European invasion, that we can allude to it in many indirect ways; its pervasive presence creates a sense of sorrow in even the funniest tales.

Mary Randle TallMountain, Athabascan poet born in the Koyukon village of Nulato, Alaska, writes of a wolf companion in her poem "The Last Wolf." The speaker is lying in a hospital in a devastated San Francisco, waiting for the last wolf to make his way to her through the "ruined city." She hears

> his baying echoes
> down the steep smashed warrens
> of Montgomery Street
> . . . and at last his low whine as he came
> . . . to the room where I sat
> I watched
> he trotted across the floor
> he laid his long gray muzzle
> on the spare white spread
> and his eyes burned yellow
> his dotted eyebrows quivered.
>
> Yes, I said.
> I know what they have done.[2]

The question that the writers face again and again, pose in a multitude of ways, answer in a multitude of ways, is this: How does one survive in the face of collective death? Bearing witness is one solution, but it is singularly tearing, for witnessing genocide—as with conversion—requires that someone listen and comprehend.

The American Indian poet is particularly bereft of listeners. The Indian people, who form a tiny subpopulation in the United States and who don't buy modern poetry or literary novels in large numbers, are very busy trying to preserve the elements of culture and tribal identity that are left them, while accommodating these elements to the larger American society around them. Audiences for the American Indian writer from among other Americans are sparse because of the many large and trivial differences in assumptions, expectations, experiences, and symbol structures between Indian and non-Indian. The American Indian writer has difficulty locating readers/listeners who can comprehend the significance of her work, even when she is being as clear and direct as she can be, because these differences in experience and meaning assigned to events create an almost impossible barrier.

What we bear witness to is not easily admissible into the consciousness of other Americans, and that inadmissibility causes us difficulty in articulation and utterance signified by Hogan's plaint and by these lines from "I expected my skin and my blood to ripen" by Hopi-Miwok poet Wendy Rose:

I expected my skin and my blood
to ripen,
not be ripped from my bones;
like green fruit I am peeled
tasted, discarded; my seeds are stepped on
and crushed
as if there were no future. Now
there has been
no past.
My own body gave up the beads,
my own hands gave the babies away
to be strung on bayonets . . .
as if the pain of their birthing
had never been.[3]

Perhaps the knowledge of the real possibility of total extinction spurs one to perceptions that transcend the usual political, sociological, psychological, or aesthetic response to pain or rage. Certainly the knowledge of continuance is difficult to cling to. We cling to it nevertheless; for as Rose writes at the end of her poem, the speaker would have protected the baby:

if I could, would've turned her
into a bush or rock if there'd been magic enough
to work such changes. Not enough magic
to stop the bullets, not enough
magic to stop the scientists, not enough magic
to stop the money. Now our ghosts dance
a new dance, pushing from their hearts
a new song.[4]

The new song our ghosts push from their hearts is a song of bitterness and grief, to be sure; but it is also a song of sanity, balance, and humor.

Humor is widely used by Indians to deal with life. Indian gatherings are marked by laughter and jokes, many directed at the horrors of history, at the continuing impact of colonization, and at the biting knowledge that living as an exile in one's own land necessitates. Thus, Leslie Marmon Silko updates Coyote tales to reflect modern life at the pueblo of Laguna, an eastern pueblo that is a crossroads of southwestern Anglo, Chicano, and Indian cultures:

> Some white men came to Acoma and Laguna a hundred years ago
> and they fought over Acoma land and Laguna women, and
> even now
> some of their descendants are howling in
> the hills southeast of Laguna.[5]

This short story tells the tale that what is important at Acoma is land, and at Laguna it is women (said to be some of the most attractive women around) and that mixed-bloods are likely to be howling around in the hills because they are the offspring of the wily and salacious Coyote. Indeed, "coyote" to many Hispanic Americans refers to a half-breed, and that idea is also present in this poetic joke.

Coyote is a tricky personage—half creator, half fool; he (or she in some versions) is renowned for greediness and salaciousness. Coyote tales abound all over native America, and he has been taken up by contemporary American Indian poets as a metaphor for all the foolishness and the anger that have characterized American Indian life in the centuries since invasion. He is also a metaphor for continuance, for Coyote survives and a large part of his bag of survival tricks is his irreverence. Because of this irreverence for everything—sex, family bonding, sacred things, even life itself—Coyote survives. He survives partly out of luck, partly out of cunning, and partly because he has, beneath a scabby coat, such great creative prowess that many tribes have characterized him as the creator of this particular phase of existence, this "fifth world." Certainly the time frame we presently inhabit has much that is shabby and tricky to offer; and much that needs to be treated with laughter and ironic humor; it is this spirit of the trickster-creator that keeps Indians alive and vital in the face of horror.

The stance of bitter irony characterizes the poetry of Crow Creek

Sioux poet Elizabeth Cook-Lynn, as this excerpt from her poem "Contradiction" indicates:

> She hears the wolves at night
> prophetically. Put them behind,
> the legends we have found,
> care not a bit,
> go make a night of it! . . .
> She wonders why you dress your eyes
> in pulsing shades of Muscatel,
> while wailing songs of what-the-hell
> make essences to eulogize.[6]

When the traditions that inform the people with life and inform that life with significance are put behind, not much but Muscatel and "songs of what-the-hell" are left. Aside from the obvious emotional, social, and psychological considerations implied in the observation, the interesting thing about the use of humor in American Indian poetry is its integrating effect: it makes tolerable what is otherwise unthinkable; it allows a sort of breathing space in which an entire race can take stock of itself and its future. Humor is a primary means of reconciling the tradition of continuance, bonding, and celebration with the stark facts of racial destruction. It is used in that way by many Indian poets, as in nila northSun's poem "moving camp too far":

> i can't speak of
>   many moons
>   moving camp on travois
> i can't tell of
>   the last great battle
>   counting coup or
>   taking scalps
> i don't know what it
>   was to hunt buffalo
>   or do the ghost dance
> but
> i can see an eagle
>   almost extinct
>   on slurpee plastic cups

i can travel to pow wows
    in campers & winnebagos
i can eat buffalo meat
    at the tourist burger stand
i can dance to indian music
    rock–n–roll hey–a–hey–o
i can
    & unfortunately
    i do[7]

Surely this poem is a mourning song, as it is one of a stunted and trivialized vision made to fit a pop-culture conception of Indian, earth, and extinction; certainly it highlights some of the more enraging aspects of American culture as they can appear only to an American Indian: among Indians, a Winnebago is a member of a tribe that lives in Iowa; among non-Indians it is a recreation vehicle—aptly enough. An eagle is a symbol of the spirit, of vision, of transcendence to many American Indian traditionals, but it is also an emblem that bedecks a plastic cup. And the buffalo signified an entire culture, a way of life for numerous tribes once upon a time; now it is a consumer curiosity one can purchase at a tourist foodstand.

Many of the poems written by American Indian women address the stark fact of extinction directly, with a vigor and resilience that does not merely bewail a brutal fate but directs our attention to a kind of hope born of facing the brutal and bitter facts of our recent history and present condition. This sense of hope is characteristic of the peoples whose history on this continent stretches beyond the dimmest reaches of time, winding back through history to time immemorial; it is a hope that comes about when one has faced ultimate disaster time and time again over the ages and has emerged stronger and more certain of the endurance of the people, the spirits, and the land from which they both arise and which informs both with life.

The metaphors that most appeal to American Indian poets are usually those that combine elements of tribal tradition with contemporary experience: thus the poetry of Creek poet Joy Harjo finds itself entwining ancient understandings of the moon, of relationship, of womanhood, and of journeying with city streets, rodeo grounds, highways, airports, Indian bars, and powwows. From the meeting of the archaic and the contemporary the facts of her life become articulate, and the fact that modern American Indians are both Indian and American becomes very clear, as in the wry, laconic lines from "3 AM":

> 3 AM
> in the albuquerque airport
> trying to find a flight
> to old oraibi, third mesa
> TWA
>   is the only desk open
> bright lights outline new york,
>
>   chicago
>
> and the attendant doesn't know
> that third mesa
> is a part of the center
> of the world
> and who are we
> just two indians
> at three in the morning
> trying to find a way back.[8]

A contemporary American Indian is always faced with a dual perception of the world: that which is particular to American Indian life, and that which exists ignorant of that life. Each is largely irrelevant to the other except where they meet—in the experience and consciousness of the Indian. Because the divergent realities must meet and form comprehensible patterns within Indian life, an Indian poet must develop metaphors that not only will reflect the dual perceptions of Indian/non-Indian but also will reconcile them. The ideal metaphor will harmonize the contradictions and balance them so that internal equilibrium can be achieved, so that each perspective is meaningful and that in their joining, psychic unity rather than fragmentation occurs.

Fortunately, modern life, like modern poetry, provides various means of making the dichotomy clear and of reconciling the contradictions within it. Airports, traveling, powwows, burger stands, recreation vehicles, and advertising layouts all provide ways to enter the contradictions and resolve them. The increasingly common images from the more arcane aspects of western traditions—alchemy, postindustrial science, electronic technology and the little-changing chores of housework and wifery—provide images that are common denominators in the experiences of Indian and non-Indian alike, making unitary perception and interpretation possible. The poetry of Oneida (Wisconsin) poet Roberta Whiteman Hill exemplifies this reconciliation, as in this fragment from "Leap in the Dark":

> —Then she sealed her nimble dreams
> with water from a murky bay. "For him I map
> this galaxy of dust that turns without an answer.
> When it rains, I remember his face in the corridor
> of a past apartment and trace the anguish around his mouth,
>   . . . With the grace that remains
> I catch a glint around a door I cannot enter.
> The clock echoes in dishtowels; I search love's center
> and bang pans against the rubble of my day, the lucid
> grandeur of wet ground, the strangeness of a fatal sun
> that makes us mark on the margin of our loss,
> trust in the gossamer of touch, trust in the late-plowed field.
> I hug my death, my chorus of years, and search
> and stretch and leap, for I will be apprentice to the blood
> in spite of the mood of the world
> that keeps rusting, rusting, the wild throats of birds.[9]

Transformation, or, more directly, metamorphosis, is the oldest tribal ceremonial theme, one common to ancient Europe, Britain, and America. And it comes once again into use within the American Indian poetry of extinction and regeneration that is ultimately the only poetry a contemporary Indian woman can write. Poets who have located a means of negotiating the perilous path between love and death, between bonding and dissolution, between tribal consciousness and modern alienation must light on the transformational metaphor to articulate their experience. Or as Whiteman writes:

> . . . Oh crazy itch that grabs us beyond loss
> and let us forgive, so that we can answer birds and deer,
> lightning and rain, shadow and hurricane
> Truth waits in the creek, cutting the winter brown hills:
> it sings of its needles of ice, sings because of the scars.[10]

And, in a recent poem, "Morning: The World in the Lake," Linda Hogan uses the metaphor of transformation to celebrate the duration and persistence that are the basic characteristics of continuance and of love:

Beneath each black duck
another swims
shadow
joined to blood and flesh.
There's a world beneath this one.
The red-winged blackbird calls
its silent comrade down below . . .

And then it rises, the blackbird
above the world's geography of light and dark
and we are there, living
in that revealed sliver of red
living in the black
something of feathers,
daughters all of us,
who would sleep as if reflected
alongside our mothers,
the mothers of angels and shadows,
the helix and spiral of centuries
twisting inside.
Oh the radiant ones are burning
beneath this world.
They rise up,
the quenching water.[11]

Reconciling the opposites of life and death, of celebration and grief, of laughter and rage is no simple task, yet it is one worthy of our best understanding and our best effort. If, in all these centuries of death, we have continued to endure, we must celebrate that fact and the fact of our vitality in the face of what seemed, to many, inevitable extinction. For however painful and futile our struggle becomes, we have but to look outside at the birds, the deer, and the seasons to understand that change does not mean destruction, that life, however painful and even elusive it is at times, contains much joy and hilarity, pleasure and beauty for those who live within its requirements with grace. I have written a series of poems about assimilation and colonization, laying these against arcane and land-centered understandings, trying to articulate the balance between despairing reality and the hope that continued existence requires, as in these lines from "Transformations":

> Out in the light or sitting alone,
> sorting, straightening tangled skeins
> (they're always tying lives in knots)
> I would like to be sleeping. Not
> dreaming, just blacked out:
> no one bumping around in my brain—
> no tangles, no deaths, just quiet
> empty nests, just threads
> lying straight and ordered and still.
> Outside the window I can see
> sweet winter birds
> rise up from tall weeds
> chattering. They fly
> into sunrisen sky that holds them
> in light.[12]

The information and the patterns of continuance are all around us, if we will accept them for what they can signify and use them to lend vitality and form to our life. Certainly in the long ago that's what they did, and that's what they can do now as well.

The Style of the Times in Paula Gunn Allen's Poetry

Elaine A. Jahner

As poet, novelist, teacher, critic, and editor, Paula Gunn Allen has been an undeniably major player in the varied scenes of contemporary Native American artistic and academic life. Yet, to date, surprisingly little sustained criticism of her poetry has been published, even though the 1997 volume of collected poems, *Life Is a Fatal Disease,* gave us her own selection of works written over a thirty-year span.[1] The sequencing of poems in this book is designed to show Allen's consistent thematic concerns. Fortunately, many items are notated with the year of their initial publication, because the thematic arrangement of the book obscures the chronology of her stylistic development and the style implies its own story. If we follow through with what style implies, we can piece together a rather different critical narrative from what we might deduce by concentrating primarily on thematic content. I propose that the progression revealed through style is finally the one that speaks most cogently about Allen as a feminist identifying with her Native American heritage while experimenting with poetic strategies in a manner she viewed as directly analogous to the way physicists test their hypotheses about energy and matter. The comparison of poetry to science points to the foundational nature of the doing and making required by Allen's poetics. She has aimed for nothing less than alternative models for thinking about relationships between time and space and their effects on perception. All of this radical experimentation, though, has also been part of a political agenda that has developed in uneasy but consistent relationships with the imagistic quest. Therefore, poetic representation has been held to a critical coherence with socially representative political expression. The differences between these conjoined projects set up a politics of subjectivity that Allen's writing both structures and brings into general critical focus.

Allen's autobiographical statement for her contribution to *Reinventing the Enemy's Language* gets directly to the foundational and, by now, resolutely popular nature of her agendas. She characterizes her career as one of gaining increasing authority to influence the dynamics of cultural definition. Encouraging Native Americans to join in the production phases of media-generated virtual reality, she states, "We must get control of those definitions, those contexts, and those images of ourselves." In reference to her own work, she restates a standardized set of assumptions about power aptly reducible to direct political statements: "I write because I am aware that whoever controls the image controls the population; that those who define us determine not only our lives, but our concept of our very selves, and that colonization begins and ends with the definer, the contextualizer, and the propagandist."[2] All of this has a very nineties resonance. Allen, though, has been using the act of constructing poems as a means of resisting inappropriate definition since her first publications. *The Blind Lion* includes a poem entitled "Definition," which is set up as a hypothesis about how individuals give defining force to each other's statements and "move" so that what is at the beginning is

> recapitulated
> in every step,
> bringing forward
> whatever of meaning
> was before
> each step[3]

Like Coyote, the wandering mythic inventor of language to whom she gestured when she entitled another early volume *Coyote's Daylight Trip,* Allen set out to make the most of evasive action within language that still finally manages to achieve social reference; and that paradoxical combination of evasion and reference sets up the struggle that characterizes her poetics. More specifically, she has tried to devise a poetics that would communicate a tribal sense of self-conceptualization as a "moving event in a moving universe." Appropriately, this phrase comes from a passage in which she explains why she uses the theoretical models of physics as strategic analogies for her own work. "Years ago Fred Young, the Navajo mathematician and physicist, explained to me the essential movement of time and space. He said that if you held time constant, space went to infinity, and when space was held constant, time moved to infinity. That was why it was not possible to determine the exact location of a particle on a grid. The tribal sense of self as a moving event within a moving universe is very similar to the physicists' understanding of the particle within time and space."[4]

There is good ethnographic and ethnolinguistic evidence for the tribal sense of self as moving event in a moving universe.[5] But documenting that facticity has not been Allen's goal. She wanted to do something much more difficult. She wanted to bring this idea of self as moving event into the way she situated a poetic persona within poetic structure, and that goal implies so much movement within movement within movement that the logic of structure easily gets lost even if one stays concentrated on the self as acting within a single tribal context. And Allen had to take much more than a single tribal context into account. She has never backed away from the fact that her own experience has been conditioned by so many different cultures and languages that she has laughingly but accurately dubbed herself "a multicultural event."[6] So, the woman whose own experience proved the inadequacy of any convenient identity labels, the woman who has been extremely critical of the potentially discriminatory consequences of any definition, is also the poet who discovered that she had to set up linguistic experiments to test ideas of time and space and the strategic limits that a poet might devise for the rapidly multiplying possibilities of signification that go with poetic reflection on her own several cultural positions. Allen's distinctive style derives from those early experiments when she was just discovering how she could use poetry to find "what will stay in line" ("Locus"). "Style" in the context of this essay refers to the pervasive effects of a set of strategies devised to establish a unifying position (a unifying subject) within poetic language. My use of the progressive tense for "unifying" is an attempt to keep Allen's notion of self as moving event in critical juxtaposition with various theoretical models of the subject-in-process. Allen's particular strategies have varied somewhat from stage to stage of her writing career, but each new phase has been a consistent development of what came before, so that we can legitimately speak of signature moves making up her distinctive style.

The first poem in *Life Is a Fatal Disease* lets us glimpse the entire progression of strategies, in a poem about historical characters. This monologue, the first of several in the collected works, is structured as La Malinche's address to Hernando Cortés. La Malinche speaks from an unspecified but definitely modern temporal position that allows her to review the course of history and pronounce her triumph over Cortés, saying,

I now stand, silent, still,
and watch with great Cihuacoatl
as your time runs out.[7]

At least two of Allen's characteristic strategies are at work in these verses, even though their subtlety proves that Allen has naturalized technique to the point where it no longer draws attention to itself. We get evidence of the first when the speaker refers to her own silence even as she speaks her judgment. As I will illustrate, this device harks all the way back to Allen's earliest poems about words that could be "kept waiting" in atemporal space until the right temporal structure might be in place and the right addressee might be ready to hear.

The second strategy is more pervasive in Allen's writing, and we note it through La Malinche's reference to "your time," an implication that the speaker's time and the conqueror's are not the same. The single most persistent set of stylistic strategies in Allen's poetry derive from experimentation with multiple temporal perspectives. While the stylistic effects of such experiments are easily overlooked in the context of a single poem chosen for illustrative purposes simply because it is the first one in the collected works, the study of the entire body of poetry proves how fundamental diverse temporal figures are to the patterns of effects that establish the subject in Allen's poetry. Proliferating temporal perspectives also constitute a major thematic strand in her poetry. If we go from the first to the last poem in the collected works, one entitled "Trinity: 50 Years Gone Return," we can see how her particularly constituted categories of time and space can do comparable thematic work in a poem that is otherwise completely different from the one previously quoted. In this final framing poem, she evokes the apocalyptic image of nuclear disaster in terms of time, space, and light all achieving annihilating conjunction. In that imagined dissolution of all the differences she has been writing about and writing in order to bring about for an entire lifetime, we witness the collapse of matter itself:

the light of annihilation
the time into the sky
a matter of location
dismattering[8]

Moving from the framing poems in the collected works to the initial poem in Allen's first published chapbook, *The Blind Lion,* we discover the original outlines of the experiments with temporality. This poem, appropriately entitled "Overture," turned out to be a genuine overture to what was to come, setting forth the main lines of development, even hinting at the many complications that followed from them. This poem has never been republished, undoubtedly because it falters as a poem. It is more accurately characterized as the statement of a problem that points toward solutions but is not in itself part of the solution. Given the complexity that Allen has always sought to sort out by way of the act of writing, critics have reason to be grateful that some of her early trial-and-error poems were published, so that we can trace the beginning stages of a progression that is startling in its complexity.

"Overture" mimes the situated dialogism of speech acts, and through it we get drawn into the first, often frustrating intricacies of Allen's conditional temporality, which she constructed early in her career to protect herself from a whole series of perceived dangers that this poem does not name, cannot name, because the persona experiences them all as vague unspecified threats. The first word of this poem, standing as an entire verse in itself, states the single most cogent and daunting of all human imperatives: "Speak." That one-word injunction loops back and around all personal symbolic activity to order to demand constantly renewed entry into time across the threshold of language. If such critical commentary seems inflated, its extreme scope is, nevertheless, in keeping with the way the intricate metaphoric problem is set up to deal with the simple and unarguable, hence foundational, fact that as soon as words achieve utterance, their interpretation belongs to others and the impacts of time and history on their comprehension. As her critical and novelistic writings attest, this commonplace observation about the fundamental nature of speech acts was a source of genuine anxiety for Allen; and that fear is easily comprehensible if we pause and think about the ordinary tensions between intentionality and interpretation and then project that reflection into conditions where politics accentuate all the ordinary tensions. This simple imagined projection points toward most of the political motives for Allen's experiments with temporality. What can protect poetic agency and intentionality (which Allen always tries to keep in textual play) when political circumstances lead to distortions that threaten agency? Allen's initial answers to this question predict her career. Therefore this early poem deserves some attention as evidence of an elementary stylistic economy, and it is certainly evidence of some amazing moves away from ordinary commonsense understandings of temporality.

Speak
as in a second
that doesn't
ask

as the people say:
as if words could wait
kept
warm in the crazed cooing
of a loony wind

as if you spoke
three days ago
with meaning

as if I
just now
replied.[9]

The poetic command to speak is immediately followed by the disconcerting reference to time that "doesn't / ask." Simple poetic artifice separates time from its inevitable role of contextualizing and thereby imposing meaning and definition on speech. The next verse ("as the people say") makes the hasty assumption that traditional speech acts collaborate with poetic language in fashioning conventions that cheat time out of its power to control contextual meaning. In this fantasy, "the people" set up the multiplying options implied by "as if," and the poet's own as-if dream is about words that can be freed from any and all conditionality implicit in their actually being spoken in real time. That same move shifts poetic agency away from an acting and speaking self to a contemplative self who can move in and out of the time frames implied by the acts of speaking and hearing.

Allen eventually modified the extreme artificiality of this attitude toward language's temporal conditionality, but she never completely abandoned the effort to use poetic artifice as a way to create "a space of now" that subverts linear temporality, to which she has occasionally assigned the impossible burden of the entire negative ideological weight of rampant rationalism. One poetic effect of Allen's attempt to separate speech from the rules of pragmatic temporality has been that her most characteristic dialogic structure removes both speaker and addressee from the immediacy of any face-to-face speech context. What is spoken is heard only when reflected back through the mediation of the imagined "as if" set of conditions, which is of the poet's making, the poet's privilege, and the poet's responsibility. What I am characterizing as an "as if" set of conditions is Allen's favored device for keeping any postulated unifying self in a shifting, moving relationship to any other defining factors. We find the features of this reflexive temporal structure (effects of what occurs in time are reflected back into time by a consciousness outside the temporal structure) recurring in every phase of Allen's poetry. But her skills in implementing the style and her capacity to control how elements of it might relate to her political goals have changed so much that it is sometimes hard to recognize the continuity in it all.

Initially, the stylistic structure was evidence of fearful indecision represented by paradoxical and contradictory moves away from any kind of control, including the poet's artistic control over form. No tradition has definitive power at this early stage. Allen has reprinted few of the poems that emerged from this early struggle in which the symbolic nature of language itself seemed the enemy. There would be no point even in referring to this work if it were not for the way this early stage presages mature stylistic patterns and sets up questions about how multiple traditions can interact in poems that retain a unifying subject. The developmental stages of this pattern give us the basis for comparison with other poets and with different theoretical understandings of reciprocal relationships between poetic language and identity. Any approach to comparison or theorizing that sidesteps this developmental emphasis is fundamentally flawed.[10] Allen's ethical and political beliefs meant that she could not just arbitrarily establish a collage of references that would work for the momentary task. She viewed herself as ethically bound to finding a locally legitimated point of entry to traditional knowing and language, and having found that threshold, she tried to chart a journey that accounted for the social facts of her varied positions. Her poetry and her novel are alternative records of this same process. Reflecting on the novel, she has summed up its autobiographical themes with the cool precision of the critic.

> Ephanie spends much of her time alone . . . trying to discover the history, the ritual traditions, and the family and personal events that led her to this lonely life and that will, perhaps, enable her to take

charge of her fate. . . . She finally uncovers the source of her despair and isolation and is drawn into the spiritual life of the women of her people. . . . As a breed Ephanie is raised outside of the formal tradition of her people, but inwardly she is ritual-oriented. Her difficulty . . . is finding a point of entry into the ritual patterns of her people.[11]

The critic's language, though, does not convey either the psychological or the political dilemmas that attend that process of finding an honest point of entry into identity as a woman whose early life brought her partway into many traditions. None of these traditions are a unitary source of symbolic structures for her own development because the guidelines for how to think about entry into any tradition are, for Allen, shaped by her Laguna Pueblo heritage.[12] And Laguna, like other Native American communities, has its own ritualized pace and custom-defined approach to structuring the stages of identity formation. Moving among different identity positions, Allen has had to try to find appropriate ways to represent a process as it was paced by events in her own life but not necessarily ritualized in any traditional way. She knew that to take shortcuts would forfeit an integrity informed by the Native American traditions to which she remains always loyal if not always literal in her practice.

The politics of subjectivity dominate our time, but they take on particular configurations in any Native American context.[13] Within any of today's many Native American cultures, individual approaches to these politics inevitably come back to Allen's questions about how the subject achieves that crucial point of entry to the communal, with its associated social, linguistic, and even spiritual requirements, and then pursues a lifetime of responsible participation. Historically, individual entry to the symbolic resources of cultures and individual progress toward increasing levels of political responsibility have been structured by ceremonial means. Obviously, though, contemporary life multiplies individual options for group identifications while complicating responsibilities to any single community, and the question of how that relates to traditional means of structuring the individual's relationship to the communal is seldom answered with easy formulas. Literature has charted the moral and psychological impact of what we are currently labeling "identity politics," although we might get closer to what is at stake with a more process-oriented term. Whether or not such a term ever achieves currency, novelists and poets are mapping the contemporary spiritual and psychological terrain as they speak from their particular positions in relation to communities. One consequence of this exceptionally difficult act of mediation on the part of any creative writer or critic is that auto-biographical writing of any kind—including interviews and poetry—has had, and no doubt will continue to have, a particularly central role in the development of Native American critical thought. The autobiographical dimension in all of Allen's writing presents the stylistic evidence of the difficulties inherent in the quest for an honest position in relation to traditional histories.[14]

Literary and cultural critics who work from within different Native American contexts have their task, too. We have been operating from the premise that the critical way forward has to start with careful descriptive work, as free as possible from prescriptive suppositions. Only after de-scription has established a reasonably adequate contextualizing frame that arises from awareness of how little most readers outside the Native American world understand the political diversity within, ought we try to evaluate or supplement the critical effectiveness of individual attempts to articulate the conjunction between their subjective quest and their per-ceived responsibilities to tribal communities.

Most of Allen's early poems illustrate the preliminary position of some-one who instinctively knows that when it comes to the social facts of any traditional subjective positioning, the intellect dare not claim for its own what has not been earned step by traditionally defined psychological step. So when the poet says in "Word Game" that her lines

> become bridges
> from void to void,
> from undefined to unknown,
> from error to disbelief,[15]

we know that the solution to all this abstraction is not just a matter of some good professional advice about what makes for strong poetry. To get beyond these hopelessly tentative, asymbolic gestures, Allen had to get at some specific sociocultural motives for the strange but honest distances she had constructed between addresser and addressee, aligning them with specific points in her imagined grids of time and space. As she did the necessary hard poetic and cultural work, she gradually achieved a linguistically constructed journey that is simultaneously a rehearsal of the stages of psycholinguistic development and a discovery of how to make her reflexive temporality do some genuine work in a recognizable social context. That, in turn, led to a poetic confrontation with real violence in real places and with all the telling detail that any good poet needs.

Allen was among the first Native Americans to write about the urban Indian experience. The poem "Locus," written in 1973, then republished in *Life Is a Fatal Disease,* shows how her disruptions of conventional notions of time and space gradually helped her envision an urban setting for her understanding of self as "moving event in a moving universe." In "Locus" the poet presents a lacerated self, a fragmented subjectivity whose local sources impact consciousness through images reflected on urban windows and bright surfaces.

> Fragments,
> Sudden surfaces mix and shatter, out
> of touch. I am deranged by seeing, need
> what will stay in line—sights, smells, sounds
> so strong that mind becomes unreal, body
> a shredded surface, plane and line
> led and obscene. There
> is a voyage on the streets, burrowed
> in parks and brothels,
> peering from windows of flats
> and loitering in doorways of cheap hotels
> (which is not allowed). Where
> are you going, city?[16]

The persona of "Locus" has been reduced to a hallucinatory aware-ness of self as controlled by the institutions whose windows let her glimpse the image that proves she really has some actual existence in this strange place. Those opaque windows reflecting the materialistic ac-coutrements of the urban cultural background for the image of self can-not, however, display the epistemological or psychological "terms" for the persona who knows she needs "what will stay in line" if she is to escape the narcissistic nightmare in the streets. The quest for these "terms" continues throughout Allen's career to date, and it becomes increasingly definite in the more recent poems. "Locus," though, marks a point at which social contexts begin to enter the figurations of time and space that typify Allen's style. Its persona may be down and out and screaming her sharp pain, but in spite of it all, she is neither overwhelmed nor defeated. She can still read her streets with remarkable pragmatic acuity that allows her to see their potential. The images reflected from the architectural artifacts of a definite locale give social content to spatial figurations, of which the self is the primary one. Time comes into the poem as the movement implied by the notion of a voyage. The poem ends on a thoroughly modernist note that echoes Yeats even as it shows evidence of Allen's continuing stylistic experiments with temporality. In fact, the Yeatsian echoes are so strong that they all but overpower Allen's own voice in the last verses. Nevertheless, the recurring image of shifting winds as guide to time and place and sense of self has to be noted as further evidence of how Allen tries to sidestep the defining impact of any one set of distinctions within time and space in order to draw attention to a contrasting but still concealed set of alternatives. The figure for time is expanded in mid-poem. Time may be on a voyage toward the new urban significance that the persona seeks, but the voyage has to begin with the spatially imaged mother. Time waits to be born; the images discovered on urban streets are finally presented as atemporal presences mothering the symbolic dimensions of historical temporality. These figurations gave Allen one of her more frequently repeated lines: "the image is where the action is begotten." "Locus" continues,

I know myself in terms of boundaries,
horns, glimpses of good times and helpless
age decaying in windows, at intersections,
through public arch and private lock on door:
institution.

So this is final, this hallucination:
although I am alone, and so, alive,
I play it close to my chest, look down
and out, look inside, in city, in street,
in body, both ways before I cross. Wind
becomes a scurrying guide
to time and place and sense
of self: the image is where
the action is begotten, and undreamed

centuries lurk in every darkened alley,
around every corner,
across every intersection,
behind every pane of glass,
waiting to be born.[17]

In "Locus" the death that the poet contemplates is her own. That finality is an outer limit against which to test awareness of continuing life. But death acquires more incisive poetic force at this stage of the poet's life and writing. One of her infant twin sons died a crib death. Her son's death becomes the catalyst that forces distinguishing finality into a dynamics of representation that had previously gone as far as language can go without specific reference. The experience of death ended the poetic experiments that staged a one-sided retreat into undecidability or a passive reflexivity, keeping as many options as possible in constant but generally unproductive play. The death of a loved one, especially a child, lances the psyche, requires recognition of the inevitability of limits that clearly do mark some kind of temporal progression, even if poets, mystics, and physicists might think about alternative markings for such progression. Following a developmental trajectory that is certainly not logical but emotional, the individual comes to know—truly and fully to know—that separations and limits will take on their necessary role in the ongoing life of survivors, and necessity itself feels real as it marshals its impacts on the psyche. Spoken words do inevitably take on predetermined signification; time does inevitably have its linear impact. The process that mainstream psycholinguistic theory calls Oedipal does occur, even though its matriarchal mythic markings, maybe even its dynamics, may vary from the patriarchal mythic labels and dynamics. And it all adds up to the awareness caught in the title of Allen's collected works: "life is a fatal disease."

The short poem "Elegy for My Son" is a simple and direct recognition of how death ended narcissistic dreams of rearranging time and unsaying words:

I wanted to write 1968 for today's date—as though
somewhere between then and
then, some step taken could be untaken, or a word
spoken be unsaid
some little thing done
not

wouldn't lead into
where with bewildered hands I sit
holding your small body dead.[18]

The poet says "I wanted," and her experience of that achieved past-
ness gives the lie to the dream of being able to rearrange time. Nevertheless, the dream still creates a reflexive distance even though the mother
has crossed a temporal boundary that imposes the firm past tense of that
"I wanted." The reflexive subjective distance, always setting the style of
Allen's poetic positioning, now begins to accommodate more definite
temporal distinctions, and the purpose of any subsequent reflexive with-
drawal on the part of the subject is called into question by the poem itself,
thereby opening the way to greater political efficacy. "Elegy for My Son"
speaks to what cannot be undone as it achieves a turn toward what might
be done. This is increasingly a turn to political imagining. Watching and
waiting begin to come into Allen's poetry as themes paired with ideas of
balancing and momentary rather than permanent withholding. We find
references to time as precisely calibrated, calculated, and artistically
used, not rejected. The poem "On the Street: Monument" directly links
the death of her son, Fuad, to the observing, judging political intelligence
that Allen began to incorporate into her poetic style during this period.

On the day Fuad died the heat
glittered and melted the asphalt; someone
in Cambridge thought Marx understood the plight
of streets and watered poor hearts of brown, black and gold
masses: proletariat, confined to non-photographic modes
of thought.

.　.　.　.

On the street
the commonplace is ideologue: so little time
spent hanging out, romantic shadows hide ivied eyes from spit
on the sidewalk, ground-in shit, sickening heat
a street is going
someplace. . . .[19]

After the revisions forced by a new understanding of death, Allen
writes poems in which the streets are going to a real "someplace." Allen's
artistic reworkings of street imagery become evidence of her own psycho-

logical journey outward from the constraints of fear to the courage of social action. There is still mediation, but it no longer serves to deflect action. Rather it is a way of seeking an appropriate response to the maternal, mythic engendering of active imagery that allows her to trace a developmental process in relation to specific mythic traditions with their own histories. We might say that the poetry begins to take place in real time. Nevertheless, it is still not the poetry of direct social activism. The mythic dimension that simultaneously allows for the marking of a psychological progression and for identification with a specific historical community guarantees that we have temporality with a difference and myth that is being put to work in new ways. The force of all that drove Allen to her descent toward psychological origins, and her poetic reconfiguration of the most basic orientations to time and space and language gets redirected as creative and hence disruptive energy, which is quickly salvaged from anarchy through its alliance with mythic reference. At this stage, we also find significant and controversial occasional shifts in the way Allen situates the unifying subject (the persona) of the poem. She definitely retains a believer's position in relation to the entire realm of the sacred as it has structured the ceremonial and social life of distinctive Native American communities, but as she adopts and poetically strategizes the teleological perspective of the mystic, she occasionally uses it with considerable comparative leeway, going quickly from one Native American tradition to another and occasionally even recruiting non-Native mystics to help her say her piece. Among other stylistic effects, all this provides poetic occasion for the humor that is a fortunate contrast to the dominating seriousness of so much earlier work. One can argue that "American Apocalypse" is among those of her poems that most consistently meet criteria for poetic excellence. In spite of its title and its quite serious cast of characters: William Blake, Isaiah, and Ezekiel, it is a richly humorous evocation of what might happen if William Blake ended up in Chicago's Grant Park with all its equestrian statuary, complete with generals in the saddle:

> Well, whaddya know, and there's old Billbelly Blake
> sitting inside a horse's mouth, eating an onion-and-pastrami
>   sandwich,
> farting on the lilacs he piled up on the beastie's tongue to make
> a couch, and spouting piss & vinegar through every follicle of his

steaming skull.
Aha, old master prophet,
voice of the pentecost wind,
old crooked-tongued mouther of forgotten words—
there you are![20]

Allen's freedom to compare traditions is a consequence of working at a level of abstraction that provides a contemplative distance from different traditions without denying the specific detailed impact of any of them. She might seem to have circled back to where she started, uniquely distanced from any tradition; but that assumption would deny her stylistic development. She has spiraled around from her starting point in abstractions, keeping her unique distance but incorporating more and more of the detail of actual traditions with each spiraling turn. She has been trying to find the right distance between subject and traditional source that would give her a point from which to comment and make something of her own. As her more recent poetry shows, she now appreciates how the historical detail of each tradition constitutes "the law," and she knows that "the law binds" as she seeks to articulate what that binding means to her as an artist, moving from one tradition to another even as her emphasis on the general aspects of the process still sometimes holds her to an abstract perspective. One of the best poetic illustrations of abstract positioning that reveals the poetic subject operating in relation to local specificity is entitled "Transformations."

Brain wraps fibers of fantasy
around the spindle of thought.
Turning
Old weaver hands steady, intent
mattering. The law binds:
There is a way often untold to require
the filaments of dream to enter
the pitch and spin of atoms. . . .[21]

Her poetry still depends on "the fibers of fantasy" for its starting points. Only now she has faced up to all that is implied when the stuff of dreams enters dense but mobile materiality, "the pitch and spin of atoms," the active historical precision of linguistic denotation and connotation. The law that binds also defines, and Allen no longer perceives this condition as oppressive. Rather, she works with "old weaver hands" that rhythmically, consistently, realize the conjunction between dream and artistic product in a traditional manner, continuing a time-honored process that employs individual creativity in the service of communal identity.

In Allen's early work, abstractions about time and space might have overwhelmed the capacity of any poetic structure to bestow even the transitory credibility that form instantiates for a reader. Mythic structures, though, grow out of human awareness that there are always possibilities that establish a collective need for images with maximum elementary referential range. Within this view of myth, we could substitute the adjective "scientific" for "mythic" without losing the force of the statement, and all of this formulaic switching between the two terms could then summarize what has been an honest, complex, and highly informed journey on Allen's part. Subjective needs could be expressed and understood as the individualized point of entry to a communal ritual context. But the sociohistorical facts of many different communal traditions multiplied and redefined the subjective needs and the repertoires of communal responses. Allen went from one political agenda to another, from civil rights struggles to feminism to antinuclear and ecological struggles, consistently adapting her poetic strategies to the task at hand. The consistency was established once she had worked her way to an honest understanding of "the eternal game: / manifestation." The game uses a concrete image, uses ordinary materiality to shrink immensity to what is poetically (and politically) manageable. The image is a "point" that can be "thought." She also works the inverse sort of magic, the kind that situates what is manageably immediate so that it points to the immensely unmanageable that is always behind Allen's style. And she has kept on trying to make the process serve communal advantage, showing how ethnic and gender distinctions set up a grid that allows the poet to show how "moving events in a moving universe" can be related to each other. Addressing the feminine divinity of Laguna culture, Allen repeats her basic positions in "Affirmation."

> moving as the light
> the wind
> plays the eternal game:
> manifestation.
>
> So, grandmothers,
> your gifts still go with me

unseen.
To reach.
Slowly
to go
(as the tree makes its way through the earth)
the simultaneous thought of this
and other
makes the distance between each point disappear.[22]

"Simultaneous thought of this / and other" is, of course, impossible within a narrowly rational, linear framework. Simultaneity belongs to a different register of linguistic experience, one that can be explored only through awareness of metaphoric polyvalence. The dream of simultaneity emerges from the prelinguistic, and the attempt to give it a place and rhythmic signifying force within language is always a usurpation that undermines and shifts stable signification, which depends upon linear temporal structures. Simultaneity finds its truest externalized semiotic equivalent in musical harmonies. Allen has understood this, and she labels rhythm and harmony as maternal qualities even as she has tried to expand her repertoire of poetic rhythms:

the Mother raises her luminous dark head

. . . .

moon rising over the heavy-leafed trees
and brings me striding the rhythm, the heartbeat of a continent
beating in my ears, throbbing in my skull.[23]

Critics can trace Allen's strategies, her rhythms, her way of listening to "the heartbeat of a continent." The specific detail of all this proves Allen's technical competence as a poet. But eventually, the poems themselves direct us back to the way Allen, the literary critic, sets up the terms of a debate that is necessary to our era and the identity politics we cannot yet avoid. Allen's critical writing has given us her own take on this political necessity. As David Payne has pointed out in a review of her most recent critical writing, "Gunn Allen describes a distinction between the solo/solipsistic nature of much of Western literary criticism, and the relational nature of criticism she would hope for, as essentially cultural."[24] With goals as ambitious as hers, shortcuts are inevitable. But her poetry is more nuanced, subtler than her criticism. In the poetry she has more to say about what is required as a condition of a relational exchange among different positions in American life. Allen has assumed the role of public intellectual and teacher, and those roles are invitations to responsible critique. The debate should address the options and distinctions that create her stylistic position, which is the undergirding and the generative source of the thematic dimensions of all the other writing.

One way to sum up the mature status and function of those stylistic distinctions is to go to the title poem of *Life Is a Fatal Disease,* a poem that is obvious about matters the early poems treated obscurely, that is materially detailed where early poems were excessively abstract, whose persona is involved and related whereas the early persona was detached and fearfully separated. Yet for all these developed differences, there is still the same concern with time, space, and the way these categories guarantee that "no association is ever free." The most obvious stylistic device at work in this poem is its multilingualism. All the languages from all the cultures that have been part of Allen's autobiographical experience create the stride rhythms of this poem. The isolated subject of early work is gone. The subject of this poem is shaped by a family structure represented by proper name, by kinship connection complete with ethnic clarifications and sometimes even endearing quirky touches.

> last time I saw Isabel was the day Wendy on the Lebanese side
>   though his
> father was German American from somewhere in the east died too
>   young
> no, at her birthday when pop picked a fight with the dude serving
>   us. today
> uncle's gone, aunt's widowed for I can't remember how many
>   years.[25]

This poem is kinship theory in half a dozen languages and cultures. The minimal autobiographical narrative line in the poem, though, advances along Allen's consistent route as it links politics with myth by narrating a flight from a familial home and landscape now poisoned by atomic radiation. We find echoes of several earlier poems in the way this one conjoins apocalyptic endings of time and space with mythically designated beginnings of another time and space. She says that "no association is ever free," and she shows that she would not want it to be. The kinship network is clear and continuing evidence of social worlds making the generational turn as something new comes into being. Like the personified figures of so many Native American myths about entering a new world because an old era has ended, the members of this poetically placed family wander in quest of defining qualities for their new time and place. The fatal limits of life come into this poem as artistic attachment to memorized (hence transposable) material detail bound to the relational structure of kinship, which overrides those same fatal limits as long as and only as long as the progression implied by journeys to new worlds (new spaces) is materially possible. The self as moving event in a moving universe is, within this poem, precisely individualized and marked by historical contingencies, but it is still a self determined by mythic action. The multilingual poetic presentation accents those historical contingencies in the strongest possible way. But a notion of some force outside this temporal structure remains, addressed through the historical accident of real names like "Gottlieb." Families are the texts of time, and the generations distinguish stages in time in relation to what Allen always places outside of time. It took a long poetic journey to make this stylistic stance work as a way of chronicling the stages of a personal development that could bring so many different histories and so many different languages into art as family history, in which multiple elements rhythmically come together in a single poetic language. Finally Allen could write:

> kifik. grossgott. everyone. and synce ye're gaun, vaya con dios.
> tante Anna and Bob the Bruce's family's name was Gottlieb
> god dear or maybe dear god.
> saalem u khalem, du–wih shatz, mine schatz[26]

Herbs of Healing

American Values in American Indian Literature

Carter Revard

Minority/Majority Considerations

The history of empires is a funny thing, whether we are talking of literary or political empires. Six thousand years ago, two small "tribes" dwelt at the far margins of great empires, and unknown elders within those tribes fashioned stories made to create and preserve those tribes as communal wholes, to keep them in a good relation to the transhuman powers of the universe, and to give them strength to handle the great forces of empire that would destroy the special separate cultures of those tribes. Versions of the stories which they fashioned have survived the fall of the great empires—and those tribes, having canonized their stories and stayed themselves by keeping them alive, now dominate Planet Earth economically and culturally. One of those tribes, of course, was "Indo-European," the other was "Hebrew." Much revised, reinterpreted, added onto in astonishing ways, the Hebrew stories are now the "Judeo-Christian Bible," while the Indo-European ones include those of Homer, Shakespeare, Karl Marx, Charles Darwin, and Mark Twain. I wonder which of the marginal tribes of this last decade of the Twentieth Century of the Christian Messiah may now be composing the poetry which, six thousand years from now, will energize our galaxy—and I wonder whether those tribes now dwell on Planet Earth.

Culture-Wars

There are some Big Guns of American culture and politics who aim to shoot down "Minority Literature," claiming that it is trash unworthy of our classrooms, that conversing with it corrupts and keeps students from the uplifting morality of the "classical" books they ought to be spending time with.[1] Well (Gentle Readers), I want to introduce you to a few members of this family of monsters, so you can judge whether they are fit company for the next generation of Americans, to whom we stand *in loco parentis*. I will do this by setting certain "classic" poems beside others by contemporary American Indian writers, hoping this critical look will prove that the true values of American are just as vividly and richly present in the "ethnic" as in the classic poems. I think the comparison will show why American culture is enriched, not weakened, by opening the curriculum to these "new" regions of our heartland—regions which the Big Guns want us to think are deserts, but which I see as *lands of plenty, filled with herbs of healing*. To show this, I hope, may help end the war fomented by those old Gunslingers between "Minority Literature" and "Great Books." They want, being Gunslingers, to divide and conquer—but (I would ask) why shouldn't we unite, and live in freedom and plenty? Think what Columbus found, five hundred years ago, upon which we now feast, or with which we doctor ourselves: corn, potatoes, chocolate, pumpkins, potatoes, quinine, curare, *as well as* European wheat and whiskey; coyotes, raccoons, bison *as well as* imported Black Angus, Norway rats, and Arab steeds; bluejays and scissortails *as well as* English sparrows, starlings, and pigeons for the shoulders of our bronzed panjandrums. Don't we want an *All-American* curriculum?

Family Values

To begin, we will set a much-anthologized poem, a "modern classic" by Wallace Stevens (1879–1955), alongside one by Simon Ortiz (1941–) of Acoma Pueblo. These are small poems but they hold huge ideas: versions of America itself. Stevens's "Anecdote of the Jar," first published in 1923, has been given much commentary.[2] No such attention has yet been given "Speaking," published in the 1970s.[3]

Anecdote of the Jar	Speaking
I placed a jar in Tennessee,	I take him outside
And round it was, upon a hill,	under the trees,
It made the slovenly wilderness	have him stand on the ground.
Surround that hill.	We listen to the crickets,

The wilderness rose up to it,
And sprawled around no longer wild.
The jar was round upon the ground,
And tall and of a port in air.

It took dominion everywhere.
The jar was gray and bare.
It did not give of bird or bush,
Like nothing else in Tennessee.[4]

cicadas, million years old sound.
Ants come by us.
I tell them,
"This is he, my son.
This boy is looking at you.
I am speaking for him."

The crickets, cicadas
the ants, the millions of years
are watching us.
My son murmurs infant words,
speaking, small laughter
bubbles from him.
Tree leaves tremble.
They listen to this boy
speaking for me.

Stevens's poem is a terse fable, a kind of bonsai version of how Art conquers and indeed enslaves Nature, or Reality. It is hard to say whether Stevens approves, disapproves, or takes an ironically detached view of this conquest. The poem certainly speaks in a Conqueror's voice, saying just what many American historians have said (with no irony intended) about "civilizing" the "American Wilderness," and compelling deference from its natives. Round, tall, and with an important air, this non-natural Jar defines Wilderness as *slovenly*, effortlessly tames it so that it "sprawl[s] around, no longer wild," as the jar assumes imperial power "everywhere." Only in the last three lines does Stevens seem to turn his irony against the Jar, describing it as "gray and bare," as not allowing any sense of Nature or Vegetation, and showing up the whole of "Tennessee" as being UNlike the Jar—which indeed is "like nothing else in Tennessee."

There is, then, an Idea of Art and America in this poem—and the idea, I think, is as purple, showy and poisonous as loco-weed. Perhaps Stevens is himself appalled or ironically critical of this Empire of Abstract Ideas and the Jar which is their Centurion—yet the poem exalts the magic of Abstraction and Power which enslaves Tennessee and its creatures. One of the poem's crimes, indeed, is its dandiacal condescending to the great abstract "state" of Tennessee—which, before that Jar arrived, was some sort of Tabula Rasa, but after its arrival is cowed into cooliedom, kowtowing to the Imperial—nay, the DIVINE!—Artist. Just one bit of European Craft, wrought by a single sly-and-handy poet, has turned an entire country into a subdued and self-alienated place, where his Viceroy refuses all resemblance to any "native" being!

It is of course a "classic" European notion that setting a Jar—or a Cross, or a Crown, or a Writ—upon a hill allows one to "take possession" of the whole "territory" surrounding that artifact. What bothers me most, I think, is that Stevens does not really put any America around his Jar. It was Gertrude Stein who wittily complained about Oakland, "There is no THERE, there!" In Stevens's poem, there is no Tennessee in Tennessee: what's "there" is an Easterner's idea that "culture stops at the Hudson" (a phrase actually spoken to me once, with amused seriousness, by a professor of German at Amherst College).[5] Here the European Modern has throned itself at the continent's center, destroying any possible alternative: has, in short, "civilized" America.

But there IS an alternative, and Simon Ortiz has given us an Acoma story that counters this "classic" one. His poem, "Speaking," like Stevens's "Anecdote," is short and profound. Its ideas of America, of Art, of Nature and Humanity, are no less heroic in size, but lack the pompous arrogance, the neurofibromatosis of the artistic ego, which mask the Stevens poem.

One crucial difference is that Ortiz puts two humans into his poem, a father and his son. The poet himself is just as powerfully "there" as in Stevens—but whereas Stevens makes the Jar his Viceroy, Ortiz acts as Intercessor for his son, speaking "for" the infant to the powerful, ancient, and enduring beings whom this poem calls to our awareness. Then Ortiz is in turn "spoken for" by his infant son, whose language is after all older than that of his father, and whose "speaking" is listened to by those future generations to whom, eventually, he will indeed "speak for" his father.

And here we touch the nub of our comparison: it is FAMILY VALUES which dominate the Ortiz poem, *and the family in question is more than human.* "Anecdote of the Jar" narrates conquest, enslavement, culture-wars, class alienation, war between the Civil and the Natural, all as a result of the poet's imagined action. In "Speaking," the poet is not alone, not alienating himself by language or art, but using speech within a family, introducing his new son to other members of that family: trees, ground, crickets, cicadas, ants, and—in a startling leap—Time itself, the "millions of years." As the title tells us, this poem is about the human act of speaking, not just the high-culture *art* of speech or poetry, which is only one part of that more profound act. Here, the act of speaking and the art of listening work together in a mutual effort to gain understanding, support, and blessing for a fruitful life on earth. More remarkably, the poem discovers for its composer that his son's first speech to this great family is as deeply meaningful and important as anything his father can say. That a child's voice utters itself, that it is heard, is after all the most important human truth celebrated in the poem: to continue, to keep the human race alive, is more important than whatever the father might have uttered at that point. Implicitly, the poem humbles its poet AND us, tells us that our best speaking begins with, depends upon, is like that of the tiniest infant in this great universe.

So the idea of America in Ortiz's poem is truly a healing reminder of what is amiss in the remarkable poem by Stevens, where abstraction disdainfully dominates nature. The English of Ortiz is no less metaphysically sophisticated than that of Stevens, but it is "ordinary" English not "artful," it sounds like plain speech, not highfalutin rhetoric. As Wordsworth said in his Preface to the *Lyrical Ballads,* it is the language of real men speaking with deep feeling and not falling into "poetic diction." The result is a sense that Ortiz is just telling us a real story, what happened, what he did, what was said. In the poem, the poet stands not imperiously but humbly, not as lord of all he surveys but as an Acoma father, one member only of this realm of beings, conscious and respectful of those others we might scarcely notice "outside" our homes, including Time itself listening to the child as well as the father. This is no "taking possession" but a ritual of acknowledging smallness and dependency, fellowship and community, shared natural being. Stevens diagnoses an illness; Ortiz enacts a cure.

Speaking of Massacres

Human beings, however, do not always "share natural being" so nicely as the Ortiz poem shows them doing. John Milton (1608–1674), for instance, lived in interesting times, when one tribe of Europeans was apt to massacre another on religious grounds if no strictly economic or political excuse came handy. In 1655, certain Catholic troopers in the Savoy Alps slaughtered a large number of Protestant men, women, and babies, whereupon Milton—a Protestant—wrote a magnificent sonnet of protest, saying some pretty nasty things about the Pope and his forces.[6] Three and a half centuries afterwards, in 1890, a slaughter of similar brutality was carried out in Wounded Knee, South Dakota, by troopers of the U.S. Seventh Cavalry (George Custer's regiment)—their motive for massacre being also, in part, religious: the Lakotas slaughtered there were engaging in a forbidden religious ritual (the "Ghost Dance"), and the Lakota were not merely "heretics" but "heathens." In the 1970s (some four-score and seven years later), the Hopi/Miwok poet Wendy Rose wrote a protest, Miltonic in its eloquence though not in its rhetoric, against the Wounded Knee Massacre. Let's see what we can learn from these two poems, starting with John Milton's sonnet.[7]

On the Late Massacre in Piedmont

Avenge, O Lord, thy slaughtered saints, whose bones
Lie scattered on the Alpine mountains cold—
Even them who kept thy truth so pure of old,
When all our fathers worshipped stocks and stones!
Forget not: in thy Book record their groans
Who were thy sheep, and in their ancient fold
Slain by the bloody Piedmontese, that rolled
Mother with infant down the rocks; their moans
The vales redoubled to the hills, and they
To heaven. Their martyred blood and ashes sow
O'er all the Italian fields, where still doth sway
The Triple Tyrant: that from these may grow
A hundred fold, who having learnt thy Way,
Early may fly the Babylonian woe!

When I talk with students about this poem, I speak of its biblical majesty of sound, of the history that lies behind and within it, its political commitment, the effective propaganda in its picture of mother and baby as they are brutally, callously, sadistically ROLLED down the steep Alpine slopes on those rocks. I marvel at how vividly we hear what happens in these mountain vales, the echoing moans of pain and screams of terror as women clinging to their babies are jerked, thrown, shoved over the precipices to fall down and down onto rocks below, how precisely Milton recreates in the poem's rhythm and cadences what the soldiers did. Then I try to say how much more powerful the poem becomes, how its words light up, when we connect them to their biblical reservoirs of prophetic rage, the thunderous lines of Isaiah, of the Psalms, of the book of Revelations. But I make sure we all remember, in all this, where the poem "comes out" in the end: not in a call for God to slaughter the Catholics in return for their slaughter of Protestants, but in a call for God to REC-ORD the martyrdom and SPREAD THE NEWS of it, so that the blood of these martyrs will become the seed of a hundred times as many new believers converted by such unjustified suffering. These new Protestants will thereafter, having learned God's true Way, FLEE the coming destruction of the Roman church, which Milton refers to as a *Babylonian woe*—that is, the kind of woe suffered by the citizens of ancient Babylon when it fell, as described in Old and New Testaments. Milton expects his readers to know both the canonical books of the Bible, and the contemporary political uses of that canon. It is a very beautiful poem, majestic in its wrath, angelic in its compassion, apostolic in its looking toward an ultimate triumph of the despised and suffering minority to which its writer belongs.

For let me repeat: though the poem seems at first to call down the wrath of God upon the Roman Catholics, in the end it steadfastly awaits God's grace to draw these criminals into the faith of those they are murdering, and expresses hope that the converted people will then manage to flee the inevitable destruction which (Milton implies) will strike down this "Babylon"—this great imperial city of the Triple Tyrant. We have to see that Milton's great flashing thunderclouds call a gentle rain of mercy down from heaven, not just the thunder and lightning of prophetic wrath.

And now let us look at Wendy Rose's poem of protest:

I Expected My Skin and My Blood to Ripen

When the blizzard subsided four days later . . . , a burial party was sent to Wounded Knee. A long trench was dug. Many of the bodies were stripped . . . to get the ghost shirts . . . the frozen bodies were thrown into the trench stiff and naked. . . . only a handful of items remain in private hands . . . exposure to snow has stiffened the leggings and moccasins, and all the objects show the effects of age and long use. . . ." [There follows:] Moccasins at $140, hide scraper at $350, buckskin shirt at $1200, womens' leggings at $275, bone breastplate at $1000.—Plains Indian Art: Sales Catalog by Kenneth Canfield, 1977

I expected my skin and my blood
to ripen,
not be ripped from my bones;
like green fruit I am peeled,
tasted, discarded; my seeds are stepped on
and crushed
as if there were no future. Now
there has been
no past.   My own body gave up the beads,
my own arms handed the babies away
to be strung on bayonets, to be counted
one by one like rosary stones and then
to be tossed to each side of life
as if the pain of their borning
had never been.
My feet were frozen to the leather,
pried apart, left behind—bits of flesh
on the moccasins, bits of papery deerhide
on the bones. My back was stripped
of its cover, its quilling intact; was torn,
was taken away, was restored.
My leggings were taken like in a rape
and shriveled to the size of stick figures
like they had never felt
the push of my strong woman's body
walking in the hills.
It was my own baby whose cradleboard I held.
Would've put her in my mouth
like a snake
if I could, would've turned her
into a bush or old rock
if there'd been enough magic
to work such changes. Not enough magic
even to stop the bullets.
Not enough magic
to stop the scientists.
Not enough magic
to stop the collectors.[8]

Rose's poem differs much from Milton's. His is spoken in the poet's own voice; hers is a dramatic monologue spoken a long time after the Wounded Knee massacre by one of the women killed there. Milton's poem says nothing of the economic forces involved in the Catholic/Protestant wars, though his *Lycidas* and prose tracts had shown his keen awareness of ecclesiastical corruptions in his time. But Wendy Rose prefaces her poem with a prose bit taken from a sales catalog written as guide to buyers and sellers of "Indian artifacts," some of which apparently were taken from corpses at Wounded Knee in 1890. The catalog offers quite a perspective on the teaching of American History in our schools. That the items described could be displayed, bought and sold on the open market, has its own grisly interest. To ask a controversial but (I think) relevant question, would it be possible to catalogue and sell a collection of souvenirs from Belsen, Dachau, or Auschwitz, and not draw a firestorm of outrage from a wide range of United States citizens? The answer to that question might explain why we may build in Washington, D.C., a monument to the Holocaust carried out in Europe by the Germans, but none to the many exterminations on this continent by the United States.

Though Rose's poem has for remote ancestor the biblical laments, it seems closer to the Martyr's Speech, particularly the Lament of Mary, Mother of Jesus. Perhaps the Middle English *Stond well, mother, under Rood* would have been the nearest "classic" poem for comparison—but it goes better with the historically parallel sonnet by Milton, which likewise concerns a particular slaughter for religious (and politico-economic) reasons of a minority group. One great difference between Rose and Milton is that she does not have his confidence that the martyrs' cause will prevail. Her speaker is defeated and lacks the tacit consolation apparent in Milton that from each of the martyred persons there will grow a multitude of "descendants" who will keep to the right way until the Apocalypse. She lacks, too, any sense that this painful death will allow her people to gain some sort of paradise, or regain America as the Ghost Dance had promised. Behind Rose's poem, no Scripture looms; it forms its own canon. Milton calls on God; Rose's unvoiced appeal is to her readers, to do the right thing to those who acted and still act against her people.

Rose expects her readers to know the history of Wounded Knee, and to have some remaining belief that what we call Art is linked in some way to the ethical and spiritual aspects of life, not solely to the monetary. As a medievalist, I know that cathedrals were built, in considerable part, by money drawn from saint-seeking tourists: religion, art, money are not separate from each other in Christian history. But it is less clear how the sufferings of women and children at Wounded Knee are related to the ART of that sales catalog, that "history" of the Collectors, the Museums, the Archaeologists and Scientists. And the only word Rose has for the Indian side of the encounter is MAGIC—not just that of the Ghost Dance, though including it. When I talk about this poem with students, one of the things I point to is the power of her final section's repeating the phrase, "not enough magic to stop . . . ," and how the "enemy list" builds to that final horror, from *bullets* to *scientists* to *collectors*. And with that last term, the poem has come full circle from its epigraph and made its point with the most poignant irony.

Men and Women: Garden and Wilderness

For our third pairing we have a complex sonnet by Robert Frost ("Never Again Would Birds' Song Be the Same") and a vivid, disturbing poem by Louise Erdrich ("Jacklight"). They are subtle in different ways about the relations between men and women: Frost puts a spin on the myth of Eden and our First Parents Adam and Eve, while Erdrich begins with the macho world of deerhunters (who use jacklights to mesmerize their prey) and turns it into the mythic world of Deer Woman (who lures men into a kind of Underworld). Here, first, is Frost's sonnet:

Never Again Would Birds' Song Be the Same

He would declare and could himself believe
That the birds there in all the garden round
From having heard the daylong voice of Eve
Had added to their own an oversound,
Her tone of meaning but without the words.
Admittedly an eloquence so soft
Could only have had an influence on birds
When call or laughter carried it aloft.
Be that as may be, she was in their song.
Moreover her voice upon their voices crossed
Had now persisted in the woods so long

That probably it never would be lost.
Never again would birds' song be the same.
And to do that to birds was why she came.[9]

And here, next, is Erdrich's poem:

Jacklight

[The same Chippewa word is used both for flirting and hunting game, while another Chippewa word connotes both using force in intercourse and also killing a bear with one's bare hands.—R. W. Dunning, Social and Economic Change among the Northern Chippewa (1959)]

We have come to the edge of the woods,
out of brown grass where we slept, unseen,
out of knotted twigs, out of leaves creaked shut,
out of hiding.

At first the light wavered, glancing over us.
Then it clenched to a fist of light that pointed,
searched out, divided us.
Each took the beams like direct blows the heart answers.
Each of us moved forward alone.

We have come to the edge of the woods,
drawn out of ourselves by this night sun,
this battery of polarized acids,
that outshines the moon.

We smell them behind it
but they are faceless, invisible.
We smell the raw steel of their gun barrels,
mink oil on leather, their tongues of sour barley.
We smell their mothers buried chin-deep in wet dirt.
We smell their fathers with scoured knuckles,
teeth cracked from hot marrow.
We smell their sisters of crushed dogwood, bruised apples,
of fractured cups and concussions of burnt hooks.

We smell their breath steaming lightly behind the jacklight.
We smell the itch underneath the caked guts on their clothes.

We smell their minds like silver hammers
cocked back, held in readiness
for the first of us to step into the open.

We have come to the edge of the woods,
out of brown grass where we slept, unseen,
out of leaves creaked shut, out of our hiding.
We have come here too long.

It is their turn now,
their turn to follow us. Listen,
they put down their equipment.
It is useless in the tall brush.
And now they take the first steps, not knowing
how deep the woods are and lightless.
How deep the woods are.[10]

Frost's sonnet, as I read it, is a love poem, delicately praising the way the natural unfallen voice of one human being has given the whole world a hidden reservoir of partly human, partly animal music.[11] Erdrich's is a poem about sexual confrontation as well as the conflicts in American culture between human and animal, technological and natural—and it may hint at whites "preying on" American Indians as well.

In Frost's sonnet, someone (the poet? A son of Adam and Eve?) "reports" to us what Adam used to say about the way Eve's voice has become "an oversound," which lives on in the song of birds now that (the reporter implies) Eve herself is no longer with us. As Adam asserts in the poem's last two lines, "Never again would birds' song be the same. / And to do that to birds was why she came." Frost has carefully distanced himself, not only from the Adam who thus reminisces, but from whichever daughter or son of Adam reports the reminiscing. More subtly, Frost has that reporter keep his or her own distance, remarking with wry amusement that HE (Adam, not the reporter) would declare such things. And even Adam seems to be mildly skeptical, since we are not told he *actually believed,* but only that he *could himself believe* what he is saying. So the reporter seems to be hinting wry disbelief or even cynical doubt of any truth in Adam's fancy: it was, well, the sort of thing Adam *would* say when he was going on about how wonderful things were in the *good* old days. In short, Frost's poem hedges Adam's fancy with so many thickets of skepticism, amused doubt, lightly patronizing headshakes, that the reader must suspect this Adam is pretty well past it, an old man telling tall tales that he has begun to take more seriously now that he is growing senilely sentimental.

Yet through all these ironic thorns, so carefully planted by Frost around his adamant fancy, there wafts a certain Edenic fragrance. The rhetorical hedges have been planted to guard a private space, not to institutionalize Adam as a loony old liar. Frost is a very subtle and tricky poet and easier to under-read than his sunlit words make it seem. His poem, however wondrous its spins and twists and leaps of poetic rhetoric, is charged with intense and yearning love for a woman who has changed the way the whole universe presents itself to him. This most shy and private man gets it both ways: any sensitive reader who has tried to celebrate his beloved without being a kiss-and-tell fool or (worse) a senti-mental pretender, will admire Frost's managing to tell the whole world what he feels with such humorous indirection that he could walk out of any courtroom unconvicted even though the jury would know the poem's "He" is really the poet's "I" in ambush. "He would declare," the poem begins: only after a rereading or two do we realize that this "He" is Adam speaking of Eve, and only after a few more readings do we understand that it is also Robert Frost speaking of his wife.[12] I know no more poi-gnant love poem in English than this, and I would forgive any mistake in tone this poet might have made anywhere—and critics are fond of finding them, or inventing if necessary—for this wonderful sonnet. At any rate—so it seems to me—Frost gives us a beautiful and comforting reminder of what love in the Western tradition might once have been like.

Erdrich, in contrast, gives us a vivid and disturbing reminder of how unlike this ideal the relations between men and women too often are. Her poem's speakers seem to be the animals (for simplicity I will call them "deer") being hunted by humans with the help of a jacklight—illegal but effective, since the deer are hypnotized and come slowly and hesitantly out of the dark woods toward the hunters' guns. But when the deer get close enough to smell the hunters, what they learn is not just about these male hunters, but about their women, families, relationships. The deer smell guns, mink-oiled boots, beer-tainted breath; but they also smell the oppressed mothers of these men, their overworked and defeated fathers ("teeth cracked from hot marrow" suggests that the fathers too were hunters, but that the excesses have damaged them), their abused sisters. Something sinister (from the point of view of the hunters) is going on here: the deer are "walking in their souls," learning the nature of their lives beyond this hunting relationship. Even though the deer are sensing the cocked guns, it is to those cocked minds ("like silver hammers"), ready to send a bullet into the first deer to step into the open, that the deer are paying sharpest attention.

And now the poem, and this relationship, begin to turn around. When the speaker, for the third time, says, "*We have come to the edge of the woods,*" and describes once more, as if hypnotized, where they have come from, "out of our hiding," this time she follows with a very different assertion: "*We have come here too long.*" For anyone reading this poem aloud, here is the place to change the voice from tranced to grimly alert, here is where the speaker begins to take charge of the situation. "It is their turn now, / their turn to follow us," the woods-creature says—and if I were reading this aloud, I would want it to sound like the Godfather making an offer not to be refused: a quiet, deadly, utterly assured tone is what we should hear in these last sentences as the deer describe how the mesmeric hunters have themselves been hypnotized.

And at this point we may wonder just what these "woods" ARE, into which Erdrich's creatures are luring the hunters. Recalling Stevens's "slovenly wilderness," we may think these woods are that very wilderness, rising up like Tecumseh against its "possessors"; and there is partial truth to this. That is, Erdrich's hunters, though more honkytonking Cowboys than hoity-toity Conquistadores, are "talking dominion" just as arrogantly as did Stevens's Jar. It is clear from Erdrich's epigraph that a main theme of her poem will be ways in which male contempt for women is shown in both language and customs of hunting, whether practiced at deer-stand or bar-stool, with jacklight or strobe lights. So luring deer to the jacklight becomes a figure for the luring of women to the sexual encounter, in both cases to "score," or as one might say in Chippewa (according to Dunning as cited by Erdrich in the epigraph to "Jacklight") to "use force in intercourse" or to "kill a bear with one's bare hands"—we need not try to cite the English slang equivalents of these Chippewa terms, but if we recall macho terms for dealing sexually with women we know there are such equivalents.

I have not paired Frost and Erdrich to put down one or the other, but I do think that alongside Erdrich's Honkytonk Horror-Babes we may see Frost's Edenic portrait of Woman—her voice so "soft" that only when she is calling out or laughing does it reach the birds in the treetops—as offering a few too many sweets to the sweet. But it is perhaps also true that Erdrich's Life-on-the-Rez portrait of Macho Man Unmanned is less a poem of healing than a celebration of power, and power used to capture and control—a reversal rather than finding a good way. Still, I like the way each poem does its thing, and the thing each poem does.

Old English, New English: Unriddling America

I want now to do something immodest: to show that it is possible for a contemporary poet—in this case, myself—to use the "classical" forms of English poetry to "say things" about this world, now, and yet (I hope) be readable. It happens that my Irish and Scotch-Irish mother's father, shortly before he died, told me to go to college (he himself had got only into the third grade when he had to drop out and work on his father's farm in the Ozarks). I admired and loved my grandfather greatly—he was always good to me, good to work alongside, good to go on walks with, a man who never lied, and though he could act a fool when he drank too much, a man whose judgment was trusted by everybody most of the time and whose heart was trusted at all times. So when Aleck Camp told me to go to college, they would have had to kill me to prevent it; and of course nobody tried to stop me, everybody did what was possible to help me. But we had no money, nobody in the family had been to college, and getting there was no sure or easy thing.

Still, I made it. That is, a lot of people lifted me up to that dazzling window and cheered me for climbing through it. And once I got to college and jumped through the necessary hoops to clothe myself in a sheepskin, the great teachers at the University of Tulsa put me up for a Rhodes Scholarship and that was given me and so I got over to Oxford University, and to get the B.A. in English Literature there I had to study Old English language and literature, had to learn how the Old English alliterative meter works, had to memorize accidence and morphology and phonology and all that, so we could read *Beowulf* and *Dream of the Rood* and other poems. Later, in Yale Graduate School, I wrote a dissertation on Middle English alliterative poetry, and since then have taught History of the English Language and medieval literature a lot.

And one semester—you probably wondered where all this was going, and here I hope you will see it is getting to the point—I had to fill in for a younger teacher, Tom Goodman, who is much better at Old English than I am, when he was called out of town that day, and the class that day happened to be considering some of the Old English poems called Riddles. With these I had a nodding acquaintance, had worked through some of the less tough ones. But now suddenly I had to face a group of students and not disgrace myself while talking with them about the "Book" and "Swan," and others of the Riddles in which whatever creature the poet taps must tell the listener/reader in enigmatic ways its life story. Here, for instance, is the magnificent "Swan," who speaks to us from the *Exeter Book* (written around A.D. 950–1000), as I translate its chant:

The Swan's Song

Garbed in silence	I go on earth,
dwell among men	or move on the waters.
Yet far over halls	of heroes in time
my robes and the high	air may raise
and bear me up	in heaven's power
over all nations.	My ornaments then
are singing glories	and I go in song
bright as a star	unstaying above
the world's wide waters,	a wayfaring soul.

It would be a grave mistake to think one had "solved" the riddle of this poem by saying, "Swan!" The Old English poet surely meant us not just to listen to each clue as the poem unfolds, and gradually deduce who is speaking to us here. We certainly are meant to go through that process, to observe that this creature telling its life story lives in silence among human beings or on the water; but then it takes to the air, rises far above human habitations and looks down from that height on those, even the most heroic of them, dwelling below; and when it moves at that height its ornaments (which the Old English original implies are the same as its "robes") "sing" and "shine," so that in flight it moves in glory that is beyond the mortal heroes on earth. And we are surely meant to see with astonishment in the poem's last few words that this earth-mute, heaven-musical traveler is a pilgrim soul. That is, everything in the poem comes together in those last few words, and we see this "swan" is an emblem of the immortal soul which in its flesh is relatively mute and slow and likely to be held of little account, but when it rises to its heavenly destination makes part of the angelic choir, going in glorious music toward the throne of God, its wayfaring at last reaching that place of power and beauty far beyond the palaces and thrones of human monarchs and heroes.

In translating, I have pretty much kept Old English alliterative meter: each line has two half-lines, each half-line has two strong stresses. So every line will have at least four stresses, and at least two of these must alliterate. It is the number three stress—that is, the first stress of the second half-line—which is the key to any line: stress 3 *must* alliterate with either 1 or 2, or with both of them. In "The Swan," for instance, line 1 alliterates on the /g/ of stresses 1 and 3: *GARBED in Silence I GO on earth.* In line 8, the alliterative stresses are 2 and 3 *(bright as a STAR unSTAYing above)*, although there is extra alliteration also between stresses 1 and 4 *(BRIGHT, aBOVE)*, an effect I like more than did Old English poets, probably.

But now comes the immodest part: I want to show that this old Anglo-Saxon poetic form is still alive, will still blossom and fruit if planted deep and watered from Indian springs. What has to be done is the same as with any ancient form: treat it with respect, not as entertainment but as revelation. I have said elsewhere that the Old English poems usually called "riddles" are meant to call before the reader certain astonishing created beings in this universe and let them speak their spiritual dimensions, cleanse the doors of perception and bare the witty ligatures by which things are put together, held together, pass into and out of human comprehension.[13] The Old English poet gives them their voices and lets them re-member themselves for us, coax us into recognizing them. If we want to write a "New English" Riddle, we need to try and give the creatures of our time such voices and dimensions, we have to realize that in our everyday life there are amazing and mysterious convergings of power and mystery: as Wordsworth said in his great Immortality Ode, we are "moving about in worlds not realized." If a house spoke its being, it would tell of its power to summon the dead Beethoven's majestic music, or the ghosts of dead movie stars to dance or machine-gun or sing us to sleep; any house could tell us how within it the great rivers rise to our lips in drinkable water, spray over our heads in cleansing coolness, flush away the grime and filth of our daily lives. Or we could ask a Television Set—say a Sony from Japan—to speak its mundane mysteries to us:

On this azure eyeball   where hell twice raised
its monstrous mushrooms,   my mind's eye opened
as the holster hardened   for its hot ghost-gun
from barrels of black   dinosaur-blood; shortly,

on floating steel,   men steered me eastward
through a gate of gold,   gave me then
to an iron horse   that hauled me here,
unpacked me and pinned   upon my backside
a long tail, tipped   with metallic teeth.
A woman acquired me,   carried me home,
set me high on an altar   for adoration,
drove Dracula teeth   into tight joyholes,
touched me until   she turned me on—
I reached into heaven   and handed her down
from its ether Caruso's   heart in a clown-suit,
spread time at her toes   like a tiger's skin
until she yawned,   touched me again,
and I went blind.   I bless FAR-SEERS
who know my name   and now will speak it!

I have followed the Old English poets in using enigmatic metaphors ("kennings") like *azure eyeball* for Planet Earth, and *monstrous mushrooms* for the bomb-clouds over Hiroshima and Nagasaki. I "transfigured" the TV's cathode-ray tube as a "hot ghost-gun"—it "shoots" arrays of electrons at a "target" screen and evokes "ghosts"; in fact, since actors and historical figures on our TV screens often are long dead, their TV icons are ghosts as nearly "real" as we can live with. And since the TV case or frame is made of plastic from polymerized petroleum, I figure it as "holster" for a "ghost-gun," and call the oil "dinosaur-blood"—not much of a far-fetch, considering the old green dinosaur on the Sinclair signs: advertising people are more poetic than plenty of our poets.

The poem won't "work" unless readers have fun figuring it out—not only as a kind of game but as a way of getting into what marvelous magical things a TV set really is and does. Poems, like jokes, work best if they don't need explaining, but unlike jokes they can be effective more than once (though differently)—and even, I would claim, *after* being explained.[14] The old *Reader's Digest* pieces are not so far from the Old English Riddles: "I am Joe's Kidney," for instance. And the poem ought to do something else besides give a Nintendo-like play-pleasure; it ought to be informative, the reader ought to come away saying: Well, that's true, I see some things now better than before, and maybe some things I didn't see before—things look a little different, a little clearer and interlocking now. Teach and delight, as Horace said: that's what I sort of hoped would happen once the reader got through the more simple "floating steel" (the paradox of those huge steel ships, which we forget "ought" never to float) and Golden Gate and Iron Horse, and fetched up on that tail and its teeth. I hoped the teasing and fun of what the woman was doing was like what some of the Old English poets did with their double entendres, and I hoped those Dracula teeth in "joyholes" would be clear enough metaphors for the plug and socket. After all, we get a lot of joy—or we expect to—from those electric outlets in our living rooms.

Then I "reversed" the usual direction of the metaphoric shift when the TV says the woman "touched me until she turned me on"—to "turn on" somebody was a cliché of Beats and Hippies, so I had fun letting a TV speak it literally of itself. And once "turned on" a TV does literally "reach into heaven" to collect its images, it "hands down" from the "ether" an old recording of, say, Caruso singing in *I Pagliacci,* so that a TV set "kills" time, makes a "trophy" of it like a tiger-skin. I thought that notion might justify the TV's saying it "spread time like a tiger's skin" at the feet of the woman viewing such old scenes. (Yes, the old rhyme about Elinor Glyn was running through my head at that point: "Would you rather sin / With Elinor Glyn / On a tiger skin . . . ?") And last, I had fun translating the Greek/Latin TELE-("far") VISION ("seeing") into FAR-SEERS, telly-viewers. The in-joke here is that an Old English poet might "give away" the solution to one of these "riddles" by writing its name in ancient runes instead of the Latin-derived alphabet used for most of the poem. So FAR-SEER in capital letters is a clue to this riddle's "solution"—*TV SET.*

But Old English poetic form will hold less technology-driven points. So let me end this essay with one short and one slightly longer example of how I have tried to use the alliterative Riddle genre, adapting WAS poetics for American Indian themes and purposes.[15] Here is the short piece, which I hope needs no commentary:

Birch Canoe

Red men embraced   my body's whiteness,
cutting into me   carved it free,
sewed it tight   with sinews taken
from lightfoot deer   who leaped this stream—

now in my ghost-skin   they glide over clouds
at home in the fish's   fallen heaven.

And finally, I have tried to compose one Riddle in gratitude for the gift of eagle feathers, given me by Bob and Evelyne Voelker when I was elected to the Board of Directors of the American Indian Center of Mid-America. I asked a friend, Dale Besse, to bead these into an Eagle Fan, which I carry when I dance; since the late 1970s I have been a Gourd Dancer. The poem tells how an eagle in flight pierces clouds just as a beadworker's needle goes through beads and the white buckskin of the fan's handle, spiralling round sky and fan; and how the eagle flies from dawn to sunset, linking colors of day and night as they are linked on a Gourd Dancer's blanket (half crimson, half blue), and just as they are beaded onto the handle of the Eagle Fan. In the poem, ordinary things are given mysterious names: tree leaves are green light-dancers, wood is tree-heart or ash-heart, clouds are thrones of thunder-beings. Readers may like to name for themselves what I have called a "one-eyed serpent with silver-straight head."

What the Eagle Fan Says

(For the Voelkers, the Besses, and all the Dancers)

I strung dazzling thrones   of thunder beings
on a spiraling thread   of spinning flight,
beading dawn's blood   and blue of noon
to the gold and dark   of day's leaving,
circling with Sun   the soaring heaven
over turquoise eyes   of Earth below,
her silver veins,   her sable fur,
heard human relatives   hunting below
calling me down,   crying their need
that I bring them closer   to Wakonda's ways,
and I turned from heaven   to help them then.
When the bullet came,   it caught my heart,
the hunter's hands   gave earth its blood,
loosened light beings   and let us float
toward the sacred center   of song in the drum,
but fixed us first   firm in song-home

that green light-dancers	gave to men's knives,
ash-heart in hiding where	deer-heart had beat,
and a one-eyed serpent	with silver-straight head
strung tiny rattles	around white softness
in beaded harmonies	of blue and red—
lightly I move now	in a man's left hand,
above dancing feet	follow the sun
around old songs	soaring toward heaven
on human breath,	and I help them rise.

Herbs of Healing

Not all healing herbs are sweet, and I have had some bitter observations to make in the discussions above. But I hope that it will be with us as with Peter Rabbit and his siblings: the camomile tea on the one hand, and the fresh blackberries and bread and milk on the other, are surely the right medicine in each case. I hope readers will have found the sweet and nourishing, the bitter and healing, in some measure in this essay. We are talking about a so far undiscovered country, five hundred years after Columbus mistook it for Japan or China or India or the Earthly Paradise. We are talking about some undiscovered writers whose work is good for this America. I wish you the joy of it.

Carter Revard's Angled Mirrors

Janet McAdams

Osage poet Carter Revard has said that his poems should be read, not in a chronological fashion, but rather like "angled mirrors, so that full-face, profile, and rearview versions of their subjects may be seen together."[1] These "angled mirrors" are present throughout Revard's work, in strategic juxtapositions of not only seemingly divergent poems but of certain sets of binaries, such as Western literary traditions and Native ones, technology and the earth, and local and global—even cosmic—cultures. Revard's central poetic task is the destabilizing of these binaries, often by transforming one into its *other*. In this essay, I assess what Joysa M. Winter has called the "amazing paradoxes" of Revard's life and career, and I use these "amazing paradoxes" to theorize more broadly about contemporary Native poetics, drawing upon certain key theoretical tropes from the field of postcolonial studies to argue that Revard's poems constitute what Mary Louise Pratt has described as "contact zones" and to demonstrate how, through the juxtaposition of these textual "angled mirrors," a new space is mapped.[2] "Contact zone" is Pratt's term for "social spaces where cultures meet, clash, and grapple with each other, often in contexts of highly asymmetrical relations of power, such as colonialism, slavery, or their aftermaths as they are lived out in many parts of the world today."[3] I look closely at three of Revard's poems, "Coyote Tells Why He Sings," "What the TV Said," and "Homework at Oxford," whose strikingly different elements generate the contact zones where the different traditions that inform Revard's work encounter each other, interact, conflict, come together.

Born in Pawhuska, Oklahoma, in 1931, Revard is the author of three collections of poetry: *Ponca War Dancers* (1980), *Cowboys and Indians, Christmas Shopping* (1992), *An Eagle Nation* (1993), as well as a collection of essays, *Family Matters, Tribal Affairs* (1998), and a memoir, *Winning* the Dust Bowl (2001). The focus of this essay will be on three of Revard's poems: "Coyote Tells Why He Sings," from his early *Ponca War Dancers*, and two more recent poems, "Homework at Oxford," from *An Eagle Nation*, and "What the TV Said," which first appeared in *Cowboys and Indians, Christmas Shopping* as "Something Indoors" and was reprinted in *Family Matters, Tribal Affairs*. However, because Revard's three volumes of poetry overlap, with each containing poems from previous books, it is difficult—and perhaps not especially useful—to characterize Revard's body of work in a linear fashion. Rather, his poems as a group form a matrix, in which they connect and interweave and reverberate off each other. These juxtapositions of different poems and different voices—and their engagement with different traditions—generate an infinite number of representations and reflections. While I discuss only these three poems, they are significant ones for their attention to certain key issues in the poet's work: communally constructed identity, politics and personal experience, and—as will be my focus here—the meetings of, encounters between, and juxtapositions of different worlds.

In the works of Revard these juxtapositions constitute poetic maps that comprise, transform, and rewrite seemingly distinct "Old World" and "New World" formulations. These revisionary cartographies depend upon and make possible the plurality of voices that speak in Revard's poems. In this essay, I am especially not arguing that Revard and other contemporary Native poets who draw upon non-Native traditions of writing are somehow caught or trapped in the in-between; that is, my concern is not with the by now overworked critical trope of mixed identity. My interest here is the new space the text itself maps out, a performed site, always dynamic. Perhaps because I am both a poet and a critic, I remain tied to certain notions of authorial agency. Native poets, I believe, in making use of Western forms, no more lose their "authenticity" than they do by writing on computers. My focus, thus, is on the textually staged encounters in Revard's work among different elements, since he characteristically introduces a third element (and sometimes a fourth or fifth one) into these received binaries that destabilizes their binarism, setting things in motion and generating the shifting, conversant dynamics that characterize many of his poems.

These disruptions are in part effected by the complex manner in which voice is constructed in Revard's poems. The voicings in his poems continually interrogate the singular "I" through ironic displacements and a questioning of who is reading and who is being read. These different manifestations of voice can be closely tied to the poet's lived experiences in Oklahoma and Oxford, England; the tension between the different traditions that emerge from these locales has produced some of Revard's most significant work.[4]

The Different Voices

I am naming as I go, as I approach the House of Mystery, those who have cast themselves into our star and are walking with us here. I am Carter Revard (Nompehwathe), at Buck Creek, Oklahoma.

In "Seeing with Another 'I': Our Search for Other Worlds," Eugene C. Eoyang writes:

> In the major intellectual movements in this century . . . a recurrent theme runs throughout the various discoveries and insights in different fields, from relativity theory to quantum mechanics to the Heisenberg principle to phenomenology to semiotics to deconstruction to chaos theory. Different as these paradigms are, they all highlight the relationship between the object and subject, between the knower and what is known. In each of these mind-sets, the traditional opposition of bipolar thinking is undermined, and a dialectic model of knowledge has been posited.[5]

Eoyang goes on to suggest that in order to uncover "what we take for granted," we should "examine some of our most familiar reference points."[6] Revard's poems undermine "bipolar thinking" by forcing us to examine the limits and boundaries we take for granted. Transformations are of crucial importance in Revard's work; often, these transformations occur in the contact zones between binaries, when one familiar polarity is re-visioned as its opposite and vice versa.

These binaries are articulated and disrupted through seemingly different voices; however, "voice" is a complex trope when subjectivity is constituted relationally, within a matrix or web of relationships. With Revard, as with many, if not all, Native writers, communally constructed identities influence and inform the speaking voice in the literature. Revard's own desire to speak to and for his extended family and larger community is evident from the prevalence with which these family anecdotes and stories appear in his poetry, from the many dedications to family members, and even from the "author photo" that appears on *Ponca War Dancers,* which defies convention by depicting the Revard/ Camp/Jump family and not a solo image of the author himself. Revard writes, "Poetry is not just what is unique to an author, an 'I,' it is mostly about what is shared, what is common to authors and readers."[7]

In his essay "History, Myth, and Identity among Osages and Other Peoples," Revard writes about Geronimo:

> Something strange appears when we look at certain autobiographies of Indian people: the notion of identity, of how the individual is related to world, people, self, differs from what we see in "Euro-american" autobiography. . . . It is only after [a] Genesis-like history of his world's creation, his people's creation and deliverance, of their land's creation, of why they are called *Apaches,* of what it means to be taken from the land created particularly for his people, that Geron-imo speaks of himself.[8]

According to Revard, the essential facts of Geronimo's autobiography range "from cosmic through geologic to tribal, subtribal, family, and then only, last and in full context, the 'individual' self that was Geronimo."[9] I quote at length from Revard's essay not only to underscore the impor-tance of rethinking the "I" in his work and that of other American Indian poets, but because these particular elements—geologic, tribal, cosmic, familial—are omnipresent touchstones of identity-making throughout his work. This relational constitution of identity as especially Native American has been written about by many Native authors.[10] Yet, it is also important to bear in mind that so-called individual identity, despite its high visibility in contemporary U.S. society, is anomalous, for, as Eugene Eoyang writes, "the concept of the individual self, as a separate, priv-ileged entity set apart from the community, is a fairly recent develop-ment, even in the West. Its pervasiveness blinds us to other notions of existence which stress the contiguity of humanity rather than the atomis-tic autonomy of each individual."[11]

In an interview with Joseph Bruchac, Revard mentions the "different voices" that have arisen from his "amazing and paradoxical life," as an Oklahoman from a mixed Osage, Ponca, and white family, and as a Rhodes scholar and professor of medieval English literature.[12] Born in 1931, Revard and his twin sister Maxine attended a one-room school, working part-time as school janitors and graduating valedictorian and salutatorion. One of his high school teachers encouraged him to enter a radio quiz show called *Going to College,* which resulted in a scholarship to the University of Tulsa. As a Rhodes scholar at Oxford, he studied English literature, and eventually went on to Yale for a Ph.D. in medieval English literature. Revard became a professor at Washington University in St. Louis, where he taught medieval literature and Native American literature until his retirement in 1998.

Because these different voices constructed in Revard's poems can be tied closely to his biography, it is crucial not to collapse "voice" and identity into a single category of literary investigation. Revard juxtaposes and sets into the play the different voices available to him, voices he traces as emerging directly from his experiences growing up in Oklahoma and as an Oklahoman transplanted to Oxford. Revard's earliest experiments with poetry were written within the parameters of traditional English verse. "Once I got in college," he explains, "I got stuck with the idea that I would write in traditional form."[13] The intersection of two experiences from either side of the paradox helped Revard discover a different voice:

> I was teaching at Amherst after I got through the Yale graduate school. I discovered one morning, up in the Emily Dickinson house, that I could talk about something. . . . I was in the top half of that house and it was raining, and I woke up in the morning about 6:00; it was starting to get dawn. I heard that dripping sound. . . . Then I remembered when I was about fourteen, hiking up Buck Creek Valley. . . . We were up there and a thunderstorm came up, so we got under the rocks. Under there were things we took to be coyote sign.[14]

Revard's realization that coyotes take in sounds and bring them back out as "song" prompted him to take "the coyote's voice," resulting in his breakthrough poem, the sonnet "Coyote Tells Why He Sings."[15] Thus, two events occurred through the conception and writing of the poem: the ability to move beyond the limitations of traditional English verse, while still drawing upon it, and a reclaiming of his Oklahoma voice, which, he explains, he lost his second year at Oxford. "Then, when I needed the Oklahoma voice, the coyote gave it to me."[16] "Coyote Tells Why He Sings" is one of Revard's most frequently anthologized and quoted poems. It is a terse illustration of the paradoxes he lives and writes:

Coyote Tells Why He Sings

There was a little rill of water, near the den,
That showed a trickle, all the dry summer
When I was born. One night in late August it rained—
The Thunder waked us. Drops came crashing down
In dust, on stiff blackjack leaves, on lichened rocks,
And the rain came in a pelting rush down over the hill,
Wind blew wet into our cave as I heard the sounds
Of leaf-drip, rustling of soggy branches in gusts of wind.

And then the rill's tune changed—I heard a rock drop
That set new ripples gurgling, in a lower key.
Where the new ripples were, I drank, next morning,
Fresh muddy water that set my teeth on edge.
I thought how delicate the rock's poise was and how
The storm made music, when it changed my world.

The poem is a significant one in Revard's oeuvre not only for its liberat-
ing effect on its author. In its fourteen lines are many of the concerns that
characterize his work: the recognition of "voice" constructed outside the
dominant mode of individualized subjectivity; the intersection of Native
subject matter and a traditional English verse form; and transformation,
in particular, transformation on a world scale. The title is key to the first
of these concerns, since the story being told is that of the coyote's, who
gives the poet his voice, so that the "I" is both coyote and poet. Revard
has said:

> I was thinking what it would be like to be a coyote pup, and it hadn't
> rained all day, and the puppy gets up and all of a sudden this thun-
> derstorm comes along. I'm thinking of what it would hear.
>   When water starts rising, the streamlet makes little sounds. Then
> when it rises a couple of inches in a half hour, it goes down a pitch.
> The storm made music. When the coyotes are singing at night, they
> hear all kinds of things like this. Maybe that's one of the ways they
> learn how to sing. So I put that in the poem. When it changed, there
> was pitch. It's like when the drum changes or the singer changes.
> The coyote learned how to sing, and all of a sudden there was music.
> The coyote had given me my voice.[17]

This "voice" that the poet has been given is that of the coyote, but the coyote is imitating the sound of water, translating it into his own language. The poet, in turn, takes the coyote's voice into his own, translating these sounds into his language. However, all these voices, these sounds, originate in the storm's music, the sound of the rain and wind and, most important, the thunder. Revard's family clan is the Thunder, which suggests that this voice is less a borrowing than an inevitable transition from thunder, the source of his clan's power, through water to the coyote through the poet. It would not be accurate to say that the poem yokes the poet's inner and outer landscapes or that it brings together voices from inside and outside him, even though that might seem apparent at first glance. Such characterizations presuppose the existence of these as separate entities. Rather, what occurs in the poem is the revelation of the continuous and intertwined nature of the landscape, the coyote, and the poet as another being, as an Osage person and member of the Thunder Clan.

The second of the concerns outlined above, the exploration of a Native subject through a fixed form, is one instance of a supposed binary being deconstructed and its polarities transformed. "Coyote Tells Why He Sings" is a sonnet, divided into the octave and sestet of the Italian, or Petrarchan, sonnet; however, the poem's form is not a rigid container into which a conflicting subject matter is poured. The poem's content cannot be clearly divided from its form: the voice of coyote, which is the voice of the water and becomes the voice of the poet, disrupts the metrical pattern of the sonnet. Revard's intention in this poem was to write a sonnet not in iambic or dactylic meter but with "six beats, a variable number of syllables," and no rhyme, so that it would sound like "talk."[18] The resulting poem, though, continually makes stylistic reference to the sonnet. It does not, in fact, rhyme, except for slant rhymes such as "den," "rained," "sounds," and "wind." Interestingly, even these slight rhymes occur only in the octave, disappearing as the poem makes its traditional turn at the opening of the sestet. Thus, while the poem may not follow the exact specifics of the Italian sonnet with its hendecasyllables and traditional rhyme scheme (abba abba, etc.), the sonnet form is organically present throughout.

The poem's closer adherence to the traditional form in the octave is significant. The division of the Petrarchan sonnet into octave and sestet is not just a line count but indicates as well a division in thought, with a shift at the opening of the sestet. This is the poem through which Revard found his voice, the Oklahoma voice he reclaimed, and began to write past the limits of traditional English verse. Structurally, as well as in terms of content, the poem documents this shift, as the language in the octave rhymes slightly and is more literary—"stiff blackjack leaves, on lichened rocks" and "Of leaf-drip, rustling of soggy branches in gusts of wind"—and the octave is the part of the poem just prior to the poet discovering his voice, the Oklahoma voice that sounds like talk. At the opening of the sestet, the poet hears the rock drop into the pool of water and the language becomes plainer: "I drank, next morning, / Fresh muddy water that set my teeth on edge." The poem not only explains this transformation of voices but also enacts them through language.

Revard has said that the last line "is a line I didn't get until the end of the day. I had thirteen lines, and I realized if I had another it would be a sonnet. And that last line turned out to be the theme of the whole thing, it summed it up."[19] With this, Revard's "play" with the sonnet form takes on another dimension, since it is traditionally the English sonnet—Shakespearean or Spenserian—that ends with a summarizing couplet. Thus, Revard's Petrarchan sonnet with its two distinct waves of thought ends with the "English" couplet: "I thought how delicate the rock's poise was and how / *The storm made music, when it changed my world.*" The transformation of the poet's voice is, clearly, a transformation of the poet himself. As well, his world has changed profoundly, which is most evident if we compare the opening line of the poem with its delicate "little rill of water" to the closing line's forceful "The storm made music."

Yet it is not so simple. I have noted earlier that Revard keeps these binaries in play by introducing additional elements, and thus sets up a dynamic field where categories cannot remain static. The sonnet form has been disrupted by the many revisions Revard makes, but there is no easy transformation from sonnet to plain style or "English" to "Okla-homan." For the last two lines, the summarizing couplet of the poem, in which this profound transformation is most clearly delineated, are the most traditional lines in the poem. The penultimate line is one stress away from exact iambic pentameter, which emphasizes the last line's strongly accented, perfect iambic pentameter. The added comma before the dependent clause creates a slight caesura that makes the following word, "when," more emphatic. The emphasized words in the resulting line, then, are "storm," "music," "when," "changed," "world." Thus, even as the transformation from one voice to another occurs and the poet's world changes from England back to Oklahoma, the poem circles back on itself and keeps these different traditions—and worlds—in play. And this, of course, is the third pursuit: the linking and transformation of different worlds.

Like the hybridized sonnet "Coyote Tells Why He Sings," Revard's reworkings of Anglo-Saxon riddle poems pair contemporary subject matter with traditional English verse forms, in order, he writes, "to use the 'classical' forms of English poetry to 'say things' about this world, now, and yet (I hope) be readable."[20] In these poems, Revard has maintained the alliterative metrics that characterize riddles: a four-beat line with a strong, central caesura. In the riddle poem, "whatever creature the poet taps must tell the listener / reader in enigmatic ways its life story."[21] Interestingly, these riddle poems are grouped in *Cowboys and Indians, Christmas Shopping,* but dispersed throughout the later *An Eagle Nation,* suggesting a fuller merging of different writing styles in the poet's work.

"What the TV Said" is one of these contemporary Anglo-Saxon riddle poems. It employs a number of traditional tropes, a four-beat, caesured line, and many kennings, such as "azure eyeball," "monstrous mushroom," and "iron horse":

> On this azure eyeball   where hell twice raised
> its monstrous mushrooms,   my mind's eye opened
> as the holster hardened   for its hot ghost-gun
> from barrels of black   dinosaur-blood; shortly,

Through these kennings, the complexity of this encounter is apparent, as each renames objects of the technological age, lacing these descriptions with irony and horror. The "azure eyeball" is the earth viewed twice through the lens of technology: the spaceship that photographs it and the television that mirrors the earth back to itself. The "monstrous mushroom" tells the horrific ineffability of nuclear destruction. The "barrels of black dinosaur-blood" are oil, modern-day fuel; the dinosaurs are ostensibly extinct, but in fact survived by becoming birds. "Iron horse" seems a play on so-called Tonto-speak for the train.[22] Revard's use of this phrase to describe a present-day automobile is both accurate and ironic, as it invokes earlier encounters, earlier namings.[23]

"Homework at Oxford" also juxtaposes the poet's different worlds of Oklahoma and England. In this long meditative poem, the speaker, displaced from his native Oklahoma while a student in England, is prompted by a long night of studying to remember his home. The poem opens in the speaker's rooms at Merton College: "Crouched and shivering, here on the soft blue-velvet sofa, / So mangy with wear it sags. . . ."[24] It is not only the sofa that is worn, but also the world itself. Ancient, the old world is rife with treasures but tainted with weariness. Furthermore, as Revard points out,

> It is not just "Oxford" and "Home" that are set up in opposition to each other in the poem; rather, it narrates one search for a good natural/supernatural overlook from which to view the world and myself in it, and it begins by posing a contrast between the Via Negativa of the medieval friar-mystic Meister Eckhart, whose "black book" I have been reading all through the dark night, and Breughel's painting of the Epiphany (which means the Making Apparent of Deity, the Showing to the Three Kings) of that very God for whom Eckhart is looking in deepest darkness. Eckhart preaches that one must leave behind every worldly sensory perception to find Deity; but Breughel pictures the Three Kings who, having followed a Star through the dark Night, arrive to find an ordinary "everyday" scene, a stable-and-animals scene, with an ordinary family and baby in it.[25]

The room's objects lead the speaker into further meditation, for example, the Breughel painting on the wall, in which everything in the landscape is accorded equal weight: "so many things alive as Christ, / Pigeons, rooster, ramshackle thatch of the roof." The speaker leaves the closed space of the room and ventures out into the garden where he sees cattle, which precipitates his "homework," his imaginative journey back to Oklahoma and childhood memory. He leaves his chilly sitting room and walks out into "the darkness of Merton Meadows" where he hears "the sighs of cattle bedded in the lush grass." This familiar presence triggers the speaker's remembrances of Oklahoma:

> I know
> The muffled drooling grind of teeth, long swallowing throbs.
> I hold my face to the herd, testing for warmth on eyes
> And forehead: only the smell of hot grass, bodies, manure,
> The ghost of milk; it might be morning darkness in Oklahoma.

There are two kinds of "home *work*" being performed in the poem: the "fifty lines of *Beowulf*" the speaker is studying and the detailed remembering of "home" that takes place in the long, italicized, middle strophe of the poem. The speaker, who has "read all night," is prompted by "this black book / Of Meister Eckhart's," to journey, as the book describes, "deep in the soul's darkness / To the sweet fountains of life."[26] These static representations of nature in the book and painting contrast sharply with the rich, full landscape of Oklahoma in which the speaker encounters crawdads, persimmons, blackbirds, geese, cattails, and herons. The heron wings on the classroom wall are linked to the Breughel painting. Each leads the speaker somewhere—in Oxford, out of the chilly and dark building; in Oklahoma, into another sequence of memories.

"Oxford" and "Home" are set up in opposition to each other in this poem, and the italicizing of the Oklahoma section emphasizes the opposition. In this way, the poem is atypical of Revard's work. Old and New World juxtapositions rarely remain as stable as they do in "Homework at Oxford." About the poem, Revard notes: "I had not thought of the poem as showing homesickness, but rather, to use a fairly awkward term, home-healthiness. After all, here in Oxford the light brings a version of Oklahoma back, and nothing Oklahoman is alien here. The two places work together—this is symbiosis, not death of a transplanted memory."[27]

In "Homework at Oxford" the shift and play between places is further signified by stylistic changes. The Oxford portions of the poem are smooth and melodious, meditative, emphasizing the quiet of the speaker's solitude (and aloneness), while the home portions are noisier and crowded with other people, with animals, with constant motion. The enjambment in the Oxford section slows down the lines, as does the frequent assonance and long vowels. They are stylistically a different point on a continuum rather than a radical shift. The lines are end-stopped almost throughout, and the major changes have to do with diction, the use of words such as "yank," "wobbled," "scrabbled," "shriek," and "jerked" in the Oklahoma section. The Oxford section is in present tense; the Oklahoma part is in conditional/past imperfect, implying events that take/took place on a regular basis, and is signaled by the conditional sentence: "it might be morning darkness in Oklahoma." The memory that follows, we come to understand, is one typical yet memorable morning. The speaker's homesickness is evident almost throughout the poem. In his essay "History, Myth, and Identity among Osages and Other Peoples," Revard has written of Geronimo: "He knew who he was and where he came from, and he was sure that removal of the Apaches from their *homeland* meant, for him and for all of them, the loss not just of a 'way of life' or a 'home,' but a change in, perhaps a loss of, their *beings*, or, as we might say, their *identities*. In his story, the notions of cosmos, country, self, and home are inseparable."[28]

While Revard's essay focuses on Geronimo and the Chiricahua Apaches, he theorizes from them to include Native people in general (acknowledging, of course, that such generalizations are ultimately impossible). In this sense, then, "homesickness" is also a sickness for one's self. Because the self is constituted through others, to long for home is to long for them. In this poem, the speaker is away from himself, because he is away from the landscape of Oklahoma and from the people who populate the italicized section of the poem.

To complicate things further, the poem is fully nostalgic. One senses the speaker's longing for both these worlds, even though the poem's strategy is for a displaced speaker to describe his longing for the warm and fertile Oklahoma that is home as he writes from a cold and dark room in England. For this is the England of the conquest. The Europe that conquered the author's nation and killed his people. It is the Europe he claims for the Osage Nation in "Report to the Nation: Repossessing Europe," a satirical essay in Revard's collection *Family Matters, Tribal Affairs*. His feeling for Oxford is not so much contradictory as it is doubled, multiple, complex.

Yet it is too easy to cast Oxford as "bad," Oklahoma as "good" in this poem. It is more complicated, for after all, education—clearly located at Oxford—is a "dazzling window," and certain subtle links between Oxford and Oklahoma are suggested. His grandfather is a hero in the poem just as Beowulf is a hero in a story in the poem. The poem ends mentioning "warriors who voyaged on foam-throated / Seabird over the waves to this wan shore," reminding us that the poet, too, has ventured across the waves. Still, the poem may make subtle connections between the two, but it does not equate them. England is "wan" in comparison with the rich and fertile Oklahoma, and *Beowulf* is finally just a story in comparison with the poet's genuinely heroic grandfather who is struggling to feed his family during hard times.

These deepest meanings are revealed in Revard's poems through challenges to categories that appear both "obvious" and inevitable. Thus, these meanings are not effected through closure but rather through the full articulation of questions about what, to use Eoyang's phrase, "we take for granted." The not-obvious history revealed in "Homework at Oxford" is the heroism depicted in the domestic scenes from Oklahoma. While the binary opposition between Oxford and Oklahoma is a strong one and one the poet keeps reminding us of, this poem, as with all Revard's work, disrupts and infiltrates this opposition.

When voices, traditions, experiences sit at angles to each other, representations are never fixed; they are always changing, transforming, being made. The poems do not imitate a separate reality but "re-present" it, revising and shaping it continually. In this sense, their use of language is performative; they make a world even as they describe one. As such, they forge connections to the oral culture that informs them, because language, meaning, and texts tend to exist in full context within oral cultures, as opposed to literate ones where texts and language circulate widely and often out of context. We as readers receive Revard's poems as written text; however, because the poems strategize, map, and construct a world, their use of language is as much performative as it is statement.

This new world made manifest in Revard's poems is a dynamic one, existing in the charged relationships and movements between and among the supposed polarities he engages. Thus, Revard delineates borders even as he crosses and erases them; his poems constitute "contact zones" where heterogeneous and dissimilar forces encounter each other.

Poetry seems an especially powerful medium in which to document and construct these contact zones. As Elaine Jahner has written, "Poetry's metaphoric impetus is toward limits of all kinds in order to reach beyond them; but as it reveals the limits of culture, it also emphasizes the originary energy channeled through these limits."[29] Revard's poems not only emphasize this "originary energy" but unleash it. Thus these poems, these zones, do not—and do not attempt to—reconcile difference. Instead, they map a new space, which exists dynamically, that is to say, which is always performed and never static.

I have noted that certain binaries are disrupted by being juxtaposed and shown to be linked and interrelated rather than in full opposition. Another gesture the poet uses to belie oppositional thinking is to introduce an additional element (or elements) into the binary. The juxtaposition of Old and New Worlds, for example, is complicated and undermined in "Homework at Oxford" by subtle links between these worlds. In other poems, the horizontal binary of Old World / New World—mapped out on either side of the ocean—is disrupted by the poet's introduction of worlds above, beneath, and within. In this way, the "cosmic" and "geo-logic" aspects that constitute identity, place, and, hence, the world itself are articulated.

Conclusion

So, like that mockingbird, I have more than one song, but they are all our songs.

For Native peoples, Michelle Cliff insists, "Everything is contiguous. Everything is connected in time, space. Therefore, there are no bound-aries. The petroglyph and what it signifies exists with the mobile home and what it signifies."[30] The world is always being written into being, and the voices that emerge from it, because they exist and speak relationally, necessarily do not speak from a priori static and discrete locations, but are always being generated and articulated. The voice of Coyote is a voice full of irony, the voice of the trickster. It is a voice that keeps us guessing, one that we can never fully fix or pin down, so that it is always changing and shifting. The collective nature of this voice arises from the very motion of these shifts.

Like many American Indian writers, Revard emphasizes the impor-tance of telling stories in his work. "Stories" do not seem exclusively Indian even as the poet emphasizes their importance in his own heritage and individual experiences. His poems do not collapse the distinctions between these traditions and cultures. Instead, they draw on a rich plu-rality. In Revard's poetry, no action is apart from the world in which it is performed; no being is separate. Instead, the world itself is a room of angled mirrors where every act is reflected and multiplied, where every-one's reflection is captured numerous times, in looking glasses filled with others.

"Dawn / Is a Good Word"

Naming an Emergent Motif of Contemporary

Native American Poetry

Robert M. Nelson

Three decades ago, in 1973, about the same time Kenneth Lincoln was heralding a "Native American renaissance"[1] in prose and poetry, a child named Rainy Dawn was born to Joy Harjo and Simon Ortiz, both of whom were already becoming powerful voices in the then-young field of published contemporary Native American poetry. Almost twenty years later, in 1992, the nearly four hundred established and emerging Native American writers at the Returning the Gift festival in Norman, Oklahoma, celebrated five hundred years of endurance and survival of their cultures and literary traditions. Here, a generation of writers who were themselves emerging or becoming established in the early seventies welcomed those of a new generation just emerging or becoming established in the early nineties. In this year also, Rainy Dawn became a mother herself, thereby promoting her parents Simon and Joy to the family rank of grandparent and elder, a rank both had long since achieved in the field of poetry.

In that same year, another elder of Native American poetry, Carter Revard, celebrated the birth of Rainy Dawn's daughter, Krista Rae, in "When Earth Brings," a poem that appeared first as the final poem of his 1993 collection *An Eagle Nation* and again in the *Returning the Gift* anthology published a year later. "When Earth Brings" is a handsomely crafted text that stands perfectly well in its own right without any reference to the foregoing story. Still, I think it is good to take this historical and familial context into account when reading it, for at least two reasons. For one, Revard directly invokes this context by naming "Joy," "Simon,"

"Rainy Dawn," and "Krista Rae" in the dedicatory epigraph to the poem.[2] A second reason is that Revard has crafted the poem's controlling motif and core term, "dawn," to function as what I want to call a *merge site*. By this I mean that, in Revard's use of the term, dawn becomes a place where, and a time when, Harjo's Creek and Ortiz's Acoma and Revard's own Osage origin traditions not only intersect but also merge in the image of a grandchild who is both metaphorically and literally Dawn's offspring, the next living generation of the People.

I think Carter Revard's use of the term "dawn" in this poem may represent and reflect the emergence and establishment of a new inter-tribal origin motif, that is, a motif that combines elements of several otherwise disparate Native origin stories. I'm proposing that this motif, itself conceivable as a child of the Native American renaissance, figures particularly strongly in the birth-celebration poetry of several major contemporary poets whose own traditional backgrounds (which include Chickasaw, Acoma, Creek, Navajo, and Osage) are otherwise about as diverse as they could possibly be. Seen against this backdrop, Revard's poem "When Earth Brings" represents the latest phase in the develop-ment of a motif that is tribally nonspecific but nevertheless resonantly Native American by both emic and etic criteria, a motif that combines the ideas of emergence, survival, return, and renewal in the image of dawn.

One of the earlier manifestations of this dawn motif, in which the con-cepts of sunrise, the birth of an individual, and the rebirth of cultural awareness and collective identity come to function as metaphors for one another, occurs in Linda Hogan's "Celebration: Birth of a Colt." This poem is one of her earliest, appearing in her collection *Calling Myself Home* in 1978, twenty-five years ago, when Hogan's now honored and distinctive poetic voice was still coalescing out of her probes into the tangles of mixed-blood identity. In the introduction she wrote for these poems when they were republished in 1991 in the volume *Red Clay,* Hogan implies some such formative significance:

> For American Indian people the journey home is what tells us our human history, the mystery of our lives here, and leads us towards fullness and strength. These first poems were part of that return for me, an identification with my tribe and the Oklahoma earth, a deep knowing and telling how I was formed of these two powers called

ancestors and clay. . . . In these poems live red land and light. . . .
They are home speaking through me. Home is in blood, and I am still
on the journey of calling myself home.[3]

Central here is Hogan's sense of her own formation out of "these two
powers called ancestors and clay," a doubled siting of "home" that is
replicated formally in the subsequent organization of her book. Part 2 of
the two-part *Calling Myself Home* is in fact subtitled "Heritage," and the
poems in that section tend to deal with family members and connections.[4] The first section, though, is subtitled "By the Dry Pond" and is
characterized by poems in which a more solitary narrative vision attempts to animate a lifeless, dry landscape. "Celebration" is the final
poem of this first section; in it, rather than attempting to animate the
landscape, the narrative vision is animated *by* it, learning finally to see
past the dry pond and dust to the redness of the clay, the "blood" that
home is in. I think it is also important here to note Hogan's 1991 assertion
that "the journey home," one way of recovering Chickasaw identity, is
also a viable strategy for recovering American Indian identity of *whatever*
tribal background: the antecedent of "us" in the passage is "American
Indian people" before it is the people of a particular tribe. This claim
about the existence of a real basis for pan-Indian identity would probably
have surprised few members of the choir in 1978, when Native authors
and savvy critics of their work alike were still struggling to convince
academe that a field of contemporary Indian literature even existed. But
it comes as some surprise to the choir in the first decade of the twenty-
first century, when increased sensitivity to issues of national sovereignty
has been accompanied by a tendency to write and critique in terms of
tribal rather than pan-Indian identities. My own sense of Hogan's claim
is that it points to what the dawn motif has come to signify in the past
quarter century: the general recognition that it is becoming possible to
confirm and celebrate individual and tribal identity within the context of
an idea of Indianness that, in turn, has been communally constructed to
emic specifications rather than to the usual etic ones.

But let me return to the proposition that Hogan's poem "Celebration" represents, as it were, the dawn of the dawn motif as a tribally
nonspecific merge site. From first line to last, the emergence event being
celebrated—the birth of the colt—is both formally and temporally embedded within the context of another, equally significant emergence

event. This is the event of sunrise, which is already under way in the first lines of the text and which is completed in the last ones, making it possible for the young persona of the poem to finally see

> . . . the land
> with pollen blowing off the corn,
> land that will always own us,
> everywhere it is red.

Combined with these events, and informing her narrative representation of them, is a third emergence of sorts, namely the persona's own dawning awareness that she is a *part* of the story she has been watching: on differing timescales the birth of the black colt, the generation of the yellow pollen, and the evolution of the persona's consciousness are all parts of a more singular and subsuming event. This event is sunrise, the time when the sun appears to emerge from the earth and, in the process, reveals the land's redness, its "blood." And in almost all of these early poems of hers, as in work of the "renaissance" period generally (Carroll Arnett's "Early Song" is a strong example), images of "blood" and "redness" signify Indianness.

In its infancy, then, the dawn motif is strongly constellated with the concept of *discovery,* and specifically discovery of Native identity. Early on, the motif also incorporates a second tribally nonspecific element: the idea of Native identity becomes grounded in place, in the land. Hogan's "Celebration" celebrates the first element over the second; in the early work of Joy Harjo, notably in "3 AM" and "last song,"[5] the second element begins to come into its own. In "3 AM" Harjo, though herself Muskogee Creek, generates a first-person narrator who claims "old oraibi, third mesa" as "home" in Hogan's *Red Clay* sense, a term that evokes both "ancestors" and "clay," one's people of origin and one's place of origin. In the narrator's present, "home"—Indian country, represented in the text by two ancient sites, "old oraibi" and "acoma"—lies west of where they are. The villages of Old Oraibi and Acoma are generally considered to be the two oldest continually occupied sites in North America. Early in the poem, Oraibi functions as a generic Native American origin place, recognizable as such to Hopis but also to Creeks (though not to TWA attendants). Readers sensitized to issues of tribal sovereignty may agree that the apparent interchangeability of Hopi and Creek here is problematic, but again it is important to keep in mind how *early* 3 A.M. is, on several metaphorical axes. On one axis, 1973, the year of this poem's composition, is a time when the possibility of reassembling an idea of Indianness consistent with emic criteria is only just becoming entertainable. And by the end of the poem, Harjo's pan-Indian vision of return is anchored to the remembered image of a small but promising surrogate sunrise, a memory of

> that time simon
> took a yellow cab
> out to acoma from albuquerque
> a twenty five dollar ride
> to the center of himself.

By the end of the poem, that is, 3 A.M. has become a time when either a Creek or a Hopi[6] can learn, from the remembered example of "simon," whose beloved Acu was always "the center of himself," that "3 AM is not too late / to find a way back" to a basis for personal and collective Native identity. But to get there, or more precisely to get *back* there, the narrative "we" need to re-envision their location in time as well as place. At 3 A.M., the hour hand of the analog clock in the Albuquerque airport points due east, directing attention toward the sunrise that, already in motion, will emerge in a few hours: what seemed "too late" now seems, rather, a few hours early.

In this short poem we can also see Harjo expanding the connotational set of the dawn motif by making *return* to identity a component of *discovery* (or re-discovery) of identity: the "just two indians" constituting the narrative presence in the poem are "trying to find a way back" to "part of the center / of the world," a destination that by the end of the poem is clearly coterminous with "the center of [one]self." To achieve this return by whatever means (even if it involves using such etic vehicles as TWA planes and yellow cabs) is to effect a transformation from a state of alienation and insignificance to one of identity and centeredness. In "last song," Harjo explores further the elements of discovery and recovery of identity associated with dawn. In this poem, she personifies these two motions in a sort of narrative duet, reversing the order of presentation from that in "3 AM" to give the impulse to return first voicing and, like Hogan in "Celebration," anchoring these elements to a vision of identity with particular place. But by locating Native identity more specifically than Hogan in terms of both geographic and ancestral origins, Harjo in effect introduces an element of tribal specificity to the element of return.

As I have argued elsewhere,[7] geographies as different as those of north-central New Mexico and Oklahoma give rise to different visions of life and how it is to be lived. Such differences of vision are the basis of differences in cultural identities, and in "last song" such a difference underlies the dialogue between the male and female voices about how life gets lived in northeast Oklahoma. From "the last song" of the man, we learn only that he is a native of New Mexico who feels out of place, a man who cannot "stand" the

> hot oklahoma summers
> where you were born
> this humid thick air is choking me
> and i want to go back
> to new mexico.

The identity of the female speaker, on the other hand, is one with this climate and milieu, and has been from birth:

> it is the only way
> i know how to breathe
> an ancient chant
> that my mother knew
> came out of a history
> woven from wet tall grass
> in her womb

Harjo's wording here repeats the idea of human identity with the land that so strongly informs the works of Native American poets from other regions. She invites us to read "her"—the source of both the "ancient chant" and the very breath of the narrating "i" of these lines—as either the speaker's biological mother or the earth, whose womb holds a "history" that some humans cannot help but call their own. And, while the male presumably goes on to try to return to his natal New Mexico, the female already knows that "oklahoma will be the last song / i'll ever sing."

In these early works of Hogan and Harjo we can see the emergence of two interesting correlatives to the development and maturation of the dawn motif that continue to figure in other, later dawn poems: the relative maturity of the narrative personae and the expansion of an implied community, a community held together by shared vision, in which these personae are embedded. The narrative perspective in Linda Hogan's dawn poem, for instance, is that of a child (not an adult)[8] who comes to see the red relation between herself, the land, and all that moves at sunrise. Even though the subject of the poem's sentences is "we," suggesting some degree of community in which the narrator is embedded, still the persona's vision comes as more of a private epiphany, a personal revelation of the significance of the event she has both experienced and become part of. By comparison, the narrative perspective in Harjo's early work is more matured, and her parent-aged, tribally specific personae discover common cause (and even a degree of identity) with coevals from other nations, in the process establishing the image of sunrise as a merge site for those differing identities and traditions and also incorporating the idea of *return* into the motif. Still, the perspective in these poems of Harjo and Hogan is that of a relative newcomer, one who is just discovering the way that tradition and renewal become a single motion at sunrise. In contrast, Simon Ortiz's early (1973) dawn poem "To Insure Survival"[9] is a dramatic monologue narrated by an adult male, a father who already knows something of what Hogan's and Harjo's narrators learn about the relation between self, the land, all that is in motion there, and sunrise. In one sense, then, the narrator of Ortiz's poem can be read as an older, male version of Hogan's narrator, who has survived to become a progenitor of the next generation. In another, equally important sense, Hogan's young female narrator is re-presented in Ortiz's text also by the narrator's newborn daughter,[10] who is as yet too new to the Fifth World to have seen, let alone come to understand, what her father tells her is there, waiting to be seen "in five more days." Here, Hogan's nonspecific, vaguely communal "us" takes on more solid shape as two people, the narrating persona and his newborn audience of one, together representing two genders from two generations in very private, but also very audible, communication one to the other. Here, too, the child in the poem represents a *second* generation of Native identity, one that coexists with a representative of the previous generation who is present and able to *tell* her about her identity's Indian underpinnings.

According to the narrator in stanza one, what the child will *see*, at sunrise, is the transformation of the land's own life from immanence to visibility,

> . . . a stone cliff
> at dawn,

> changing colors,
> blue to red
> to all the colors of the earth.

This is also the sequence of colors that the parent is watching his own daughter's body go through at birth. And because this is the very first thing he tells his daughter about her identity, we might anticipate that her new name, sign of her identity, would bespeak her kinship to, and identity with, the sandstone mesas whose colors during the motion of emergence are identical with her own. But Ortiz models a narrative vision that has survived and grown beyond this first light and first principle of Indian identity. Embedding the story of his daughter's emergence within the context of his own Acoma origin traditions, the narrator, like the story he goes on to give his daughter, asserts that she is born into identity with more than the land. In the second stanza he introduces the Keresan creatrix figure Spider Grandmother,[11] who, he tells his daughter, has been weaving an identity for her newest granddaughter to grow into ever since the beginning of time and place; in the third stanza the narrator emphasizes the child's kin identity with her own mother, whose blood the newborn child still wears, and by extension the child's identity with her mother's people and traditions; and finally, in the fourth stanza, he tells his daughter of her kin relationship to the katsinas, "the stones with voices, / the plants with bells," who will gather at sunrise in five more days to dance welcome to the newest member of the congregation of Acoma life. For the poet/parent, as for Spider Grandmother and the katsinas, his daughter is the latest incarnation of the ageless project of Acoma cultural survival and renewal, and her survival insures this joint project of Spider Grandmother, the katsinas, and the People for at least one more generation. And as the poem's dedicatory epigraph gives us to understand, the best single word for "all these, all these," a term that encompasses the need to insure survival of Native identity in the current and coming years, a name as strong and ancient as the stone cliffs and as fragile and new as a child still wet with her mother's blood, is "Dawn."[12]

In Ortiz's poem "To Insure Survival," then, we can see a merging of Hogan's and Harjo's uses of dawn—functioning as a vehicle for the interrelated concepts of ancestry and place of origin, of discovery and return—with the use of dawn as a *name* as a means of insuring the survival of native identity. Harjo, too, seems to be working with this aspect of the development of the dawn motif in her 1986 prose poem "Rainy Dawn," the fourth piece in the second section of *In Mad Love and War*. Like "To Insure Survival," "Rainy Dawn" is cast as a dramatic monologue; but whereas Ortiz's text is addressed to the newborn daughter, Harjo's conflates "[t]hat day so hot" when "we both stood poised at that door from the east" with the time "thirteen years later" when the words are uttered by the narrating mother to her implied immediate audience of one, her thirteen-year-old daughter. Again as in Ortiz's text, Dawn is cast as a child who carries, in her existence as in her name, the promise and the hopes of cultural tradition: as the child aligns for birth in "the bowl of my body," the narrative persona reminds her that "ancestors lined up to give you a name made of their dreams cast once more into this stew of precious spirit and flesh." In this text, as in "3 AM," the concept of an identity that one is born into tends to anchor in a Southwestern rather than Oklahoman traditional cultural milieu: the narrator's vision, like the child's name, comes from "the approximate direction of Acoma, and farther on to the roofs of the houses of the gods who have learned there are no endings, only beginnings." Still, Harjo in 1986 is careful to keep Muskogee antecedents alive and part of the dawn/Dawn story: at the time of delivery, albeit located geographically in New Mexico, "*we both* . . . listened . . . to the sound of *our* grandmothers' voices, the brushing wind of sacred wings, the rattle of raindrops in dry gourds" (italics mine). No less a child of Acoma's Grandmother Spider, Rainy Dawn here is clearly also dedicated to those other grandmothers whose "ancient chant" is reembodied in the life and song of the persona of "last song"; their life is a part of the "it" that Dawn's first breath is, according to the narrator, a "promise to take it on like the rest of us, this immense journey, for love, for rain."

A fourth major exponent of the cultural values constelled by the dawn motif is Navajo poet Luci Tapahonso. From the perspective both of a mother in "A Breeze Swept Through" and her prose poem "White Bead Girl" and from the perspective of an elder, literally a grandmother, in her birth celebration poems "Shisói" and "Blue Horses Rush In," the dawn visions of Tapahonso's personae provide a bridge between the relative naïveté of the generations represented by the personae of earlier dawn poems and the wisdom generally attributed to the elders, themselves intermediaries between the uninitiated young and the ancestors.

The title poem of Tapahonso's 1987 *A Breeze Swept Through* is inscribed "For my daughters, Lori Tazbah and Misty Dawn"; like Hogan's "Celebration," Ortiz's "To Insure Survival," and Harjo's "Rainy Dawn," it is a birth poem, formally celebrating the birth of the first daughter in the first half of the poem and the second daughter in the second. It is also a dawn poem, in which Navajo and Acoma ancestries, different as they are, are brought into delicate balance through the agency of dawn imagery. Lori Tazbah, though born at the time of an "August sunset," is introduced as "The first born of dawn woman," aligning the narrative persona with dawn and her firstborn, "named for wild desert flowers" in the Navajo way, with her mother's people, a child of the dawn despite her evening emergence time. The second daughter, Misty Dawn, is, like her cousin Rainy Dawn,[13] strongly identified with Acoma in the poem: at the moment of her mid-November emergence during "early morning darkness," as "outside / the mist lifted as the sun is born again," we are told that "east of Acoma, a sandstone boulder split in / two." Like every misty dawn, this daughter "is born of damp mist and early sun"; like every newborn Navajo girlchild, including her sister Lori Tazbah and her mother, "she is born again woman of dawn"; still, like her cousin Rainy Dawn, who "come[s] forth / the color of the stone cliffs at dawn," Misty Dawn is "born knowing the warm smoothness of rock. / She is born knowing her own morning strength." As a figure in contemporary poetry, Dawn here functions not only as a name bearing a certain ancestral cultural burden but also as a site for the amalgamation of tribal identities as disparate as those of the Diné and the Acu-meh, the people of Acu.

In her most recent collection, *Blue Horses Rush In,* Tapahonso continues to enrich the connotations of "dawn," understood as a name, an event tied in complex ways to both time and place, and a metaphor for both discovery and recovery. Nested between two poems in which a female persona celebrates newborn granddaughters, the story "White Bead Girl" bears several interesting resemblances to Harjo's "Rainy Dawn": formally, both are narrative monologues cast typographically as prose pieces; thematically, the narrators of both are mothers living through the anxiety of separation from their adolescent daughters, and in both cases the narrator anchors both the child's identity and the promise of her return in an image of dawn that is part of the daughter's name. In both, though perhaps more overtly in Tapahonso's piece, dawn is becoming a *story* as well as an emergence event. As Tapahonso makes clear elsewhere in this collection,[14] "Each morning, White Bead Girl arrives," and this is also "white dawn girl." In "White Bead Girl," the story begins with one dawn and ends with another.[15] The narrative opens with the words "This morning the sun shines bright," and during this first dawn the narrator realizes that her daughter, "just fourteen," "has run away"; in the last words of the narrative, delivered sometime after receiving a police phone call at "3:15 the next morning" and then going to bring her daughter home from the station, the narrator "pray[s] for the future that, at this moment, in the pure glow of the moon, shines on all of us like nothing I've ever seen." In between, in the spirit of story invoked by the epigraph by Li-Young Lee ("The characters survive through the telling, / the teller survives / by [her] telling . . .") and very much in the spirit of the story about a "yellow cab" that helps "just two indians" make it through the dark predawn hours in Harjo's "3 AM," the narrator retells the story of her daughter's name. We are to understand that the narrator's internal monologue is, like the Hózhójí, or "blessing ceremony," the narrator recalls having been performed over her daughter a year ago, part of a ceremony working for recovery and return. Compared to the description of the child given in Harjo's "Rainy Dawn," the identity Tapahonso's narrator attributes to her departed, and recovered, daughter is at once more densely tribally specific and more explicitly mixed blood or pan-Indian. This specificity is especially telling in the narrator's description of how her daughter's Navajo and Acoma names align her identity with both of these places and cultural traditions:

On her fourth day, my [Navajo] parents presented her to the sun, our father, and named her "At'ééd Abíní" in memory of the early winter morning that welcomed her. Her name means the billows of morning mist that fill the valley above the winding river. Her name means woman of the morning—the first spark of creativity, the first ray of sunlight, the last glimmer of the white moon before it melts in the west. Her name means the world waited for her then rejoiced, as we did at her birth. Later that month, we took her to her nalis, her father's [Acoma] parents, and they, too, had a naming for her. . . . Her name at her father's village is ceremonial and is called aloud when the katzinas and the sacred clowns present to her and the other children baskets of fruits, nuts, sweet treats, and pottery. Various katzinas call her several times a year. . . . She walks out shyly to the center of the plaza and nods thank you as the whole pueblo watches. When the dancers call her, it is to remind us all of the happiness she brings to the family. These are her names—my slender daughter who now is in a place I am afraid to imagine. . . . I think that the bright morning sun recalls naming her years ago. Watch over her, I whisper. ("White Bead Girl," 66)

Like White Bead Girl and White Shell Woman in Navajo origin traditions, the daughter's name draws attention to the eastern horizon at dawn and to the motion of airborne moisture at the moment before sunrise—in Navajo as in Acoma experience, misty dawn, a time of emergence that is also a time of reemergence, regeneration, and return. In this passage we can begin to see, too, that a term like *mixed blood* is, finally, a pale and misleading description of the state of such an identity—"enriched," or "augmented," comes closer. As Tapahonso's Hózhóji singer puts it while he is explaining "the sacred stones and the ears of corn": " 'This,' he said, 'represents Changing Woman. This represents you. It shows us that young girls like yourself are strong because you're Navajo. You have extra help, too, because of your Pueblo side,' he said" ("White Bead Girl," 69).

To the extent that every Navajo woman is Changing Woman, the narrator of "Blue Horses Rush In" can be understood as a more mature or riper version of both the runaway daughter of "White Bead Girl" and her mother. Strategically situated as the first poem in *Sáanii Dahataał, The Women Are Singing* and the last in *Blue Horses Rush In*, a formal reminder perhaps that every ending is also a beginning, Tapahonso's birth poem "Blue Horses Rush In" heralds a third generation of Navajo consciousness and identity formation. Like the father who speaks his daughter into identity with Acoma in "To Insure Survival," but also like Grandmother Spider who in the same poem "speaks" a life for her newest granddaughter to grow into, the grandmother who narrates "Blue Horses Rush In" crafts a statement that is both a prayer for the child's survival and a vision of cultural tradition—an identity—for the child to grow into. "Blue Horses" is also a text in which the sacred directional colors of Navajo tradition converge at the moment of the child's birth, harking back to the colored mountains in the four directions,[16] the boundary markers of Dinétah put in motion by First Man prior to the advent of the Glittering World. These four directions correlate also with the four stages of female identity (daughter, mother, grandmother, ancestor) through which, if all goes well, the child will sunwise move. In Navajo tradition, "blue horses" are aligned with the second stage, generative motherhood;[17] this is the phase the narrator moves beyond when she becomes *shimásani,* grandmother, and which, when blue horses rush in at dawn, becomes an immanent part of the life of her immediate audience, the newborn child, *Shisóí 'aláájí' naaghígíí* (my daughter's daughter who lives furthest away).

I want to close this essay as I began it, by drawing attention back to Carter Revard's poem "When Earth Brings." "When Earth Brings" is the most recent of all the texts discussed in this essay; it is also, I think, the most inclusive of them all. Like both Ortiz and Tapahonso, Revard begins with a dedicatory epigraph celebrating the event of individual human birth, and in the body of the poem he embeds his presentation of the event within a specific nation's emergence traditions. To be more precise: in the spirit of the 1992 Returning the Gift festival, the poem presents the 1992 birth of Rainy Dawn Ortiz's child Krista Rae, Creek and Acoma on her mother's side and Navajo on her father's, as the fulfillment also of the Washashe Osage account of the unending, constantly rehappening emergence of the People. In this way the poem celebrates birth, mixed-blood or pan-Indian identity, and specific tribal tradition simultaneously.

Formally, in a structure that echoes both Hogan's *Red Clay* and Harjo's "last song" duet, "When Earth Brings" is composed of two sentences of seventeen and sixteen lines respectively, the lines center justified on the page. Strategically located at the center of the text, on both its vertical and horizontal axes, looking all the more central because it is also easily the shortest line in the poem, is the single word "Dawn," the first word of the second sentence. In the first sentence the stars, who are also ancestors to the Osage, speak to the Little Ones, the People, whom they address as "grandchildren." They remind the Little Ones that the sun watches over them on behalf of its relatives, the other stars, until such time as earth brings the night again and the starlight that is the source of life on earth again becomes visible. In the second sentence, the poem's choral narrative voice goes on to remind us again that we come from the stars, and that "children come into a world / again and again," and that again and again the grandparents speak through the "rainy light" at dawn. Dawn, they give us to know, is one of those special times when "the earth meets heaven," a time when each child, who is also a grandchild, can see what the grandparents have prepared for each and all of them to see in "a small pool," where rain and daylight combine on earth to form a natural mirror. What is given for her, and us, to see is a vision of herself as a child in the company of the stars who, for now, are "go[ing] quietly into the / blue air" at sunrise, at dawn. It is a moment in which she is given to see herself as she truly is, as the living bridge between "the world and heaven in which [we] live / and move and have [our] being," this day as every day.

One interesting way this poem adds to the dawn motif is by incorporating a noncorporeal narrative persona into the tradition. In Hogan's and Harjo's early work, narrative personae are left to learn about their native identity pretty much on their own: that is, dawn is a time of *discovery* for them. In Ortiz's and Tapahonso's birth celebration poems, however, the story of the child's identity as one of the People is given to her as part of the event of her birth by a blood relative, either a parent or grandparent; that is, dawn is less a time of discovery than of *regeneration*, when a child's birthright is fashioned into a story that is both given to her and also, as it were, comes to be held in trust for her by her relations, human and otherwise. Now, as though to insure the survival of the People beyond even the possibility of loss, "When Earth Brings" has a whole host of ancestors, as numerous as the night-sky stars, first whispering reminders of identity to the newest Little One as she is making the transition from starlight to human life and then, in the second sentence, prophesying the day she will re-see her status for herself, at dawn, in a pool of water and light. That is, we are given to understand that, like Plato's human "soul" at its purest, the child auditor in this poem already *knows* where she comes from and how transformation and emergence are aspects of each other. Beyond discovery and regeneration, dawn for such a child brings *reassurance* of one's own immortal identity. The dawn poems of Ortiz, Harjo, and Tapahonso emphasize the tremendous importance of storytelling as a primary means of transferring Native identity, first from one generation to the next and then across two generational divides; "When Earth Brings" holds out the hope that, even in the absence of human storytellers, any child of the dawn carries the knowledge of her origins and her ancestors within her, awaiting only the moment when light, water, and vision interact to awaken her to it, and it to her. In this way, perhaps "When Earth Brings" can be read also as an interpretive gloss on Hogan's early dawn poem "Celebration: Birth of a Colt."

One final word about Revard's expansion of the dawn motif in "When Earth Brings." Like Hogan's "Celebration" and Ortiz's "To Insure Survival," Revard's "When Earth Brings" ends by relating sunrise to vision. In Hogan's and Ortiz's poems, at sunrise the land is revealed to us as the source of life, and life originates in the land in Harjo's and Tapahonso's dawn poems as well. In Revard's poem, however, the source of life is revealed to lie elsewhere: consistent with the Washashe origin story, the stars (including the earth's sun and moon) are the beings whose light becomes life, human and otherwise, when that light interacts with water and the stuff of earth in a place called *hoega*. The land, by Osage reckoning, is the vehicle, not the source, of our being as humans. But whether the source of life is Revard's starstuff or Tapahonso's earth, in contemporary Indian poetry the grandparents, the parents, and the little ones agree that the best time for illuminating our origins and all our relations is sunrise, and that for all three generations "Dawn / is a good word" for that event.

Call Me Brother

Two-Spiritness, the Erotic, and Mixedblood Identity
as Sites of Sovereignty and Resistance in
Gregory Scofield's Poetry

Qwo-Li Driskill

Gregory Scofield (Métis Cree) is a poet whose words we need. He is a writer who gives us back our tongues, who dislodges our silences and turns them into sites of resistance. Scofield's work is forcefully political. It asserts a Two-Spirit and Indian aesthetic and disrupts the hegemony of dominant culture's discourses on Native identities and lives. His poetry claims sovereignty and challenges the racism and homophobia of colonialism. Sovereignty is an issue of vital importance to Native people, not only as a right we have as independent nations within the borders of colonial governments, but also as a struggle to define ourselves outside of Eurocentric and racist notions of our lives as First Nations people. Scofield's work demands that Two-Spiritness, the erotic, and mixedblood identity be seen as sovereign. He writes us weapons and shields, weaves us blankets. Scofield's erotic is intensely political, and his politic intensely erotic. His work, ultimately, is one that heals.

My own reading of Scofield's work comes from my experiences as a mixedblood Cherokee, a Two-Spirit, and a poet who believes that poetry is a tool for social change and healing. Poetry is one of the many ways we tell our stories and encourage others to loosen their tongues—our stories are transformative. As a good Cherokee, I believe that words have an intense power to shape reality. And, because Two-Spirits are supposed to be silent or dead, our stories are necessarily political. Scofield's poetry helps me come home. There are few out Two-Spirit male poets publishing full volumes of poetry. There are few out Two-Spirit male writers being published at all. This makes Scofield's work all the more precious and necessary for a movement of decolonization and mending. Haunani-Kay Trask (Native Hawai'ian) defines decolonization as "collective resistance to colonialism, including cultural assertions, efforts toward self-determination, and armed struggle."[1]

Scofield's poetry is resistance. His use of Cree is life-giving to Native people, as it honors his Native language as beautiful and valuable. The use of Cree (and other indigenous tongues) asserts a Native identity that is sovereign from both colonial governments and from other Native people. Too often, dominant culture sees Native people as a monolithic culture. The use of our languages is a radical act, especially considering the violent history that means many of our languages are endangered or not spoken at all. By using Cree in his work, Scofield encourages other Native poets to use our Native languages in our writings and lives.

The poetry of Native (and other marginalized) people is always political and always necessary. In "Poetry Is Not a Luxury" Audre Lorde writes that poetry "is the skeleton architecture of our lives. It lays the foundations for a future of change, a bridge across our fears of what has never been before."[2] The idea that poetry should abstain from politics does nothing for struggles toward liberation. Because our work is often overtly political, it is also an idea that conveniently erases and devalues work from marginalized communities. Contemporary Native poetry is distinct from the mainstream (white, male, straight) canon because it comes from political and cultural histories often denied by a racist/colonial culture. Chrystos (Menominee) writes, "I assert that poetry without politics is narcissistic & not useful to us. I also believe that everything is political—there is no neutral, safe place we can hide out in waiting for the brutality to go away."[3]

Scofield's poetry cannot simply be seen as "Native," "Queer," "urban," "Canadian," or any of the other words one might want to use to describe it. His work must be understood within the complexities of overlapping identities.

Two-Spirit Country

Scofield's work speaks from a Two-Spirit identity that demands to be seen as separate from white Queer identities. The term "Two-Spirit"[4] was started as an act of resistance to anthropologists using the word *berdache* to describe traditional Native alternative gender roles. It is also employed to describe contemporary Queer Native people and give Native people a word to communicate traditional gender diversity in English.

Because *berdache* is still frequently employed as a term to describe Two-Spirit people, it is important to briefly address its history and its inaccuracy when discussing the sexualities and/or genders of First Nations people. In their introduction to the book *Two-Spirit People: Native American Gender Identity, Sexuality, and Spirituality*, Sue-Ellen Jacobs, Wesley Thomas (Navajo), and Sabine Lang give us a brief history of *berdache*, explaining its non-Native (Persian) origins and later European definitions as "kept boy," "male prostitute," and "catamite."[5] None of these words, or *berdache*, speaks accurately of our genders and sexualities as Native folks. Besides the derogatory connotations (and denotations) of *berdache*, it is a word that erases female and female-embodied Two-Spirits and suggests sexual abuse of children. While many Native people have asked academics and anthropologists to refrain from using *berdache*, non-Native writers such as Will Roscoe have defended its use: "As a Persian term, its origins are Eastern not Western. Nor is it a derogatory term, except to the extent that all terms for nonmarital sexuality in European societies carried some measure of condemnation. It was rarely used with the force of 'faggot,' but more often as a euphemism with the sense of 'lover' or 'boyfriend.' Its history, in this regard, is akin to that of 'gay,' 'black,' and 'Chicano'—terms that also lost negative connotations over time."[6] Yet Roscoe does not address the fact that *berdache*, regardless of its origins as "Eastern not Western," is nevertheless a colonial word brought to the Americas by "Western" invaders and enforced (like all non-Native languages) on our people. Two-Spirits have stated that the term *is* offensive to us, which negates his assertion that the term is not derogatory. Furthermore, *berdache* is not a word being readily reclaimed by our communities as a tool to build identity, community, and resistance, which is markedly different from words such as *gay*, *black*, and *Chicano*. *Berdache* continues to be an enforced word, and Roscoe's "Berdache Studies" maintains colonial attitudes about Native people.[7]

Using *Two-Spirit*, or *Two-Spirited*, rather than, or in addition to, labels such as *Trans*, *Intersexed*, *Bi*, *Queer*, *Lesbian*, and *Gay* creates a sovereign label for Native people to discuss our traditional and contemporary gender and sexual identities.[8] It helps us decolonize our bodies and minds from the homophobic, sexist, transphobic, and racist ide-

ologies that are entrenched in European occupation of Turtle Island.
Though in some ways calling ourselves *Two-Spirit* is overtly political, in
the sense that any act of decolonization is political, Anguksuar / Richard
LaFortune (Yup'ik) notes that

> the sudden appearance of Native people claiming two-spirit identity
> should not be interpreted as a strategy for acquiring political power.
> . . . Likewise, it would be a mistake to think this a recently developed
> fiction used to resituate individuals into tribal communities that
> sometimes reject them. . . . What is happening, actually, is that we are
> remembering again who we are and that our identities can no longer
> be used as a weapon against us. It is once again a source for healing.[9]

Scofield's poetry resists a racist white Gay culture that sexualizes
Native men and male-embodied people and sees us, like our homelands,
as things to be used and discarded. In his poem "Promises," Scofield
connects the reality of genocide and colonization with the ways in which
Two-Spirit men are often used by white Gay men for sexual gratification
and the internalized racism that often leads men of color to seek white
men for acceptance and validation:

> beneath the buffalo robe
>
> snuggle into him   temporary
> the famine his doeskin fingers snail
> across my lips of strawberry pleasure
>
> . . . .
>
> spread my arms, my legs
> I offer moose tongue and berries
> generations he devours in seconds

The images of famine and devoured generations speak from a history of
loss that Native people continue to endure under colonialism. The Two-
Spirit body becomes colonized. Scofield continues,

> the taste his foreign tongue snakes
> through ravines, over valleys
>
> . . . .
>
> each kiss
> history
> lolls on the tip of my tongue[10]

Two-Spiritness is understood within Native contexts and traditions. Our experiences are always entwined with histories of genocide and racism. Scofield's poetry helps us remember our traditional understanding of gender and sexuality. His Cree heritage provides him with a map to understand his Two-Spiritness. "*Âyahkwêw's* Lodge"[11] can be understood only within a Two-Spirit context.

> *êkwa êkosi, nikîwêhtatânân ôhi mistatimwak*[12]
> and gave them to our women
> who in turn
> gave them to our men.
> That night a baby was born in camp,
> eyes clenched shut,
> fist in his mouth.
>
> . . . .
>
> In the blood
> a twinning spirit was seen.
>
> . . . .
>
> At dawn, the time of prayer
> they brought the child
> to our lodge to be named—
> and so we named him twice,
> *Mistatim-awâsis /* [13]
> He Who Calls *Piyesîwak-iskwêw.*[14]

Poems such as this help us heal from colonialism. By speaking from a Cree Two-Spirit context, Scofield resists Two-Spirit invisibility that lumps us together with white Gay identities and he honors traditions that are often silenced and / or hidden. The sovereignty of Two-Spirit people is illustrated, as well, through poems dealing specifically with our stories, people(s), and issues. "Owls in the City" mourns the loss of urban Two-Spirits to AIDS. He writes,

> our *iyiniwak*[15] are dropping
> like rotten chokecherries
>
> . . . .
>
> Even owls have migrated to the city,
> perched on rooftops or clotheslines
> hooting their miserable death chant.

Tonight at the darkened window
tapping softly my drum, I think
how fortunate I am—
saved to pull up these *Âyahkwêw* songs
from my still beating heart.[16]

The owl images evoke many Native traditions in which owls signify death
and/or severe illness. AIDS is a pandemic that severely affects Native
communities, particularly because our communities are so small. AIDS
mirrors a history in which Native communities have been devastated by
disease. Profound loss is an important element in much of Scofield's
work. "Another Street Kid Just Died" mourns the death of a young Two-
Spirit to murder or suicide.[17] "Queenie" mourns the death of a former
lover.[18] Several poems (especially in *Love Medicine and One Song*) celebrate and mourn the life of Dean, who often becomes a ghost lover in
Scofield's work. These expressions of mourning are often expressed by
Queer people of color, a response to the many ways in which those we
love are lost. José Esteban Muñoz writes that melancholia "is a mechanism that helps us (re)construct identity and take our dead with us to the
various battles we must wage in their names—and in our names."[19]

Scofield's Two-Spirit poetry does not leave us stranded in "melancholia" with only the dead to take into battle, but also offers us images of
Two-Spirit people filled with life, sexuality, and rebellion against homophobia and racism.

Snag Poem

a dark lover   so clever

. . . .

want to be my nichimoose[20]
say would you be satisfied just snuggling close
would suit me fine to blow this beer joint
so just keep lookin' sweetie[21]

He offers us sexy, fierce words like these from "Unhinged":

Sure
I've slipped the curve
of your backside, slipped between
your thighs,

my seasoned lips mouthing
the peach song
beneath your scrotum.
So, sing my breather, play me
the whole black night.[22]

Poems such as this illustrate a political and powerful erotic that refuses to illustrate Queerness as shameful, tragic, or disgusting. He gives us poems such as "I Used To Be Sacred (on Turtle Island)" that incite mutiny against white Gay men who exploit Two–Spirit men.

Pissed off, he tottered along
snorting his hooked nose.
So much for brotherly turtleship
I thought
that one would make a good soup
at a Two-Spirited gathering.[23]

He gives us poems such as "Night Train" celebrating his love for both men and women, writing,

if you added
his perfect lips, her perfect arms
multiplied my heart, counted
all the sensations
I subtract and divide and
put together like so many railcars
my skeleton would stretch
a love song from here
to eternity.[24]

Scofield helps tell our stories as Two–Spirit people, celebrating the intricacies of who we are both within and outside of Native communities. His poetry is full of the humor, rage, erotic power, and sovereign identity that is needed for us to survive as colonized people living with layered forms of oppression.

The Sovereign Erotic

Sexuality is one of the many areas in which Native people are colonized. Dominant culture often asserts ideas of the erotic that are fiercely damaging to marginalized people. As Native people, especially as Two-Spirits, the act of creating and understanding the erotic as an aspect of our sovereignty is of vital importance. In *Love Medicine and One Song: Sâkihtowin-Maskihkiy Êkwa Pêyak-Nikamowin*, Scofield creates an erotic poetic that is distinctly Native in which dominant culture's fragmented understandings of sexuality are shed. Scofield roots the erotic in Cree traditions and language. His love poems become a tool for healing and erotic celebration. Beth Brant (Bay of Quinte Mohawk) writes:

> The love that was natural in our world, has become unnatural as we become more consumed by the white world and the values therein. Our sexuality has been colonized, sterilized, whitewashed. Our sense of spirit has been sterilized, colonized, made over to pander to a growing consumer need for quick and easy redemption. What the dominant culture has never been able to comprehend is that spirit/sex/prayer/flesh/religion/natural is who I am as a Two-Spirit.[25]

Perhaps decolonizing sexuality is one of the many tasks of contemporary Two-Spirits.

Scofield writes that his poems in *Love Medicine and One Song* "come from a sacred place within. I have made tobacco offerings to ask for the help and guidance of The Grandmothers and Grandfathers, and to honour my Two Spirits as well as my two loves."[26] By centering himself in Native ways of knowing, Scofield speaks from a sovereign erotic, one that is outside dominant culture's notions of the erotic, which are often accompanied by the sexism and racism infused into its fiber. He speaks from an erotic wholeness, one in which "spirit/sex/prayer/flesh/religion/natural" is expressed.

Scofield's erotic imagery in these lyric poems often draws upon Native spirituality and traditions. "My Drum, His Hands" links the erotic with Native song, dance, and spirituality. The use of drum imagery reminds us that the erotic is a life-giving, creative force. The body becomes the drum, the erotic becomes ceremony, prayer, and celebration.

over the bones, over the bones
stretched taut
my skin, the drum

softly he pounds
humming

. . . .

he carries me to dreams,
his hands wet
and gleaming

my drum aching[27]

Asserting a sovereign erotic, especially speaking honestly about loving both men and women, is a radical act against the homophobia of both
white and Native communities, the racism of the white community and
the biphobia, sexism, and racism of mainstream Gay movements. Scofield's poems are not for consumption by a dominant culture. They go
against the grain of the concepts that colonized the Americas. The fact
that he links sex between two men to his sacred traditions as a Native
person certainly rocks the boats of Native people buying into homophobia and Puritanical sexual notions.

Scofield's erotic is based in earth and nature. Images of the more-
than-human world are infused into the poems in *Love Medicine and One
Song*. Linda Hogan (Chickasaw) writes, "In the traditional belief systems
of native people, the terrestrial call is the voice of God, or of gods, the
creative power lives on earth, inside earth, in turtle, stone, and tree."[28]
Scofield listens to this terrestrial voice, understanding that the erotic is a
creative power given to us as a part of Creation. "Earth and Textures" is
an example of his poetry that puts imagery from nonhuman creation and
Native sacred traditions in the center of the erotic. In it he writes

îh, îh[29]
she is pîhtwawikamik[30]
where I come
to cry the dry stone
from my throat.

. . . . . .

pehtâw, pehtâw[31]
she is the song
of frogs and crickets
tickling my feet
so always I am rooted.[32]

Audre Lorde tells us, "The dichotomy between the spiritual and the
political is . . . false, resulting from an incomplete attention to our erotic

knowledge. For the bridge which connects them is formed by the erotic—the sensual—those physical, emotional, and psychic expressions of what is deepest and strongest and richest within each of us, being shared: the passions of love, in its deepest meanings."[33]

The People Who Own Themselves

Throughout his poetry, Scofield deals with the history and complexity of Métis people and lives. He uses his poetry to tell Métis stories and to deal with his own identity as a mixedblood Indian. He writes from what Louis Owens (Choctaw and Cherokee) calls "a straitjacket of history" that we grapple with in our lives and writings.[34] In "Divided" he deals with his feelings of exile from both white and Indian communities.

> My beigy-pink shade
> Unlike you with bronze skin
> I'm a Skin without colour; I get the brushoff
>
> . . . .
>
> Deciding if I am pure enough Red enough
>
> . . . .
>
> I am not your white whipping-boy[35]

Issues of wholeness and division are of major importance to mixedblood writers, who are often dismembered by concepts such as racial purity and blood quantum. To be Native and white often means to feel at war with your own identity. The frustration with feeling otherized by Native communities as a Métis person is also a frustration with a racist, colonial, and Indian-hating culture that otherizes him for being Indian.

> Growing up in an all-white town
> I never forgot my red half   It counted big
> Especially if you looked not right white
> But wrong white   To white people that's off-white.

Similarly, "Call Me Brother" deals with the complexity of mixed-blood identity within Native communities. It deals with Scofield's reality as a light-skinned mixedblood, and his feelings of rejection from Native communities.

> "You never know when you're talking to an Indian," he
> says wisely because I am only half which we both know

is not the real issue but the way I look which makes it
next to impossible not to spot me sticking out of a
powwow . . .[36]

Muñoz writes that "hybrid" identity practices are "spaces of productivity
where identity's fragmentary nature is accepted and negotiated."[37] Scofield creates a space to discuss mixedblood identity on the printed page,
not only pushing imposed boundaries of the concept of "race" as a mixed
person, but also the ideas of what a "real Indian" is. He continues,

>   I am a true die-hard
> Skin with blue eyes that really screws up the whole
> history book image except my roots can't be traced to
> the Bering Straight but nine months after European
> contact . . .[38]

One of the difficulties of mixedblood identity that Scofield mentions here
is that of feeling genetically colonized. "European contact" (colonization) becomes a metaphor for his conception. The ending of the poem
challenges notions of racial purity, maintaining a sovereign mixedblood
identity: "the next time / you see me up dancing call me brother."[39]

A specific Métis history and identity is asserted in his work as sovereign. He resists a colonialism that abuses Métis people. By telling his
own story and the stories of other Métis people, Scofield helps mend
Métis communities and continues Métis traditions of rebellion. "Answer
for My Brother" is a perfect example of the ways he declares a sovereign
Métis identity. The poem answers the question, "Who Are The Métis?"
Scofield gives a brief glimpse at the ways his people have been exploited
and ignored.

> There is so little written about the Métis because we
> are not one or the other but a shaded combination
>
> .   .   .   .
>   written
> right out of history except for
>
> Brief mention of our leaders who were a thorn in the
> government's ass they made it to the N section in the encyclopedia
>   under the "North West Rebellion"[40]

The entire poem speaks from a specificity of Métis history, but it is the last line
of the poem that claims Métis identity as sovereign from both "fullblood" and

white contexts: "If anything, we are Katipamsoochick."[41] *I Knew Two Metis Women* is Scofield's tribute song to his late mother and aunt, a praiseful look at the ways they learned to survive and find joy despite the harsh reality of their lives as Métis women. In "Not All Halfbreed Mothers," Scofield celebrates his mother's life by honoring her complexities:

Not all halfbreed mothers
speak like a dictionary
or Cree hymn book,
tell stories
about faithful dogs
or bears
that hung around or sniffed
in the wrong place.

Not all halfbreed mothers
know how to saddle
and ride a horse,
how to hot-wire a car
or siphon gas.

Not all halfbreed mothers

drink

red rose, blue ribbon,
Kelowna Red, Labatt's Blue.

Mine just happened
to like it

Old Style.[42]

"They Saw" is a similar tribute to his mother, one that deals with the racist and sexist gaze of dominant culture.

One time, she said, a woman
whispered behind her back,
"Just look where our tax
dollars are going."

And they saw

what all their parents said—
Indian women her age

were walking corpses
scrounging for a drink[43]

Scofield goes on to subvert this gaze and see his mother as the strong woman she was.

I saw her

my patch–quilt mother
with a hat so beat up
only a miracle
kept it on her head.
Running to meet her,
I saw her eyes charm up a smile.
"Look!" she said,
glowing in her new sweatshirt:
METIS & PROUD OF IT.[44]

The poem ends not only with a transformation of who is interpreting Scofield's mother, but also with his mother's assertion of a sovereign Métis identity.

Scofield's poetry is beautiful, sharp, and complex. It demands to be seen within the intricacies of history and identity. His poetry is a political and spiritual tool to help Native people in struggles for sovereignty, self-definition, and decolonization. By integrating his experiences as a Two-Spirit Métis Cree living under the government of Canada, Scofield brings us to a more complete perspective of the experiences of First Nations people in the Americas. His words heal and bring us home, help us understand who we are as Native peoples alive under continuing colonialism. Scofield's work demands that we call him brother.

Song/Poetry and Language—
Expression and Perception

Simon J. Ortiz

My father is a small man, in fact almost tiny. I think it must be the way that the Pueblo people were built when they lived at Mesa Verde and Pueblo Bonito. That's a long time ago, around 800–1200 A.D. One thousand years ago—this man? He's very wiry, and his actions are wiry. Smooth, almost tight motions, but like currents in creek water or an oak branch in a mild mountain wind. His face is even formed like that. Rivulets from the sides of his forehead, squints of his eyes, down his angular face and under his jaw. He usually wears a dark blue wool cap. His hair is turning a bit gray, but it's still mostly black, the color of distant lava cliffs. He wears glasses sometimes if he's reading or looking closely at the grain swirls of wood he is working with.

My father carves, dancers usually. What he does is find the motion of Deer, Buffalo, Eagle dancing in the form and substance of wood. Cottonwood, pine, aspen, juniper which has the gentle strains of mild chartreuse in its central grains—and his sinewed hands touch the wood very surely and carefully, searching and knowing. He has been a welder for the ATSFRY railroad and is a good carpenter, and he sits down to work at a table which has an orderly clutter of carving tools, paints, an ashtray, transistor radio, and a couple of Reader's Digests.

His movements are very deliberate. He holds the Buffalo Dancer in the piece of cottonwood poised on the edge of his knee, and he traces—almost caresses—the motion of the Dancer's crook of the right elbow, the way it is held just below midchest, and flicks a cut with the razor-edged carving knife. And he does it again. He knows exactly how it is at that point in a Buffalo Dance Song, the motion of elbow, arm, body and mind.

He clears his throat a bit and he sings, and the song comes from that motion of his carving, his sitting, the sinews in his hands and face and the song itself. His voice is full-toned and wealthy, all the variety and nuance of motion in the sounds and phrases of the words are active in it; there is just a bit of tremble from his thin chest.

I listen.

"Stah wah maiyanih, Muukai-tra Shahyaika,
duuwahsteh duumahsthee Dyahnie guuhyoutseh mah-ah.
Wahyuuhuunah wahyuuhuu huu nai ah."

Recently, I was talking with a friend who is enrolled in a Navajo language course. She is Navajo, but she does not know how to speak Navajo. That is the story at present with quite a number of Indian young people who use English as the language with which they express themselves. English is the main language in which they experience the meaning and the uses of language.

She made a comment about not being able easily to learn Navajo as a course of instruction. She said, "I can't seem to hear the parts of it," referring to inflections and nuances of spoken sentences and words.

I referred to a remark I made sometime before. "The way that language is spoken at home—Acu, the tribal people and community from whom I come—is with a sense of completeness. That is, when a word is spoken, it is spoken as a complete word. There are no separate parts or elements to it." And I meant that a word is not spoken in any *separate parts,* that is, with reference to linguistic structure, technique of diction, nuance of sound, tonal quality, inflection, etc. Words are spoken as complete words.

For example when my father has said a word—in speech or in a song—and I ask him, "What does that word break down to? I mean, breaking it down to the syllables of sound or phrases of sound, what do each of these parts mean?" And he has looked at me with an exasperated —slightly pained—expression on his face, wondering what I mean. And he tells me, "It doesn't break down into anything."

For him, the word does not break down into any of the separate elements that I expect. The word he has said is complete.

The word is there, complete in its entity of meaning and usage. But I with my years of formal American education and some linguistic training

—having learned and experienced English as a language—having learned to recognize the parts of a sentence, speech, the etymology of words, that words are separable into letters and sounds and syllables of vowels and consonants—I have learned to be aware that a word does break down into basic parts or elements. Like that Navajo friend who is taking the Navajo language course, I have on occasion come to expect—even demand—that I hear and perceive the *separated* elements of Indian spoken words.

But, as my father has said, a word does not break down into separate elements. A word is complete.

In the same way, a song really does not break down into separate elements. In the minds and views of the people who are singing it at my home or in a Navajo religious ceremony, for whatever purpose that a song is meant and used—whether it be for prayer, a dancing event, or as part of a story—the song does not break down. It is part of the complete voice of a person.

Language, when it is regarded not only as expression but is realized as experience as well, works in and *is* of that manner. Language is perception of experience as well as expression.

Technically, language can be disassembled according to linguistic function that mainly deals with the expression part of it. You can derive—subsequently define—how a language is formed, how and for what purpose it is used, and its development in a context. But when the totality is considered—language as experience and expression—it doesn't break down so easily and conveniently. And there is no need to break it down and define its parts.

Language as expression and perception—that is at the core of what a song is. It relates to how my father teaches a song and how a poet teaches a poem.

There is a steel vise at one end of my table my father works at. He clamps a handlong piece of wood in it. This pine is the torso of an Eagle Dancer. The Dancer is slim and his chest is kind of concave. The eagle is about to fly aloft, and my father files a bit of the hard upper belly with a rasp. Later, he will paint the dancing Eagle Man who has emerged out of the wood.

My father built the small house in which we sit. The sandstone was brought from a simple quarry near Shuutuh Tasigaiyamishrouh, on the plateau uplift south of here towards Acu. This is his workshop. It has a couple of windows and a handmade door because he couldn't find the right size door at the lumberyard in Grants where he trades. The single room is very secure and warm when he has a fire built on cold days in the woodstove which is one of those that looks like a low-slung hog.

There are a couple of chairs on which we sit and the table with his work and a bed in a corner. There is a stack of shelves against the eastern wall. My mother stores her pottery there. The pottery is covered with some cloth that formerly was used to sack flour. I think there is a box of carpentry tools on the floor below the lowest shelf. Against another wall is a bookcase that doesn't hold books. Mainly there are pieces of wood that my father is carving—some he has started and didn't feel right about or had broken and he has laid aside—and a couple of sheep vertebra he said he is going to make into bolo ties but hasn't gotten around to yet. And a couple of small boxes, one of them a shoebox and the other a homemade one of thin plyboard in which are contained the items he uses for his duties as a cacique.

He is one of the elders of the Antelope people who are in charge of all of the spiritual practice and philosophy of our people, the Acumeh. He and his uncles are responsible that things continue in the manner that they have since time began for us, and in this sense he is indeed a 1,000-year-old man. In the box are the necessary items that go with prayer: the feathers, pollen, precious bits of stone and shell, cotton string, earth paints, cornmeal, tobacco, other things. The feathers of various birds are wrapped in several-years-ago newspaper to keep the feathers smoothed. It is his duty to ensure that the prayer songs of the many and various religious ceremonies survive and continue.

My father sings, and I listen.

Song at the very beginning was experience. There was no division between experience and expression. Even now, I don't think there is much of a division except arbitrary. Take a child, for example, when he makes a song at his play, especially when he is alone. In his song, he tells about the experience of the sensations he is feeling at the moment with his body and mind. And the song comes about as words and sounds—expression. But essentially, in those moments, that song that he is singing is what he is experiencing. That child's song is both perception of that experience and his expression of it.

The meaning that comes from the song as expression and perception comes out of and is what the song is.

> Stah wah maiyanih, Muukai-tra Shahyaika,
> duumahsteh duumahsthee Dyahnie guuhyoutseh mah-ah.
> Wahyuuhuunah wahyuuhuu huu nai ah.

This is a hunting song which occurs to me because it is around deer hunting season. I look around the countryside here, the piñon and the mountains nearby, and feel that I might go hunting soon, in November. The meaning the song has for me is in the context of what I am thinking, of what I want and perhaps will do. The words are translatable into English and they are

> My helping guide, Mountain Lion Hunting Spirit Friend,
> in this direction, to this point bring the Deer to me.
> Wahyuuhuunah wahyuuhuu huu nai ah.

The latter part of the song is a chanted phrase that is included with all hunting songs. The meaning—the song for the hunt, asking for guidance and help—is conveyed in English as well. There is no problem in deciphering the original meaning, and I don't think there ever really is when a song is taken to be both expression and perception.

The meaning that it has for me is that I recognize myself as a person in an active relationship—the hunting act—with Mountain Lion, the spirit friend and guide, and Deer. It is a prayer. A prayer song. The meaning that it has, further, is that things will return unto me if I do things well in a manner that is possible, if I use myself and whatever power I have appropriately. The purpose of the song is first of all to do things well, the way that they're supposed to be done, part of it being the singing and performing of the song. And that I receive, again well and properly, the things that are meant to be returned unto me. I express myself as well as realize the experience.

There is also something in a song that is actually substantial. When you talk or sing with words that are just words—or seem to be mere words—you sometimes feel that they are too ethereal, even fleeting. But when you realize the significance of what something means to you, then they are very tangible. You value the meaning of the song for its motion in the dance and for the expression and perception it allows you. You realize its inherent quality by the feeling that a song gives you. You become aware of the quietness that comes upon you when you sing or hear a song of quiet quality. You not only feel it—you know. The substance is emotional, but beyond that, spiritual, and it's real and you are present in and part of it. The act of the song which you are experiencing is real, and the reality is its substance.

A song is made substantial by its context—that is its reality, both that which is there and what is brought about by the song. The context in which the song is sung or that a prayer song makes possible is what makes a song substantial, gives it that quality of realness. The emotional, cultural, spiritual context in which we thrive—in that, the song is meaningful. The context has to do not only with your being physically present but it has to do also with the context of the mind, how receptive it is, and that usually means familiarity with the culture in which the song is sung.

The context of a song can be anything, or can focus through a specific event or act, but it includes all things. This is very important to realize when you are trying to understand and learn more than just the words or the technical facility of words in a song or poem. That means that you have to recognize that language is more than just a group of words and more than just the technical relationship between sounds and words. Language is more than just a functional mechanism. It is a spiritual energy that is available to all. It includes all of us and is not exclusively in the power of human beings—we are part of that power as human beings.

Oftentimes, I think we become convinced of the efficiency of our use of language. We begin to regard language too casually, thereby taking it for granted, and we forget the sacredness of it. Losing this regard, we become quite careless with how we use and perceive with language. We forget that language beyond its mechanics is a spiritual force.

When you regard the sacred nature of language, then you realize that you are part of it and it is part of you, and you are not necessarily in control of it, and that if you do control some of it, it is not in your exclusive control. Upon this realization, I think there are all possibilities of expression and perception which become available.

This morning my father said to my mother and me, "On Saturday, I am going to go hunting. I am telling you now. I will begin to work on Tuesday for it." He means that he will begin preparations for it. He explained

that my brother-in-law will come for him on Friday, and they are going to hunt in Arizona. This is part of it, I knew, the proper explanation of intention and purpose. I have heard him say that since I was a boy.

The preparations are always done with a sense of excitement and enjoyment. Stories are remembered.

Page was a good story teller. I don't know why he was called Page—I suppose there is a story behind his name but I don't know it. Page was getting older when this happened. He couldn't see very well anymore, but he was taken along with a group of other hunters. He said, "I was to be the kuusteenehrru." The camp cook sticks around the camp, sings songs and makes prayers for the men out hunting, and waits, and fixes the food. Page got tired of doing that. He said, "I decided that it wouldn't hurt if I just went out of camp a little ways. I was sort of getting tired of sticking around. And so I did; I wasn't that blind."

He walked a ways out of their camp, you know, looking around, searching the ground for tracks. And he found some, great big ones. He said, "It must be my good fortune that I am to get a big one. I guess I'm living right," and he reached into his cornfeed bag and got some meal and sprinkled it with some precious stones and beads and pollen into the big tracks. He said, "Thank you for leaving your tracks, and now I ask you to wait for me; I am right behind you." And putting his mind in order, he followed the tracks, looking up once in a while to see if the larger deer he could already see in his mind was up ahead.

"I was sure in a good mood," Page said, and he would smile real big. "Every once in a while I sprinkled cornfeed and precious things in the tracks. They were big," he said and he would hold out his large hand to show you how big, "and I would sing under my breath." He followed along, kind of slow you know because he was an old man and because of his eyes, until he came down this slope that wasn't too steep. There was an oak brush thicket at the bottom of it. He put his fingers upon the tracks, to let it know that he was right behind, and the tracks felt very warm.

He said, "Ah haiee, there you will be in the thicket. There is where we will meet," and he prayed one more time and concluded his song and set his mind right and checked to make sure his gun was ready—I don't know what kind of rifle he had but it was probably an old one too. And he made his way to the thicket very carefully, very quietly, slightly bent down to see under the branches of the oak. And then he heard it moving around in the thicket, and he said quietly, "Ah haiee, I can hear that you're a big one. Come to me now, it is time, and I think we are both ready," just to make sure that his spirit was exactly right. And he crouched down to look and there it was some yards into the thicket and he put his rifle to his shoulder and searched for a vital spot, and then it turned to him and it was a *pig*.

"Kohjeeno!" Page said, his breath exhaling. He lowered his rifle, cussed a bit, and then he raised his rifle and said, "Kohjeeno, I guess you'll have to be my Quuyaitih today," and shot the pig. He cut the pig's throat to let the blood, and then on the way back to camp he tried to find all the precious stones he had dropped in the tracks of the pig.

After that, until he went back North—passed away—his nephews and grandsons would say to him, "Uncle, tell us about the time the kohjeeno was your Quuyaitih." And Page would frown indignant a bit, and then he would smile and say, "Keehamaa dzee, we went hunting to Brushy Mountain. . . ."

The song is basic to all vocal expression. The song as expression is an opening from inside of yourself to outside and from outside of yourself to inside, but not in the sense that there are separate states of yourself. Instead, it is a joining and an opening together. Song is the experience of that opening, or road if you prefer, and there is no separation of parts, no division between that within you and that without you, as there is no division between expression and perception.

I think that is what has oftentimes happened with our use of English. We think of English as a very definitive language, useful in defining things—which means setting limits. But that's not supposed to be what language is. Language is not definition; language is all-expansive. We, thinking ourselves capable of the task, assign rules and roles to language unnecessarily. Therefore, we limit our words, our language, and we limit our perception, our understanding, our knowledge.

Children don't limit their words until they learn how, until they're told that it's better if they use definitive words. This is what happens to most everyone in a formal educational situation. Education defines you.

It makes you see with and within very definite limits. Unless you teach and learn language in such a way as to permit it to remain or for it to become all-expansive—and truly visionary—your expressiveness and perceptions will be limited and even divided.

My father teaches that the song is part of the way you're supposed to recognize everything, that the singing of it is a way of recognizing this all-inclusiveness because it is a way of expressing yourself and perceiving. It is basically a way to understand and appreciate your relationship to all things. The song as language is a way of touching. This is the way that my father attempts to teach a song, and I try to listen, feel, know, and learn that way.

When my father sings a song, he tries to instill a sense of awareness about us. Although he may remark upon the progressive steps in a song, he does not separate the steps or components of the song. The completeness of the song is the important thing, how a person comes to know and appreciate it, not to mark especially the separate parts of it but to know the whole experience of the song.

He may mention that a particular song was sung sometime before or had been made for a special occasion, but he remembers only in reference to the overall meaning and purpose. It may be an old, old song that he doesn't know the history of, or it may be one he has made himself. He makes me aware of these things because it is important, not only for the song itself but because it is coming from the core of who my father is, and he is talking about how it is for him in relationship with all things. I am especially aware of its part in our lives and that all these things are a part of that song's life. And when he sings the song, I am aware that it comes from not only his expression but from his perception as well.

I listen carefully, but I listen for more than just the sound, listen for more than just the words and phrases, for more then the various parts of the song. I try to perceive the context, meaning, purpose—all of these items not in their separate parts but as a whole—and I think it comes completely like that.

A song, a poem becomes real in that manner. You learn its completeness; you learn the various parts of it but not as separate parts. You learn a song in the way that you are supposed to learn a language, as expression and as experience.

I think it is possible to teach song and poetry in a classroom so that language is a real way of teaching and learning. The effort will have to be with conveying the importance and significance of not only the words and sounds but the realness of the song in terms of oneself, context, the particular language used, community, the totality of what is around. More complete expression and perception will be possible then.

Yesterday morning, my father went over to Diabuukaiyah to get oak limbs for the Haadramahni—the Prayer Sticks. After he got back he said, "The Haadramahni for hunting are all of hardwoods, like the hahpaani." The oak grows up the canyons which come out of the lava rock of Horace Mesa.

And at his worktable, he shows me. "This is a Haitsee—a shield if you want to call it that—and it is used as a guide." It is a thin, splitted strip of hahpaani made into a circle which will fit into the palm of your hand. "There is a star in the center—I will make it out of string tied to the edges of the circle. This is a guide to find your way, to know directions by. It is round because the moon is round. It is the night sky which is a circle all around in which the stars and moon sit. It's a circle, that's why. This is part of it, to know the directions you are going, to know where you are at."

He shows me a stick about the thickness of his thumb. The stick is an oak limb split in half, and he runs the edge of his thumbnail along the core of the wood, the dark streak at the very center of the wood. The streak does not run completely straight, but it flows very definitely from one end to the other. And my father says, "This is the Heeyahmani. This is to return you safely. This is so you will know the points on your return back, the straight and safe way. So you will be definite and true on your return. It is placed at the beginning point of your journey. This line here is that, a true road."

And then he explains, "I haven't gotten this other stick formed yet, and it is of oak also. It is pointed on both ends, and it is stout, strong." He holds up his right hand, his fingers clutched around the stout oak limb. "It's for strength and courage, manliness. So that in any danger you will be able to overcome the danger. So that you will have the stamina to endure hardship. It is to allow you to know and realize yourself as a man. It is necessary to have also."

He tells me these things, and I listen. He says, "Later, we will sing some songs for the hunt. There is a lot to it, not just a few. There are any numbers of prayer. There are all those things you have to do in preparation before you begin to hunt, and they are all meant to be done not only because they have been done in the past but because they are the way that things, good things, will come about for you. That is the way that you will truly prepare yourself, to be able to go out and find the deer, so that the deer will find you. You do these things in the proper way so that you will know the way things are, what's out there, what you must think in approaching them, how you must respond—all those things. They are all part of it—you just don't go and hunt. A person has to be aware of what is around him, and in this way, the preparation, these things that I have here, you will know."

My father tells me, "This song is a hunting song; listen." He sings and I listen. He may sing it again, and I hear it again. The feeling that I perceive is not only contained in the words; there is something surrounding the song, and it includes us. It is the relationship that we share with each other and with everything else. And that's the feeling that makes the song real and meaningful and which makes his singing and my listening more than just a teaching and learning situation.

It is that experience—that perception of it—that I mention at the very beginning which makes it meaningful. You perceive by expressing yourself therefore. This is the way that my father teaches a song. And this is the way I try to learn a song. This is the way I try to teach poetry, and this is the way I try to have people learn from me.

One time my father was singing a song, and this is the instance in which this—perception by/and expression—became very apparent for me. He was singing this song, and I didn't catch the words offhand. I asked him, and he explained, "This song, I really like it for this old man." And he said, "This old man used to like to sing, and he danced like this," motioning like the old man's hands, arms, shoulders, and he repeated, "This song, I really like it for this old man."

That's what the song was about, I realized. It was both his explanation and the meaning of the song. It was about this old man who danced that way with whom my father had shared a good feeling. My father had liked the old man, who was probably a mentor of some sort, and in my father's mind, during the process of making the song and when he sang it subsequent times afterwards, he was reaffirming the affection he had for the old guy, the way "he danced like this."

My father was expressing to me the experience of that affection, the perceptions of the feelings he had. Indeed, the song was the road from outside of himself to inside—which is perception—and from inside of himself to outside—which is expression. That's the process and the product of the song, the experience and the vision that a song gives you.

The words, the language of my experience, come from how I understand, how I relate to the world around me, and how I know language as perception. That language allows me vision to see with and by which to know myself.

Notes

Introduction, Dean Rader and Janice Gould

1. N. Scott Momaday, *The Way to Rainy Mountain* (Albuquerque: University of New Mexico Press, 1969), 33.

2. Joseph Bruchac, "Many Tongues: Native American Poetry Today," *North Dakota Quarterly* 55 (1987): 239.

3. Bruchac, "Many Tongues," 242.

4. Momaday, "Plainview: 1," in *In the Presence of the Sun: Stories and Poems, 1961–1991* (New York: St. Martin's Press, 1992), 8.

5. Jane Tompkins, *Sensational Designs: The Cultural Work of American Fiction, 1790–1860* (Oxford: Oxford University Press, 1985), xi.

6. Linda Hogan, *The Book of Medicines* (Minneapolis: Coffee House Press, 1993), 87.

7. Thomas Sanders and Walter Peek, *Literature of the American Indian* (New York: Glencoe Press, 1973), 103.

Poems as Maps in American Indian Women's Writing, Janice Gould

1. Kimberly M. Blaeser, *Trailing You* (Greenfield Center, N.Y.: Greenfield Review Press, 1994), 40; Anita Endrezze, *At the Helm of Twilight* (Seattle: Broken Moon Press, 1992), 13; Diane Glancy, *The Relief of America* (Chicago: Tia Chucha Press, 2000), 12; Awiakta, *Selu,* 10.

2. Native American women are not, of course, the only ones to employ the map or cartographic metaphor. In Elizabeth Bishop's "The Map," the poet becomes mapmaker. The first thing she points out to the reader is the shadowy, tense, and fluid boundary of land and water—or of child and mother—that the map metaphorically appears to record. More recently, in "Cartographies of Silence" (in *The Dream of a Common Language* [New York: Norton, 1978]), Adrienne Rich attempts to track her way through terrains of annihilating silence that have, in her view, separated women. In her later volume *An Atlas of the Difficult World* (New York: Norton, 1991), the poet binds together a series of "maps" that catalog troubling events that have been written out of history. The restoration of people, places, and events to the "atlas" allows it to bear a larger burden of pain and anger than the conventional and popular atlas of our history. Rich acknowledges that the "maps" in her poem create a "mural," but whether map or mural, what really counts, she argues, is the vantage point from which we see or read it.

3. See Denis Wood on how maps serve particular interests and how those interests are often masked. Denis Wood, with John Fels, *The Power of Maps* (New York: Guilford Press, 1992).

4. Wilma Mankiller, foreword to *Selu: Seeking the Corn-Mother's Wisdom,* by Marilou Awiakta (Golden, Colo.: Fulcrum, 1994), ix.

5. Yup'ik writer Harold Napoleon explores the debilitating effects of silence and alcoholism in Alaska Native communities in *Yuuyaraq: The Way of the Human Being,* ed. Eric Madsen (Fairbanks: University of Alaska, Fairbanks, College of Rural Alaska, Center for Cross-Cultural Studies, 1991).

6. Mankiller, foreword, ix. For more information on this topic, see Derrick Jensen, "Where the Buffalo Go: How Science Ignores the Living World—An Interview with Vine Deloria," *The Sun,* July 2000, 295. See also Paula Gunn Allen's *The Sacred Hoop* (Boston: Beacon Press, 1992).

7. Mankiller, foreword, ix.

8. Ibid.

9. Leslie Marmon Silko's novel *Ceremony* is perhaps the best prose example by a Native American writer of a (male) individual finding his way back to balance, harmony, and integration within the community after great personal suffering, disharmony, and dislocation.

10. Beck, Walters, and Francisco, *The Sacred,* 166.

11. Deborah Miranda, "Indian Cartography," in *Indian Cartography* (Greenfield Center, N.Y.: Greenfield Review Press, 1999), 76.

12. Allen, *Sacred Hoop,* 155.

13. Miranda, "Indian Cartography," 76.

14. Ibid.

15. Angelika Bammer, ed., *Displacements: Cultural Identities in Question* (Bloomington: Indiana University Press, 1994), xiii.

16. Linda Hogan, "Map," in *The Book of Medicines* (Minneapolis: Coffee House Press, 1991), 37–38.

17. Ibid., 37.

18. Ibid.

19. Hogan, "Deify the Wolf," in *Dwellings: A Spiritual History of the Living World* (New York: Norton, 1995), 64.

20. Hogan, "Map," 37–38.

21. Joy Harjo, "We Must Call a Meeting," in *In Mad Love and War* (Middletown, Conn.: Wesleyan University Press, 1990), 9.

22. Harjo, "The Field of Miracles," in *The Woman Who Fell from the Sky* (New York: Norton, 1994), 56.

23. Harjo, "A Map to the Next World," in *A Map to the Next World* (New York: Norton, 2000), 19.

24. Ibid., 20.

25. See Beck, Walters, and Francisco, *The Sacred,* 75.

26. Harjo, "A Map to the Next World," 21.

27. Ibid.

Situating American Indian Poetry, Eric Gary Anderson

1. See, for example, Gordon Sayre's discussion of ethnography as colonial genre in *Les Sauvages Américains: Representations of Native Americans in French and English Colonial*

Literature (Chapel Hill: University of North Carolina Press, 1997), 99–115, and Arnold Krupat, *Ethnocriticism: Ethnography, History, Literature* (Berkeley and Los Angeles: University of California Press, 1992), especially chapter 1, "Ethnography and Literature: A History of Their Convergence," 49–80.

2. As recent work by Sharon Holland and various others indicates, this situation is gradually beginning to change. Interested readers might begin with Holland's essay " 'If You Know I Have a History, You Will Respect Me': A Perspective on Afro-Native American Literature," *Callaloo* 17 (1994): 334–350. One of the texts Holland discusses is Leslie Marmon Silko's *Almanac of the Dead* (New York: Simon and Schuster, 1991), in which Silko reveals and theorizes various powerful links between tribal peoples of Africa and the Americas. Another, very different American Indian novel that addresses similar issues is Sherman Alexie's *Reservation Blues* (1995), while various novels by Toni Morrison, including *Song of Solomon* (1977) and *Paradise* (1997), also articulate Afro-Native situations and issues.

3. Recently, various Native scholars—Jace Weaver (Cherokee), Robert Warrior (Osage), Craig Womack (Muscogee Creek), and others—have made compelling arguments for a Native-centered criticism that would, in part, take control of the terms of the debate and turn back this Euro-American tendency to use their own yardsticks. See, for example, Weaver's *That the People Might Live: Native American Literatures and Native American Community* (New York: Oxford University Press, 1997), Warrior's *Tribal Secrets: Recovering American Indian Intellectual Traditions* (Minneapolis: University of Minnesota Press, 1994), and Womack's *Red on Red: Native American Literary Separatism* (Minneapolis: University of Minnesota Press, 1999).

4. Weaver, *That the People Might Live*, 4.

5. Ibid., 5.

6. Ibid., x.

7. Carter Revard, *Family Matters, Tribal Affairs* (Tucson: University of Arizona Press, 1998), 181.

8. Ibid., xi.

9. Kenneth M. Roemer, ed., *Approaches to Teaching Momaday's "The Way to Rainy Mountain"* (New York: Modern Language Association of America, 1988), ix.

10. Dean Rader, "Arriving Amid a Herd of Horses," *SAIL: Studies in American Indian Literatures* 10, 3 (fall 1998): 89.

11. Ibid., 90.

12. This essay is published as chapter 6 of Sarris's *Keeping Slug Woman Alive* (Berkeley and Los Angeles: University of California Press, 1993), 115–145.

13. Ibid., 70.

14. There are, of course, exceptions. Among the anthologies, see, for example, *The Remembered Earth*, ed. Geary Hobson (Albuquerque: University of New Mexico Press, 1979); *Dancing on the Rim of the World: An Anthology of Contemporary Northwest Native American Writing*, ed. Andrea Lerner (Tucson: Sun Tracks and University of Arizona Press, 1990); *Returning the Gift: Poetry and Prose from the First North American Native Writers' Festival*, ed. Joseph Bruchac (Tucson: University of Arizona Press, 1994); and *Reinventing the Enemy's Language*, ed. Joy Harjo and Gloria Bird. And among the critical texts, see Weaver, *That the People Might Live;* Kathleen M. Donovan, *Feminist Readings of Native American Literature: Coming to Voice* (Tucson: University of Arizona Press, 1998);

Louis Owens, *Mixedblood Messages: Literature, Film, Family, Place* (Norman: University of Oklahoma Press, 1998); Revard, *Family Matters, Tribal Affairs;* and Eric Gary Anderson, *American Indian Literature and the Southwest: Contexts and Dispositions* (Austin: University of Texas Press, 1999).

15. Owens, *Mixedblood Messages*, 20.

16. Weaver, *That the People Might Live*, 26.

17. Ibid., 163.

18. Ibid., 163.

19. *Reinventing the Enemy's Language: Contemporary Native Women's Writings of North America*, ed. Joy Harjo and Gloria Bird (New York: Norton, 1997), 21, 26.

20. Ibid., 23.

21. Joseph Bruchac, *Survival This Way: Interviews with American Indian Poets* (Tucson: University of Arizona Press, 1987), 317.

22. Laura Coltelli, *Winged Words: American Indian Writers Speak* (Lincoln: University of Nebraska Press, 1990), 188.

23. Ibid. 126.

24. Bruchac, *Survival This Way*, 64.

25. Ibid., 96.

26. Ibid., 226.

27. Quoted in Brian Swann, "Introduction: Only the Beginning," in *Harper's Anthology of 20th Century Native American Poetry*, ed. Duane Niatum (New York: Harper-Collins, 1988), xviii. Emphasis Rose's.

28. Weaver, *That the People Might Live*, 165.

29. *Speaking for the Generations: Native Writers on Writing*, ed. Simon Ortiz (Tucson: University of Arizona Press, 1998), 73.

30. *Reinventing the Enemy's Language*, 20.

31. Weaver, *That the People Might Live*, 168.

32. *Speaking for the Generations*, xiv.

33. Elizabeth Woody, *Luminaries of the Humble* (Tucson: University of Arizona Press, 1994), xi.

34. Ibid., xiv.

35. *Speaking for the Generations*, xii.

36. Elaine Jahner, "Knowing All the Way Down to Fire," in *Feminist Measures: Soundings in Poetry and Theory*, ed. Lynn Keller and Cristanne Miller (Ann Arbor: University of Michigan Press, 1994), 175.

37. Ibid.

38. Linda Hogan, "Crossings," in *The Book of Medicines* (Minneapolis: Coffee House Press, 1993), 28.

39. Hogan, "Map," in *The Book of Medicines*, 38.

40. Hogan, "Naming the Animals," in *The Book of Medicines*, 40–41, 41.

41. Woody, *Luminaries of the Humble*, x.

42. Bruchac, *Survival This Way*, 220.

43. Roberta Hill Whiteman, *Philadelphia Flowers* (Duluth, Minn.: Holy Cow! Press, 1996), 98. See James Clifford, *Routes: Travel and Translation in the Late Twentieth Century* (Cambridge: Harvard University Press, 1997), especially 24–25. Interested readers might also wish to consult my discussion and application of Clifford's paradigm;

see Eric Gary Anderson, *American Indian Literature and the Southwest*, particularly chapter 1, "Mobile Homes: Migration and Resistance in American Indian Literature."

44. Woody, *Seven Hands, Seven Hearts*, 13–14.

45. Ibid., 14.

46. Ibid., 16.

47. Woody, *Luminaries of the Humble*, xii.

48. Ibid., xii.

49. Ibid., xiii.

50. Woody, "Version of Moon," in *Luminaries of the Humble*, 3.

51. Woody, "Anonymous," in *Luminaries of the Humble*, 83.

52. *Reinventing the Enemy's Language*, 29.

53. Ibid., 31.

54. Leslie Marmon Silko, *Ceremony* (New York: Penguin, 1977), 13.

55. Bruchac, *Survival This Way*, 70.

56. Woody, *Luminaries of the Humble*, xiii.

Daydreaming Primal Space, Marilou Awiakta

* This essay was originally published in *The Poetics of Appalachian Space*, an anthology of essays on interior space, based on the philosophy of Gaston Bachelard's *La Poetique de l'espace*, and was reprinted in Marilou Awiakta, *Selu: Seeking the Corn-Mother's Wisdom*.

The Poetics of Appalachian Space, ed. Parks Lanier, Jr. (Knoxville: University of Tennessee Press, 1991), 193–210; Gaston Bachelard, *The Poetics of Space*, trans. Marla Jolas (Boston: Beacon Press, 1969); Marilou Awiakta, *Selu: Seeking the Corn-Mother's Wisdom* (Golden, Colo.: Fulcrum, 1993), 167–182.

1. Bachelard, *Poetics of Space*, 5.

2. Ibid., xxxii.

3. Ibid., 46–47.

4. Ibid., 18–20.

5. Ibid., 101.

6. Ibid., 51–54.

7. Ibid., 101.

8. Ibid., 144–145.

9. Ibid., 197.

Beloved Woman Returns, Daniel Heath Justice

1. Ameropean historian Sarah H. Hill, in her book *Weaving New Worlds: Southeastern Cherokee Women and their Basketry* (Chapel Hill: University of North Carolina Press, 1997), studies Eastern Cherokee history through the transformations of basketry composition, design, and function, and draws a compelling picture of the reflections that the art of basketweaving provides of Cherokee life and history.

2. *Selu*, 34.

3. "Selu and Kanati," in *Selu*, 117.

4. *Selu*, 34.

5. Wilma Mankiller and Michael Wallis, *Mankiller: A Chief and Her People* (New York:

St. Martin's Press, 1993), 20. Mankiller goes on to explain that "wrong actions could disturb the balance. . . . Sometimes when our people were not careful or let down their guard, the balance was unsettled. That is just what occurred when the Cherokee people became more acculturated and adopted more of the values of the Europeans who invaded and infiltrated their country." Sexism, racism, and viewing the world as a dead resource are all connected to the wrong actions adopted from European worldviews.

6. "Trail Warning," in *Selu,* 39. Awiakta continues this warning with the following anecdote: "I plunged past this sign without heeding its warning the first time I came this way. I also forgot what my parents have always advised, 'If you meet a copperhead—snake or person—give 'em a wide berth. If you have to go in close, take a hoe.' "

7. *Selu,* 134.

8. Ibid., 17.

9. Gretchen Legler, "(Re)Eroticizing Human Relationships with the Natural World: Native American and Anglo Women Writers' (Re)Visions," *Studies in the Humanities* 19, 2 (December 1992): 184.

10. "Dawn Birth," in *Selu,* 204.

11. "Song of the Swinging Bridge, in *Selu,* 258.

12. *Spider Woman's Granddaughters: Traditional Tales and Contemporary Writing by Native American Women,* ed. Paula Gunn Allen (New York: Fawcett Columbine, 1990), 21.

13. "Mother Nature Sends a Pink Slip," in *Selu,* 88.

14. *Selu,* 184.

15. Ibid., 6.

16. Ibid., 5.

17. Theda Perdue, *Cherokee Women: Gender and Culture Change, 1700–1835* (Lincoln: University of Nebraska Press, 1998), 13.

18. Mankiller and Wallis, *Mankiller,* 207.

19. *Selu,* 151.

20. "On Being a Female Phoenix," in *Selu,* 135.

21. Craig Lesley, "Characteristics of Contemporary Native American Literature," in *Emerging Voices: A Cross-Cultural Reader: Readings in the American Experience* (Fort Worth, Tex.: Holt, Rinehart, and Winston, 1990), 491–502.

22. From "I Offer You a Gift," in *Selu,* 8.

23. *Selu,* 195.

The Power and Presence of Native Oral Storytelling Traditions . . . , Susan Berry Brill de Ramírez

1. Kimberly M. Blaeser, *Trailing You* (Greenfield Center, N.Y.: Greenfield Review Press, 1994), xi.

2. Craig Womack, *Red on Red: Native American Literary Separatism* (Minneapolis: University of Minnesota Press, 1999), 15.

3. Arnold Krupat, "The Dialogic of Silko's Storyteller," *Narrative Chance: Postmodern Discourse on Native American Indian Literatures,* ed. Gerald Vizenor (Albuquerque: University of New Mexico Press, 1989), 62.

4. Peggy V. Beck, Anna Lee Walters, and Nia Francisco, *The Sacred: Ways of Knowledge, Sources of Life* (Tsaile, Ariz.: Navajo Community College Press, 1992), 12, 13.

5. Luci Tapahonso, interview by James Meadows, WCBU-FM, Peoria, Ill., 24 April 1996.

6. Marilyn Dumont, "The Devil's Language," in *A Really Good Brown Girl* (London, Ont.: Brick Books, 1996), 54.

7. Blaeser, " 'Native Americans' vs. 'The Poets,' " in *Trailing You*, 53.

8. Jane Caputi, "Nuclear Visions," *American Quarterly* 47, 1 (March 1995): 174.

9. Susan Berry Brill de Ramírez, *Contemporary American Indian Literatures and the Oral Tradition* (Tucson: University of Arizona Press, 1999), 223.

10. Luci Tapahonso, *Sáanii Dahataal, The Women Are Singing* (Tucson: University of Arizona Press, 1993), xii.

11. Albert Yava, *Big Falling Snow: A Tewa-Hopi Indian's Life and Times and the History and Traditions of His People*, ed. Harold Courlander (Albuquerque: University of New Mexico Press, 1978), 4.

12. Ibid.

13. Dumont, "The Devil's Language," 54.

14. Ibid.

15. "Memoirs of a Really Good Brown Girl," in *A Really Good Brown Girl*, 15.

16. "The Devil's Language," 54.

17. Keith E. Davis and Mary K. Roberts, "Relationships in the Real World: The Descriptive Psychology Approach to Personal Relationships," in *The Social Construction of the Person*, ed. Kenneth J. Gergen and Keith E. Davis (New York: Springer-Verlag, 1985), 147.

18. Dumont, *A Really Good Brown Girl*, 55.

19. "Stories, Words Finding Their Way," in *After and Before the Lightning* (Tucson: University of Arizona Press, 1994), 97.

20. Blaeser, *Trailing You*, xi.

21. Ibid.

22. Ibid.

23. "Trailing You," in *Trailing You*, 40.

24. "Sewing Memories," in *Trailing You*, 77.

25. Ibid., 75.

26. Ibid., 75.

27. Leslie Marmon Silko and James Wright, *The Delicacy and Strength of Lace: Letters between Leslie Marmon Silko and James Wright*, ed. Anne Wright (St. Paul, Minn.: Graywolf Press, 1986), 28.

28. "Sewing Memories," 76.

29. Ibid., 75.

30. Ibid., 76.

31. Greg Sarris, *Keeping Slug Woman Alive: A Holistic Approach to American Indian Texts* (Berkeley and Los Angeles: University of California Press, 1993), 40.

32. "Sewing Memories," 75.

33. Kimberly Blaeser, *Gerald Vizenor: Writing in the Oral Tradition* (Norman: University of Oklahoma Press, 1996), 27.

34. David L. Moore, "Myth, History, and Identity in Silko and Young Bear," in *New Voices in Native American Literary Criticism*, ed. Arnold Krupat (Washington, D.C.: Smithsonian Institution, 1993), 380.

35. Reed Way Dasenbrock, "Forms of Biculturalism in Southwestern Literature: The Work of Rudolfo Anaya and Leslie Marmon Silko," *Genre* 21 (1988): 313.

36. "Sewing Memories," 77.

37. Ibid., 76.

38. Sarris, *Keeping Slug Woman Alive,* 91–92.

39. Leslie Marmon Silko, "Language and Literature from a Pueblo Indian Perspective," in *English Literature: Opening Up the Canon,* ed. Leslie A. Fiedler and Houston A. Baker, Jr. (Baltimore: Johns Hopkins University Press, 1981), 72.

40. Marilou Awiakta, *Abiding Appalachia: Where Mountain and Atom Meet* (Bell Buckle, Tenn.: Iris Press, 1995), 11.

41. Ibid., 13.

42. Caputi, "Nuclear Visions," 172.

43. "An Indian Walks in Me," in *Abiding Appalachia,* 14.

44. "Prayer of the Poet-Hunter," in *Abiding Appalachia,* 15.

45. Ibid.

46. "The Coming of Little Deer," in *Abiding Appalachia,* 16.

47. "The Graphite Queen," in *Abiding Appalachia,* 59.

48. Blaeser, "On the Way to the Chicago Pow-Wow," in *Trailing You,* 13.

49. Simon J. Ortiz, *Men on the Moon: Collected Short Stories* (Tucson: University of Arizona Press, 1999), ix.

50. Ibid., viii.

Ain't Seen You Since, Patricia Clark Smith

* I would like to thank Gerri Rhoades for making me start to think about this subject, and William McGlothing for the check and balance of his sharp criticism.

1. *Editor's note:* When Patricia Clark Smith published this essay in 1983, she listed in a note (deleted from this reprinting) a number of books that, twenty years later in 2003, are out of date. Of the titles mentioned, perhaps only *The Whispering Wind: Poetry by Young American Indians,* ed. Terry Allen (Garden City, N.Y.: Doubleday, 1972) and *Voices from Wah'Kon-Tah: Contemporary Poetry of Native Americans,* edited by Robert K. Dodge and Joseph B. McCullough (New York: International, 1974) are of interest to the contemporary reader or scholar. For more recent anthologies of contemporary American Indian poetry, see the Suggestions for Further Reading at the end of this book.

2. *The Sky Clears: Poetry of the American Indians,* ed. A. Grove Day (Lincoln: University of Nebraska Press, 1964), 2.

3. "Ritual Chant for the Sick (Omaha)," in *American Indian Poetry: An Anthology of Songs and Chants,* ed. George W. Cronyn (1934; reprint, New York: Liveright, [1970?]), 57.

4. "Earth Mother," trans. Frank Gordon, in *American Indian Poetry,* 234.

5. "The Song My Paddle Sings," trans. Pauline Johnson, in *American Indian Poetry,* 241.

6. Patricia Irvina, "Sun Dancers," in *Whispering Wind,* 80.

7. Alonzo Lopez, "Eagle Flight," in *Whispering Wind,* 7.

8. A partial list of these periodicals and presses would include *South Dakota Review, Cimarron Review, Blue Cloud Quarterly, Sun Tracks, Greenfield Review, Scree, Akwasasne*

Notes, Pembroke, Indian Historian Press, Strawberry Press, A Press, Red Earth Press, Yardbird, Cold Mountain Press, the Crossing Press, the Rio Grande Writer's Association Press, Puerto del Sol. (*Editor's note:* Of course, when Smith refers to poetry appearing "during the last ten years or so," she is referring to the ten years before 1983.)

9. See Geary Hobson, ed., *The Remembered Earth* (Albuquerque, N.Mex.: Red Earth Press, 1981), 9–10.

10. Shirley Kaufman, "Mothers and Daughters," in *Tangled Vines: A Collection of Mother and Daughter Poems*, ed. Lyn Lifshin (Boston: Beacon Press, 1978), 12.

11. Sylvia Plath, "Three Women," in *Tangled Vines*, 2.

12. Judith Minty, "Waiting for the Transformation," in *Tangled Vines*, 8.

13. Judith Hemschemeyer, "The Survivors," in *Tangled Vines*, 60–61.

14. Sharon Olds, "Tricks," in *Tangled Vines*, 74.

15. Kathleen Spivak, "Daughterly," in *Tangled Vines*, 53.

16. L. L. Zeiger, "The Fish," in *Tangled Vines*, 59.

17. Nancy Friday, *My Mother / My Self: The Daughter's Search for Identity* (New York: Delacorte, 1977), 113.

18. Patricia Goedicke, "Circus Song," in *Tangled Vines*, 18.

19. Erica Jong, "Mother," in *Tangled Vines*, 52.

20. For a supporting discussion of mother-daughter relations among women in southwestern tribes as reflected in other literary genres, especially autobiography, see Helen M. Bannan, "Spider Woman's Web: Mothers and Daughters in Southwestern Native American Literature," in *Embraced and Embattled: A History of Mothers and Daughters*, ed. E. M. Bronner and Cathy N. Davidson (New York: Ungar, 1979), 268–279.

21. Friday sounds this note throughout much of her book.

22. Carter Revard, "Deer Talk, Coyote Talk, Meadowlark Territory: The Muses Dance to Our Drum Now" (paper presented at the Modern Language Association, New York, 28 December 1978).

23. nila northSun, "the way & the way things are," in *Diet Pepsi and Nacho Cheese* (Fallon, Nev.: Duck Down, 1977), 13.

24. Marnie Walsh, "Bessie Dreaming Bear: Rosebud, So. Dak. 1960," in *A Taste of the Knife*, 2d ed., ed. A. Thomas Trusky (Boise, Idaho: Ahsahta Press, 1976); reprinted in *The Remembered Earth*, 369.

25. northSun's cycle of family poems in *Diet Pepsi and Nacho Cheese* includes "what gramma said about how she came here," "what gramma said about her grandpa," "what gramma said about her kids," "what grandpa said," "what happened to grandpa," "what gramma said after," "what gramma said late at night," "what gramma said in the last story," "the way & the way things are," "how my cousin was killed," "shadow knew nothing was my cousin," "my other grandma," "grandma and burgie," "heritage," "babe," and "little red riding hood."

26. "what gramma said late at night," 11.

27. "what grandpa said," 8.

28. "what gramma said late at night" 11.

29. "what gramma said in the last story," 12.

30. "diet pepsi & nacho cheese," 26.

31. "moving camp too far," 14.

32. "the way & the way things are," 13.

33. Lyn Lifshin, "My Mother and the Bed," in *Tangled Vines, 57*.

34. L. L. Zeiger, "The Fish," in *Tangled Vines, 59*.

35. "what gramma said about her grandpa," 6.

36. Popovi Da, "Indian Values," *The Living Wilderness* 34 (spring 1970): 26.

37. "my other grandma," 20.

38. Ibid., 20.

39. "grandma & burgie," 21.

40. "heritage," 22.

41. Janet Campbell Hale, "Desmet Idaho, March 1969," in *Custer Lives in Humboldt County* (Greenfield Center, N.Y.: Greenfield Review Press, 1978), 21. For Anglo women poets' portrayals of mourners, see, for example, two poems in *Rising Tides:* Carolyn Stoloff, "For the Suicide's Daughter," 167, and Sylvia Plath, "Last Words," 217 (*Rising Tides: Twentieth Century American Women Poets,* ed. Laura Chester and Sharon Barba [New York: Washington Square Press, 1973]).

42. Joy Harjo, "White Sands," in *Southwest: A Contemporary Anthology,* ed. Karl Kopp and Jane Kopp (Albuquerque, N.Mex.: Red Earth Press, 1977), 69.

The Epic Lyric, Dean Rader

1. John Bierhorst, ed. *The Sacred Path* (New York: Morrow, 1983), 1–3.

2. Jonathan Culler, *Structuralist Poetics* (Ithaca, N.Y.: Cornell University Press, 1975), 108.

3. See the first part of Eric Anderson's essay in this collection, particularly his reading of Jace Weaver.

4. Kimberly M. Blaeser, "Native Literatures: Seeking a Critical Center," in *Looking at the Words of Our People: First Nations Analysis of Literature,* ed. Jeannette Armstrong (Penticton, B.C.: Theytus Books, 1993), 56.

5. Dean Rader, "Simon Ortiz and Luci Tapahonso: Symbol, Allegory, Language, Poetry," *Southwestern American Literature* 22 (spring 1997): 75–92.

6. Joy Harjo, introduction to *Reinventing the Enemy's Language: Contemporary Native Women's Writings of North America,* ed. Joy Harjo and Gloria Bird (New York: Norton, 1997), 22.

7. See James Nolan, *Poet-Chief: The Native American Poetics of Walt Whitman and Pablo Neruda* (Albuquerque: University of New Mexico Press, 1994), 78–135.

8. W. R. Johnson, *The Idea of Lyric: Lyric Modes in Ancient and Modern Poetry* (Berkeley and Los Angeles: University of California Press, 1982), 5.

9. Helen Vendler, *Poems, Poets, Poetry* (Boston: Bedford Books, 1997), 101–102.

10. Pound, "LXXXV," in *The Cantos of Ezra Pound* (New York: New Directions, 1970), 569.

11. James E. Miller, Jr., *The American Quest for a Supreme Fiction: Whitman's Legacy in the Personal Epic* (Chicago: University of Chicago Press, 1979), 24.

12. Oscar Williams, *A Little Treasury of American Poetry: The Chief Poets from Colonial Times to the Present* (New York: C. Scribner's Sons, 1948), xvi.

Side note: The irony of the subtitle *(The Chief Poets)* should not be lost on the reader.

13. For the ambitious and patient scholar, I would direct you to a number of useful sources on the history and characterization of the epic poem: E.M.W. Tillyard, "The

Nature of the Epic," *Parnassus Revisited: Modern Critical Essays on the Epic Tradition*, ed. Anthony C. Yu (Chicago: American Library Association, 1973), 42–52; Peter Felix Hägin, *The Epic Hero and the Decline of Heroic Poetry* (Bern: Solothurn, 1964); John P. McWilliams, Jr., *The American Epic: Transforming a Genre, 1770–1860* (Cambridge: Cambridge University Press, 1989); A. T. Hato, "Towards an Anatomy of Heroic/Epic Poetry," *Traditions of Heroic and Epic Poetry*, vol. 2, *Characteristics and Techniques* (London: Modern Humanities Research Association, 1989), 147–306; Albert Bates Lord, *Epic Singers and the Oral Tradition* (Ithaca, N.Y.: Cornell University Press, 1991); Adena Rosmarin, *The Power of Genre* (Minneapolis: University of Minnesota Press, 1985).

14. Bernstein, *The Tale of the Tribe: Ezra Pound and the Modern Verse Epic* (Princeton, N.J.: Princeton University Press, 1980).

15. Ibid., 14.

16. I am using Jane Tompkins's classic definition of "cultural work" as defined in her *Sensational Designs: The Cultural Work of American Fiction, 1790–1860* (Oxford: Oxford University Press, 1985), xiv–xv, 36–39.

Also, I would reiterate a distinction between the epic poem and the oral tradition. Many scholars have noted the connection between recent American Indian literature and the oral tradition; my interest in this study lies in the epic form, which is informed by and arises out of the oral tradition. I am not equating the epic poem or the epic genre with the oral tradition as such.

17. Carter Revard, *Cowboys and Indians, Christmas Shopping* (Norman, Okla.: Point Riders Press, 1992), 8.

18. Walter Ong, *Orality and Literacy: The Technologizing of the Word* (London: Methuen, 1982), 11.

19. Sherman Alexie, *The Summer of Black Widows* (Brooklyn, N.Y.: Hanging Loose Press, 1996), 56.

20. Deborah Miranda, *Indian Cartography* (Greenfield Center, N.Y.: Greenfield Review Press, 1999), 92.

21. Wendy Rose, *Bone Dance: New and Selected Poems, 1965–1993* (Tucson: University of Arizona Press, 1994), 82.

22. Luci Tapahonso, "This Is How They Were Placed for Us," in *Blue Horses Rush In* (Tucson: University of Arizona Press, 1997), 41.

23. Ibid., 42.

24. For a similar poem on the Hohokam sites, see Duane Niatum's "At the Hohokam Ruins," in *Drawings of the Song Animals: New and Selected Poems* (Duluth: Holy Cow! Press, 1991), 56–57.

25. Tapahonso, *Sáanii Dahataal, The Woman Are Singing* (Tucson: University of Arizona Press, 1993), 64–68; Simon J. Ortiz, *Woven Stone* (Tucson: University of Arizona Press, 1992), 196–97.

26. Paula Gunn Allen, *Skins and Bones: Poems, 1979–87* (Albuquerque, N.Mex.: West End Press, 1988), 2.

27. Joy Harjo, "Song for Thantog," in *She Had Some Horses* (New York: Thunder's Mouth Press, 1983), 36; Harjo, "Eagle Poem," in *In Mad Love and War* (Hanover, N.H.: Wesleyan University Press, 1990), 65.

28. Ortiz, "Telling about Coyote," in *Woven Stone* (Tucson: University of Arizona Press, 1990), 157.

29. Ortiz, "And there is always one more story," in *Woven Stone,* 177.

30. Louise Erdrich, *Jacklight* (New York: Henry Holt, 1984), 79, 68–69.

31. For similar lyrical reworkings of older myths, see Niatum's poems "Woman of the Moon," "Raven Dancer," "Wolves," "Klallam Song," and "Runner for the Thunder, Cloud and Rain," in *Drawings of the Song Animals.*

32. Joy Harjo, *The Woman Who Fell from the Sky* (New York: Norton, 1994).

33. Linda Hogan, "Crow Law," in *The Book of Medicines* (Minneapolis: Coffee House Press, 1993), 31.

Answering the Deer, Paula Gunn Allen

1. Linda Hogan, "Blessing," in *Calling Myself Home* (New York: Greenfield Review Press, 1978), 27.

2. Mary Randle TallMountain, "The Last Wolf," in *There Is No Word for Goodbye* (Marvin, S. Dak.: Blue Cloud Quarterly, 1981), 15.

3. Wendy Rose, "I Expected My Skin and My Blood to Ripen," in *Lost Copper* (Morongo Indian Reservation, Canning, Calif.: Malki Museum Press, 1980), 219.

4. Rose, "I Expected," 219.

5. Leslie Marmon Silko, "Toe'osh: A Laguna Coyote Story," in *Storyteller* (New York: Viking, 1981), 237.

6. Elizabeth Cook-Lynn, "Contradiction," in *Then Badger Said This* (New York: Vantage Press, 1977), 12.

7. nila northSun, "moving camp too far," in *Diet Pepsi and Nacho Cheese* (Fallon, Nev.: Duck Down Press, 1977), 14.

8. Joy Harjo, "3 AM," in *The Last Song* (Las Cruces, N. Mex.: Puerto del Sol Press, 1975); and in *What Moon Drove Me to This* (Berkeley, Calif.: Reed and Cannon, 1979), 43.

9. Roberta Hill Whiteman, "Leap in the Dark," in Dexter Fisher, *The Third Woman: Minority Women Writers of the United States* (Boston: Houghton Mifflin, 1980), 123–124.

10. Ibid.

11. Linda Hogan, "Morning: The World in the Lake," unpublished manuscript, 1981. Revised version published in *Seeing Through the Sun* (Amherst: University of Massachusetts Press, 1985), 56.

12. Paula Gunn Allen, from "Transformations," revised version in manuscript; original in *Starchild* (Marvin, S. Dak.: Blue Cloud Quarterly, 1981).

The Style of the Times in Paula Gunn Allen's Poetry, Elaine A. Jahner

1. Cynthia McDaniel has published an annotated bibliography of secondary sources on Paula Gunn Allen. See *SAIL: Studies in American Indian Literatures* 11, 2 (summer 1999): 29–50.

2. Paula Gunn Allen, quoted in her introduction to "Going Home, December 1992," in *Reinventing the Enemy's Language,* ed. Joy Harjo and Gloria Bird (New York: Norton, 1997), 151.

3. Paula Gunn Allen, *The Blind Lion* (Berkeley, Calif.: Thorp Springs Press, 1974), n.p.

4. Paula Gunn Allen, *The Sacred Hoop: Recovering the Feminine in American Indian Traditions* (Beacon Press, 1986), 147.

5. Such documentation has to be tribally specific. In a Lakota context, the fact that ultimate reality is designated as Skan, or movement, indicates the starting points for a process of documentation in one tribe that Allen recognizes as part of her heritage. Factual documentation should also address the fine distinctions in verbs of movement in the Lakota language as spoken in the nineteenth century. See James R. Walker, *Lakota Belief and Ritual* (Lincoln: University of Nebraska Press, 1980) and Franz Boas and Ella Deloria, *Dakota Grammar* ([Sioux Falls, S.Dak.]: Dakota Press, [1979]).

6. For biographical information along with critical analysis, see James Ruppert's article in *Dictionary of Native American Literatures* (New York: Garland, 1994), 395–399.

7. "Malinalli, La Malinche, to Cortés, Conquistador," in *Life Is a Fatal Disease* (Albuquerque, N.Mex.: West End Press, 1997), 4.

8. "Trinity: 50 Years Gone Return," in *Life Is a Fatal Disease,* 197.

9. "Overture," in *The Blind Lion,* n.p.

10. As it happens, Allen's stylistic development can productively be glossed by reference to Julia Kristeva's work in critical and psychoanalytic theory. Kristeva established many of the same fundamental distinctions that Allen found necessary for her poetic efforts. Anyone who has grasped the fundamental starting points for Kristeva's ever more comprehensive and demanding explorations of symbolic activity will recognize very similar starting points in Allen's poetry. Without implying any kind of direct causal explanation for the correspondences, I want to note that both women were trying to move away from the influences of positivism without abandoning social and historical accountability. Establishing comparisons between what the two women have accomplished allows me to place Allen's work in a recognized philosophical and psychoanalytic framework at the same time as I note the psycholinguistic force of the mythic and cognitive revaluation involved in Allen's bringing contrasting traditions into relationship with European ones.

An important part of Kristeva's contribution has always been her daunting knowledge of the history of literature and philosophy as the context for the writings of Freud and Lacan. Allen's general, nonspecialized awareness of European intellectual traditions has given her a sense that what she experienced as a threat to her own powers of thought and definition had a history within European philosophy. Setting Allen's images against Kristeva's descriptive categories reveals moves both women are trying to achieve in order to offset historically powerful theories about what constitutes epistemological validity. In Kristeva's early and detailed presentations of the semiotic, she stressed her differences from positions that can easily be confused with hers: "our point of view is very different from that of an immanent semiotics, anterior to language, which explores a meaning that is always already there, as in Hjelmslev. Equally apparent is our epistemological divergence from a Cartesian notion of language, which views thought as preconditioned by or even identical to natural factual data, and gradually considers it innate" (*Revolution in Poetic Language* [New York: Columbia University Press, 1984], 34).

The divergences sketched by Kristeva help account for Allen's sense of exclusion of what she called "white" ways of knowing and speaking, an exclusion that she linked to a view of temporality and linearity. Allen feared the meaning "that is always already there" because she associated it with cultural imposition. Valid as that association is, it is dangerous in the abstract precisely because what is "always already there" represents a necessary condition of meaning. Before resistance to imposed meaning can become productive, it must be refined by a highly developed attentiveness to cognitive and semantic variation. Both the need for this refinement and one woman's way of achieving it are themes at the heart of the narrative behind Allen's poetry.

Until certain distinctions between the primary functioning of the symbolic and the secondary cultural processes of meaning elaboration could become conscious pragmatic features of Allen's style, the force of rejecting what oppresses was a totalizing one that caused a recoil from any direct subject-object relationship. "No name I say can find its object here; trouble / needs no name . . ." ("Deep Deep City Blues").

A good critical study of Kristeva is John Lechte, *Julia Kristeva* (London: Routledge, 1990).

11. Allen, *The Sacred Hoop*, 100–101.

12. James Ruppert's excellent essay on Paula Gunn Allen written for the *Dictionary of Native American Literature* addresses this aspect of Allen's work. "In both her creative and critical work, Allen forges conscious connections between her life and the life of the Laguna Pueblo. Laguna was founded by people from several different pueblos, and it has always included Navajos, Mexicans, and whites. Allen sees this confluence structuring her ancestry and her life. This diversity could be a source of fragmentation, but, for her, it is more importantly a source of strength. She sees the people at Laguna functioning as mediators, and her own life as a half-breed as reflecting centuries of Laguna experience. Both her critical and creative work rise out of the necessity of talking from at least two perspectives at once—an act that is both illuminating and alienating. For Allen, the mediator's role is more than just making peace between warring factions of experience; it is an act in which the epistemological framework of one group is used to define meaning and value in another system" (Ruppert, "Paula Gunn Allen," 396–397).

13. The dominant intellectual themes of the century all derive from the impact of psychoanalytic models within social theory. Historicizing such theory for non-European cultures remains a task more honored in theory than practice, but postcolonial analysis, often following the example of Franz Fanon, has advanced this critical debate. Christopher Lane's edited book *The Psychoanalysis of Race* (New York: Columbia University Press, 1998) includes several essays that address the political consequences of how we conceptualize individual psychic organization and group identification. His introduction highlights the question asked by David Marriott: "If the act of identification produces a fractured doubling of the self, how can we distinguish what is interposed from what is properly desired?" (31). To date, theorists have not consistently addressed Native American contexts from these perspectives.

14. Michael Fischer's statements on autobiographical writing could productively be applied in relation to many Native American writers, especially someone like Allen. Fischer states that "insofar as ethnicity is a deeply rooted component of identity, it is often transmitted less through cognitive language or learning (to which sociology has almost entirely restricted itself) than through processes analogous to the dreaming and transference of psychoanalytic encounters" (M. J. Fischer, "Ethnicity and the Post-Modern Arts of Memory," in *Writing Culture: The Poetics and Politics of Ethnography*, ed. James Clifford and George M. Marcus [Berkeley and Los Angeles: University of California Press, 1986], 95).

By following Allen's story of progress from debilitating fear of a world that seemed to have no place for her to a struggle with poetic language as the way out of fear and finally to her use of mythic language to transform her understanding of cultural identity, we can learn to use autobiographical literature in ways that help us better understand the role of ethnicity in contemporary life.

15. "Word Game," in *The Blind Lion*, n.p.

16. "Locus," in *Life Is a Fatal Disease*, 142.

17. Ibid.

18. "Elegy for My Son," in *Life Is a Fatal Disease*, 75.

19. "On the Street: Monument," in *Life Is a Fatal Disease*, 17.

20. "American Apocalypse," in *Life Is a Fatal Disease*, 130.

21. "Transformations," in *Starchild* (Marvin, S.Dak.: Blue Cloud Quarterly, 1981), n.p.

22. "Affirmation," in *Life Is a Fatal Disease*, 88.

23. "The Turning Point," in *Coyote's Daylight Trip* (Albuquerque, N.Mex.: La Confluencia, 1978).

24. David Payne, review of *Off the Reservation: Reflections on Boundary-Busting, Border Crossing, and Loose Canons*, by Paula Gunn Allen, *SAIL: Studies in American Indian Literatures* 11, 2 (summer 1999): 88.

25. "Life Is a Fatal Disease," in *Life Is a Fatal Disease*, 45.

26. Ibid., 46.

Herbs of Healing, Carter Revard

1. I am thinking of Allan Bloom, George Will, Dinesh D'Souza and their sort, whose approach to literary and cultural matters reminds me of words put by clever Oxonians into the mouth of the great Plato scholar Benjamin Jowett: *Here am I, my name is Jowett: / There is no knowledge but I know it. / I am the Master of this College—/ What I know not is not knowledge.* Or, again, they are like Jim arguing with Huck Finn about whether French is a human language or not: "Is a Chicano—or Black, or American Indian—REALLY an American? Then why doesn't he SPEAK like an American?" By their standards, of course, Mark Twain had no business letting the narrator of his greatest book speak in the vulgar uneducated English of a grade-school dropout, which obviously cannot be used to communicate anything to such educated persons as our cultural guardians.

2. See, for instance, Frank Lentricchia's brilliant discussion in *Ariel and the Police: Michel Foucault, William James, Wallace Stevens* (Madison: University of Wisconsin Press, 1988), 3–27.

3. "Speaking" has been republished in Simon J. Ortiz, *Woven Stone* (Tucson: University of Arizona Press, 1992).

4. Wallace Stevens, "Anecdote of the Jar," in *Wallace Stevens: The Collected Poems* (New York: Knopf, 1954), 76.

5. What I said was, "I *had* noticed that culture stops at the Hudson, but I'm from Oklahoma—I'll bring some over to you, if Massachusetts Customs allow it."

6. Milton, it must be said, made no known protest against the slaughter by Oliver Cromwell's men of the Irish Catholic women, children, and men who surrendered the besieged towns of Drogheda and Wexford, not long before the massacre of Protestants in the Piedmont. What WE do is a military necessity; what THEY do is a massacre.

7. I have modernized spelling and punctuation of Milton's text. Though written in

1655, it was not published until 1673—a year before Milton died, by which time King Charles II was no longer trying to imprison or execute him for having helped, in 1649, to overthrow and execute Charles's father. In 1673, the sonnet would still wake echoes of the deadly Civil War of thirty years before, and its protest was highly relevant to the current political situation: Charles II was secretly Catholic and receiving illegal financial support from the French tyrant Louis XIV, while the English Parliament in 1673 would pass the Test Act by which both Catholics and Puritans were excluded from holding any civil or military office. Milton's protest against minority-bashing was thus published in a year when the restored English monarchy was conniving to make Catholicism the state religion and the restored English parliament was excluding both Catholics and Puritans from power.

8. Wendy Rose, "I Expected My Skin and My Blood to Ripen," in *New and Old Voices of Wah'Kon-Tah,* edited by Robert K. Dodge and Joseph B. McCullough (New York: International Publishers, 1985), 102–103.

9. Robert Frost, "Never Again Would Bird's Song Be the Same," in *A Witness Tree* (New York: Henry Holt, 1942).

10. Louise Erdrich, "Jacklight," in *Jacklight* (New York: Henry Holt, 1984), 3–4.

11. A colleague I respect has suggested that however Frost treats women in the poem, he does patronize the birds by suggesting that since Eve arrived all bird-music has taken on a human oversound. It's a good point, worth raising with students in an American Indian Literature class—though in Indian stories the lines between bird and human run differently.

12. I used to associate this sonnet with Frost's lyric "Come In," in which he tells of passing along the edge of the woods at dusk, hearing from the woods a thrush's final song before dark, and of being tempted to go into the dark woods himself and "lament"—but he refuses the temptation saying "No, I was out for stars, / I would not come in. / I meant not, even if asked, / And I hadn't been." I thought that in the lyric, printed not long after the death of Frost's wife, the bird sounded like the spirit of Frost's wife calling him to join her, a call which Frost, independent and skeptic to the last, held back from, both because he wanted more of life, being "out for stars," and because he rejected the thrush-call as inviting self-pity.

Recently, however, Michael Cornett has printed a transcript (*Papers in Language and Literature* 29, 4 [fall 1993]: 417–435) of a 1955 broadcast by Frost in which Frost speaks of "Come In" as a *political* poem—the last kind of reading I would have given it. He presents it as a response to the despairing "America's finished" poetry that was being written in the 1930s. Could it make indirect reference to the poetry of Robinson Jeffers, say in such poems as "Shine, Perishing Republic"? Biographers might check dates and letters to look into the notion at least.

13. See "Two Riddles," *World Literature Today* 66, 2 (spring 1992): 229.

14. Of course people *used* to treat jokes as more *like* poems, preferring old ones as best. But if I am wrong, if "explained" poems don't take effect, then why do we pay hundreds of thousands of teachers to explain poems to readers who supposedly can't figure them out? I wonder, though, if professionalizing poetry-teaching has herded poets toward sheer obscurity, driven ordinary readers away from poem-reading, and subsidized bad writing that needs explaining. Who knows, the same may be true of prose-writers—it certainly is true of legal statutes and lawyer-interpreters, and may be for novelists. The next step

might be to mystify newspapers and require a degree in reading newspapers before the voting booth is made available. I bet George Will would like that—until he saw how the teachers were demystifying his columns.

15. "WAS poetics" of course means "White Anglo-Saxon poetics"—they would not be Protestant until Henry VIII wanted to kick Queen Catherine out of bed, at which time the poetics turned *WASP-ish.*

Carter Revard's Angled Mirrors, Janet McAdams

1. Carter Revard, *Winning the Dust Bowl* (Tucson: University of Arizona Press, 2001), xiii.

2. Joysa M. Winter, "The Voice of the Coyote," *Osage Nation News,* January 1995, 14; see Mary Louise Pratt, "Arts of the Contact Zone," *Ways of Reading: An Anthology for Writers,* 3d ed., ed. David Bartholomae and Anthony Petrosky (Boston: St. Martin's Press, 1993), 442–462.

3. Pratt, "Arts of the Contact Zone," 444.

4. I especially wish to avoid suggesting a monolithic Indian tradition of writing (or an Osage one), but rather to suggest the many different cultural traditions from which a writer such as Professor Revard might draw.

5. Eugene Eoyang, "Seeing with Another 'I': Our Search for Other Worlds," in *An Other Tongue: Nation and Ethnicity in the Linguistic Borderlands,* ed. Alfred Arteaga (Durham, N.C.: Duke University Press, 1994), 93.

6. Ibid.

7. Revard, *Winning the Dust Bowl,* xvi.

8. Revard, "History, Myth, and Identity among Osages and Other Peoples," in *Family Matters, Tribal Affairs* (Tucson: University of Arizona Press, 1998), 126–127.

9. Ibid., 127.

10. See Jace Weaver, *That the People Might Live: Native American Literatures and Native American Community* (New York: Oxford University Press, 1997), especially the introductory chapter.

11. Eoyang, "Seeing with Another 'I,'" 98.

12. See Joseph Bruchac, "Something That Stays Alive: An Interview with Carter Revard," in *Survival This Way: Interviews with American Indian Poets* (Tucson: University of Arizona Press, 1987), 242.

13. Bruchac, "Something That Stays Alive," 240.

14. Ibid., 241.

15. "Coyote Tells Why He Sings" appeared in *Ponca War Dancers* (Norman, Okla.: Point Riders Press, 1980) as "The Coyote," 11. The most recent version, which I quote here, appears in *Winning the Dust Bowl,* 3.

16. Bruchac, "Something That Stays Alive," 242.

17. Winter, "Voice of the Coyote," 14.

18. Bruchac, "Something that Stays Alive," 242–243.

19. Ibid., 243.

20. Revard, "Herbs of Healing: American Values in American Indian Literature," in *Family Matters, Tribal Affairs,* 176. (The essay is also reprinted in this volume.)

21. Ibid., 177.

22. In *When Nickels Were Indians* (Washington, D.C.: Smithsonian Institution Press, 1995), Patricia Penn Hilden describes the "scholarly and ideological roots of a simple, childlike, and above all practical Indian, who expressed himself or herself in 'Tonto-speak.' Although the middle of the twentieth century continued to idealize key Native orators—especially those long dead in the Indian wars—it was generally believed that most Indians, good or bad, 'renegade' or 'hang-around-the-fort,' talked in an instantly recognizable combination of the first-person singular subject (in the objective case: 'me'), simple, present-tense verbs ('want'), single-syllable nouns ('meat'), and a variety of hand signals" (55).

23. While I don't wish to overdetermine this particular kenning, the train was especially unkind to Indian people, rapidly accelerating the "settling" of the West and the Indian diaspora. As well, the train proved a useful tool in decimating the great buffalo herds on which the Plains Indian cultures so depended.

24. Revard, "Homework at Oxford," in *An Eagle Nation* (Tucson: University of Arizona Press, 1993), 75–83.

25. Revard, e-mail to author, May 14, 2001.

26. Revard, "Homework at Oxford," 75.

27. Revard, e-mail to author, May 14, 2001.

28. Revard, "History, Myth, and Identity," 128.

29. Elaine A. Jahner, "Knowing All the Way Down to the Fire," in *Feminist Measures: Soundings in Poetry and Theory,* ed. Lynn Keller and Cristanne Miller (Ann Arbor: University of Michigan Press, 1994), 180.

30. Michelle Cliff, "Poetry Is a Way of Reaching Out to What Is Reaching for You," *American Poetry Review* 24, 4 (1995): 33.

"Dawn / Is a Good Word," Robert M. Nelson

1. The term is Lincoln's: see his *Native American Renaissance* (Berkeley and Los Angeles: University of California Press, 1983). I am aware that the term "renaissance" has recently incurred criticism from those who believe it falsely implies that Native literary production was somehow dormant prior to the boom of print-text publication beginning around the 1960s. Perhaps "efflorescence" would be a more correct term; I still prefer Lincoln's, warts and all.

2. The epigraph reads, in full, "For Joy and Daisy, grandmothers; for Simon, grandfather; for Rainy Dawn and Chris, parents; for Krista Rae, child; and for all our relatives."

3. Linda Hogan, *Red Clay* (Greenfield Center, N.Y.: Greenfield Review Press, 1991), 1.

4. Linda Hogan, *Calling Myself Home* (Greenfield Center, N.Y.: Greenfield Review Press, 1978).

5. These two poems, which appeared originally in Harjo's chapbook *The Last Song* (Las Cruces, N.Mex.: Puerto del Sol, 1975), are reprinted in *The Remembered Earth*, edited by Geary Hobson (Albuquerque: University of New Mexico Press, 1980), 109–110.

6. Or even a Laguna: see Silko's memorable poem "Toe'osh," where once again in the last lines "Simon" serves as a role model for, as Vizenor puts it, survivance. Interestingly, the date given in this poem's dedicatory line—"for Simon Ortiz, July 1973"—is the same

month and year given in the dedicatory lines of Ortiz's "To Insure Survival" as the birth date of Harjo's and Ortiz's daughter, Dawn.

7. See Robert M. Nelson, "Place, Vision, and Identity in Native American Literatures," *American Indian Studies: An Interdisciplinary Approach to Contemporary Issues*, ed. Dane Morrison (New York: Peter Lang, 1997), 261–279.

8. Or more precisely, not an adult at the time *in* the narration, as perhaps distinguishable from the time *of* the narration. This kind of narrative play between "time *in*" and "time *of*" seems to me to characterize much of what is best in contemporary Native American poetry that overtly or implicitly appeals for its authority to the idea of oral traditionalism.

9. Originally published in *Going for the Rain* (New York: Harper and Row, 1976), this poem is reprinted in Hobson's *The Remembered Earth*, 271, and, more recently, in Ortiz's *Woven Stone* (Tucson: University of Arizona Press, 1992), 48–49.

10. In case it is not obvious, I am presuming here that the antecedent of the pronoun "you," the grammatically identified audience in the text of the poem, is the subject noun of the dedicatory lines of the poem, "for Rainy Dawn / born July 5, 1973"—or, if the "you" of the subsequent lines is understood to be plural, that Rainy Dawn is part of that projected audience.

11. Readers may quickly, and correctly, recognize Ortiz's Spider Grandmother as identical with Leslie Marmon Silko's "Ts'its'tsi'nako, Thought-Woman" *(Ceremony)* and Paula Gunn Allen's "Tse che nako" (*The Sacred Hoop*, 13) or "Sussistinaku, The Spider, Old Woman" (*The Woman Who Owned the Shadows*, 207).

12. More precisely, the name "Rainy Dawn" conjures the image of dawn coupled with the blessing of rain. In the context of Acoma traditions, this rain can in turn be understood as *shiwanna*, the ancestor spiritstuff that works for growth and regeneration.

13. As it happens, Misty Dawn's father, Earl Ortiz, is brother to Simon Ortiz, Rainy Dawn's father.

14. The poem is titled "A Song for the Direction of North." In it, Tapahonso works with the propinquity of north/black/death/ancestors to east/white/birth/childhood, as constellated concepts in Navajo tradition: on a circular spectrum, the midpoints of black (night, death) and white (dawn, birth) are 90 apart, rather than 180. Compare Shelley's classic observation (in "Ode to the West Wind") regarding the relationship of winter to spring.

15. Luci Tapahonso, "White Bead Girl," in *Blue Horses Rush In* (Tucson: University of Arizona Press, 1997), 62–71; see pages 62 and 71 for the opening and closing words of the story.

16. I say this with some trepidation. There are several rather important, though perhaps minor for most critical intents and purposes, variations in the two published versions of this text. In the 1993 *(Sáanii Dahataał)* version, "For Chamisa Bah Edmo, / who was born March 6, 1991," the sequence of colors and directions from which the herds of spirit horses arrive is given as white/west, yellow/east, blue/south, and black/north; in the 1997 *(Blue Horses Rush In)* version, "For Chamisa Bah Edmo, Shisóí 'aláájí' naaghígíí," the sequence is white/east, blue/south, yellow/south, and black/north. The sequence of combinations is not only different in the two versions, but also both versions differ from the traditional (as I understand it) sequence, which would be white/east, blue/south, yellow/west, and north/black.

17. Cf. Nia Francisco's allusion to this motif in the title of her collection of poetry *Blue Horses for Navajo Women.*

Call Me Brother, Qwo-Li Driskill

1. Haunani-Kay Trask, *From a Native Daughter: Colonialism and Sovereignty in Hawai'i,* rev. ed. (University of Hawai'i: Honolulu, 1999), 251.

2. Audre Lorde, *Sister Outsider* (Trumansburg, N.Y.: Crossing Press, 1984), 38.

3. Chrystos, *Fire Power* (Vancouver, B.C.: Press Gang, 1995), 129.

4. Beatrice Medicine (Standing Rock Lakota) notes, "The use of the term 'two-spirit' as a Pan-Indian term is not intended to be translated from English to Native languages. . . . To do so changes the common meaning it has acquired by self-identified two-spirit Native Americans. Translating the word *two-spirit* into some languages could lead to misunderstandings that could have adverse effects on the person using them." See Beatrice Medicine, *Learning to Be an Anthropologist and Remaining "Native": Selected Writings,* ed. with Sue Ellen Jacobs (Urbana: University of Illinois Press, 2001), 119.

5. *Two-Spirit People: Native American Gender Identity, Sexuality, and Spirituality,* ed. Sue-Ellen Jacobs, Wesley Thomas, and Sabine Lang (Urbana: University of Illinois Press, 1997), 4.

6. Will Roscoe, *Changing Ones: Third and Fourth Genders in Native North America* (New York: St. Martin's Press, 1998), 17.

7. Ibid., 19.

8. It should be made clear that not all Native Queers identify as Two-Spirit. Similarly, people who identify as Two-Spirit do not necessarily identify as Queer, Intersexed, Lesbian, Gay, Bi, or Trans. *Two-Spirit* is one of many words we might choose to describe our genders and sexualities within Native contexts.

9. See *Two-Spirit People,* 221–222.

10. Gregory Scofield, *Native Canadiana: Songs from the Urban Rez* (Vancouver, B.C.: Polestar, 1996), 86.

11. *Âyahkwêw:* "loosely translated as a person who has both male and female spirits; also known as Two-Spirited"

12. "And so, we brought these horses home"

13. "Horse-child"

14. "Thunder-woman"; Scofield, *Native Canadiana,* 66–67.

15. "people"

16. Scofield, *Native Canadiana,* 72.

17. Ibid., 103.

18. Ibid., 68–70.

19. José Esteban Muñoz, *Disidentifications: Queers of Color and the Performance of Politics* (Minneapolis: University of Minnesota Press, 1999), 74.

20. "sweetheart"

21. Scofield, *The Gathering: Stones for the Medicine Wheel* (Vancouver, B.C.: Polestar, 1993), 56.

22. Scofield, *Love Medicine and One Song: Sâkihtowin-Maskihkiy Êkwa Pêyak-Nikamowin* (Vancouver, B.C.: Polestar, 1997), 44.

23. Scofield, *Native Canadiana,* 64.

24. Scofield, *Love Medicine*, 99.

25. Beth Brant, *Writing as Witness: Essay and Talk* (Toronto: Women's Press, 1994), 59–60.

26. Scofield, *Love Medicine*, 12.

27. Ibid., 39.

28. Linda Hogan, *Dwellings: A Spiritual History of the Living World* (New York: Norton, 1995), 85.

29. "look, look"

30. "the sacred lodge where the pipe is smoked"

31. "listen, listen (as in to hear very closely)"

32. Scofield, *Love Medicine*, 19.

33. Lorde, *Sister Outsider*, 56.

34. Louis Owens, *Mixedblood Messages: Literature, Film, Family, Place* (Norman: University of Oklahoma Press, 1998), 198.

35. Scofield, *The Gathering*, 45.

36. Ibid., 50.

37. Muñoz, *Disidentifications*, 79.

38. Scofield, *The Gathering*, 50.

39. Ibid., 50.

40. Ibid., 82–83.

41. "the people who own themselves"; ibid., 83.

42. Scofield, *I Knew Two Metis Women* (Vancouver, B.C.: Polestar 1999), 106.

43. Ibid., 96.

44. Ibid., 97.

Suggestions for Further Reading

Below is a list of books of poems by American Indian authors and articles and books on American Indian poetry and poets. Many of these texts are mentioned in this book, but we thought it might be helpful to assemble a more comprehensive list here. This is by no means an exhaustive assemblage, merely a starting point.

Collections of Poems by Native Authors

Sherman Alexie

The Business of Fancydancing. Brooklyn: Hanging Loose Press, 1992.
First Indian on the Moon. Brooklyn: Hanging Loose Press, 1993.
The Lone Ranger and Tonto Fistfight in Heaven. New York: Atlantic Monthly Press, 1993.
Old Shirts and New Skins. Los Angeles: UCLA American Indian Studies Center, 1993.
The Summer of Black Widows. Brooklyn: Hanging Loose Press, 1999.

Paula Gunn Allen

The Blind Lion. Berkeley, Calif.: Thorp Springs Press, 1974.
A Cannon Between My Knees. New York: Strawberry Hill Press, 1981.
Coyote's Daylight Trip. Albuquerque, N.Mex.: La Confluencia, 1978.
Life Is a Fatal Disease. Albuquerque, N.Mex.: West End Press, 1997.
Shadow Country. Los Angeles: American Indian Studies Center, University of California, 1982.
Skins and Bones: Poems 1979–87. Albuquerque, N.Mex.: West End Press, 1988.
Star Child. Marvin, S.Dak.: Blue Cloud Quarterly, 1981.
The Woman Who Owned the Shadows. San Francisco Spinsters, Ink, 1983.
Wyrds. San Francisco: Taurean Horn Press, 1987.

Marilou Awiakta

Abiding Appalachia: Where Mountain and Atom Meet. Bell Buckle, Tenn.: Iris Press, 1995.
Selu: Seeking the Corn-Mother's Wisdom. Golden, Colo.: Fulcrum Publishing, 1993.

Jim Barnes

La Plata Cantata. West Lafayette, Ind.: Purdue University Press, 1989.

Esther G. Belin

From the Belly of My Beauty. Tucson: University of Arizona Press, 1999.

Fred Bigjim

Sinrock. Portland, Oreg.: Press-22, 1983.

Gloria Bird

Full Moon on the Reservation. Greenfield Center, N.Y.: Greenfield Review Press, 1993.
The River of History. Portland, Oreg.: Trask House Books, 1997.

Kimberly Blaeser

Absentee Indians and Other Poems. Lansing: Michigan State University Press, 2002.
Trailing You. Greenfield Center, N.Y.: Greenfield Review Press, 1994.

Peter Blue Cloud

Clans of Many Nations: Selected Poems 1969–94. Fredonia, N.Y.: White Pine Press, 1995.

Beth Brant

Food and Spirits: Stories. Ithaca, N.Y.: Firebrand Books, 1991.
Mohawk Trail. Ithaca, N.Y.: Firebrand Books, 1985.

Joseph Bruchac

Near the Mountains. Fredonia, N.Y.: White Pine Press, 1987.

Barney Bush

Inherit the Blood. New York: Thunder's Mouth Press, 1985.
Longhouse of the Blackberry Moon. 1975.
My Horse and a Jukebox. Los Angeles: American Indian Studies Center, 1979.
Petroglyphs. Greenfield Center, N.Y.: Greenfield Review Press, 1982.

Gladys Cardiff

To Frighten a Storm. Port Townsend, Wash.: Copper Canyon, 1976.

Chrystos

Dream On. Vancouver, B.C.: Press Gang, 1991.
Fire Power. Vancouver, B.C.: Press Gang, 1995.
Not Vanishing. Vancouver, B.C.: Press Gang, 1988.

Elizabeth Cook-Lynn

From the River's Edge. New York: Arcade, 1991.
The Power of Horses and Other Stories. New York: Arcade, 1990.
Then Badger Said This. Fairfield, Wash.: Ye Galleon Press, 1983.
Seek the House of Relatives. Marvin, S.Dak.: Blue Cloud Quarterly Press, 1983.

Nora Marks Dauenhauer

The Droning Shaman. Haines, Alaska: Black Current Press, 1988.

Marilyn Dumont

A Really Good Brown Girl. London, Ont.: Brick Books, 1996.

Jimmie Durham

Columbus Day. Albuquerque, N.Mex.: West End Press, 1993.

Anita Endrezze

At the Helm of Twilight. Seattle: Broken Moon Press, 1992.

Louise Erdrich

Baptism of Desire. New York: Harper and Row, 1989.
Jacklight. New York: Henry Holt, 1984.

Nia Francisco

Blue Horses for Navajo Women. Greenfield Center, N.Y.: Greenfield Review Press, 1994.

Diane Glancy

Brown Wolf Leaves the Res and Other Poems. Marvin, S.Dak.: Blue Cloud Quarterly Press, 1984.
Claiming Breath. Lincoln: University of Nebraska Press, 1992.
Iron Woman. Minneapolis: New Rivers Press, 1990.
Lone Dog's Winter Count. Albuquerque, N.Mex.: West End Press, 1991.
Offering. Duluth, Minn.: Holy Cow! Press, 1988.
One Age in a Dream. Minneapolis: Milkweed Editions, 1986.
Traveling On. Tulsa: Myrtlewood Press, 1982.

Janice Gould

Beneath My Heart. Ithaca, N.Y.: Firebrand Books, 1990.
Earthquake Weather. Tucson: University of Arizona Press, 1996.

Janet Campbell Hale

Custer Lives in Humboldt County and Other Poems. Greenfield Center, N.Y.: Greenfield Review Press, 1978.

Joy Harjo

In Mad Love and War. Middletown, Conn.: Wesleyan University Press, 1990.
The Last Song. Las Cruces, N.Mex.: Puerto Del Sol Press, 1975.
A Map to the Next World. New York: W.W. Norton, 2000.
Secrets from the Center of the World (with Steven Strom). Tucson: University of Arizona Press, 1989.
She Had Some Horses. New York: Thunder's Mouth, 1983.
What Moon Drove Me to This? New York: I. Reed Books, 1979.
The Woman Who Fell from the Sky. New York: Norton, 1994.

Lance Henson

Another Distance: New and Selected Poems. Norman, Okla.: Point Riders Press, 1991.
Another Song for America. Norman, Okla.: Point Riders Press, 1987.
Buffalo Marrow on Black. Full Count Press, 1979.
A Circling Remembrance. Marvin, S.Dak.: Blue Cloud Quarterly Press, 1982.
Dieser kleine Klang / This Small Sound. Berlin: Institut fur Indianishe Kulturen Nordamerikas, 1987.
Keeper of Arrows. Chickasha, Okla.: Renaissance Press, 1972.
Mistah. New York: Strawberry Press, 1978.
A Motion of Sudden Aloneness. Fayetteville, Ark.: University of Arkansas Press, 1991.
Naming the Dark: Poems for the Cheyenne. Norman, Okla.: Point Riders Press, 1976.
Le Orme de Tasso / The Badger Tracks. Italy: Soconas Incomindios, 1989.
Poems for a Master Beadworker. Germany: OMBA, 1991.
Selected Poems, 1970–1983. Greenfield Center, N.Y.: Greenfield Review Press, 1985.
Strong Heart Song: Lines from a Revolutionary Text. Albuquerque, N.Mex.: West End Press, 1997.
Tepee. Italy: Cooperativa La Parentesi / Soconas Incomindios, 1987.
Tonger Ut Stiennen / Thunder from Stones. Netherlands: Fryske Nasjonale Parij, 1987.

Linda Hogan

The Book of Medicines. Minneapolis: Coffee House Press, 1993.
Calling Myself Home. Greenfield, N.Y.: Greenfield Review Press, 1979.
Daughters, I Love You. Denver: Loretto Heights Women's Research Center, 1981.
Eclipse. Los Angeles: American Indian Studies Center, University of California, 1983.
Red Clay. Greenfield Center, N.Y.: Greenfield Review Press, 1991.
Savings. Minneapolis: Coffee House Press, 1988.
Seeing Through the Sun. Amherst: University of Massachusetts Press, 1985.

Karoniaktatie

Landscape. Marvin, S.Dak.: Blue Cloud Quarterly Press, 1984.

Maurice Kenny

Between Two Rivers: Selected Poems, 1956–1984. Fredonia, N.Y.: White Pine Press, 1987.
Blackrobe: Isaac Jogues, b. March 11, 1604, d. October 18, 1646. Saranac Lake, N.Y.: North Country Community College Press, 1982.
Dancing Back Strong the Nation. Marvin, S.Dak.: Blue Cloud Quarterly Press, 1979.
Dead Letters Sent, and Other Poems. New York: Troubador Press, 1958.
Greyhounding This America: Poems and Dialog. Chico, Calif.: Heidelberg Graphics, 1988.
I Am the Sun: A Lakota Chant. Fredonia, N.Y.: White Pine Press, 1979.
The Mama Poems. Fredonia, N.Y.: White Pine Press, 1984.
North: Poems of Home. Marvin, S.Dak.: Blue Cloud Quarterly Press, 1977.
Only as Far as Brooklyn. Boston: Good Gay Poets, 1979.
Tekonwatonti, Molly Brant, 1735–1795. Fredonia, N.Y.: White Pine Press, 1992.
With Love to Lesbia. Orono, Maine: Aardvark Press, 1959.

Harold L. Littlebird

On Mountains' Breath. Santa Fe, N.Mex.: Tooth of Time Books, 1982.

Adrian C. Louis

Fire Water World. Albuquerque, N.Mex.: West End Press, 1989.

Victoria Lena Manyarrows

Songs from the Native Lands. San Francisco: Nopal Press, 1995.

Lee Maracle

I Am Woman. North Vancouver, B.C.: Write-On Press, 1988.
Sojourner's Truth. Vancouver, B.C.: Press Gang, 1990.

Deborah Miranda

Indian Cartography. Greenfield Center, N.Y.: Greenfield Review Press, 1999.

N. Scott Momaday

Angle of Geese and Other Poems. Boston: David Godine, 1974.
The Gourd Dancer. New York: Harper, 1976.
In the Presence of the Sun: A Gathering of Shields. Santa Fe, N.Mex.: Rydal Press, 1992.
In the Presence of the Sun: Stories and Poems, 1961–1991. New York: St. Martin's Press, 1992.

Daniel David Moses

Delicate Bodies. Sechelt, B.C.: Nightwood Editions, 1992.
The White Line. Saskatoon, Sask.: Fifth House, 1990.

Nora Naranjo-Morse

Mud Woman: Poems from the Clay. Tucson: University of Arizona Press, 1992.

Duane Niatum

After the Death of an Elder Klallam. Phoenix: Baleen Press, 1970.
Ascending Red Cedar Moon. New York: Harper and Row, 1974.
A Cycle for the Women in the Field. Baltimore: Laughing Man Press, 1973.
Digging Out the Roots. New York: Harper and Row, 1977.
Drawings of the Song Animals: New and Selected Poems. Duluth, Minn.: Holy Cow! Press, 1991.
Pieces. New York: Strawberry Press, 1981.
Selected Poems. Duluth, Minn.: Holy Cow! Press, 1991.
Songs for the Harvester of Dreams. Seattle: University of Washington Press, 1981.
Taos Pueblo. Greenfield, N.Y.: Greenfield Review Press, 1973.
Turning to the Rhythms of Her Song. Seattle: Jawbone Press, 1977.

Louis Littlecoon Oliver

Chasers of the Sun: Creek Indian Thoughts. Greenfield Center, N.Y.: Greenfield Review Press, 1990.

Simon Ortiz

After and Before the Lightning. Tucson: University of Arizona Press, 1994.
Fight Back: For the Sake of the People, For the Sake of the Land. Albuquerque: University of New Mexico Press, 1980.
From Sand Creek. New York: Thunder's Mouth Press, 1981.
Going for the Rain. New York: Harper and Row, 1976.
A Good Journey. Philadelphia: Turtle Island, 1977.
A Poem Is a Journey. Bourbonnais, Ill.: Pternandon, 1981.
Woven Stone. Tucson: University of Arizona Press, 1992.

Carter Revard

Cowboys and Indians, Christmas Shopping. Norman, Okla.: Point Riders Press, 1992.
An Eagle Nation. Tucson: University of Arizona Press, 1993.
Family Matters, Tribal Affairs. Tucson: University of Arizona Press, 1998.
My Right Hand Don't Leave Me No More. St. Louis: Eedin, 1970.
Ponca War Dancers. Norman, Okla.: Point Riders Press, 1980.

Wendy Rose

Academic Squaw: Report to the World from the Ivory Tower. Marvin, S.Dak.: Blue Cloud Press, 1977.
Bone Dance: New and Selected Poems, 1965–1993. Tucson: University of Arizona Press, 1994.
Builder Kachina: A Home-Going Cycle. Marvin, S.Dak.: Blue Cloud Quarterly, 1979.
Going to War with All My Relations. Flagstaff, Ariz.: Entrada Books, 1993.
The Halfbreed Chronicles and Other Poems. Los Angeles: West End Press, 1985.
Hopi Roadrunner Dancing. Greenfield, N.Y.: Greenfield Review Press, 1973.
Long Divisions: A Tribal History. New York: Strawberry Press, 1980.
Lost Copper. Banning, Calif.: Malki Museum Press, 1980.
"Neon Scars." In *I Tell You Now: Autobiographical Essays by Native American Writers,* edited by Brian Swann and Arnold Krupat, 253–61. Lincoln: University of Nebraska Press, 1987.
Poetry of the American Indian Series: Wendy Rose. American Visual Communications Bank, 1978. Multi-media.
What Happened When the Hopi Hit New York. New York: Contact II, 1981.

Ralph Salisbury

Going to the Water: Poems of a Cherokee Heritage. Eugene, Oreg.: Pacific House Books, 1983.

Gregory Scofield

The Gathering: Stones for the Medicine Wheel. Victoria, B.C.: Polestar, 1993.
I Knew Two Metis Women. Victoria, B.C.: Polestar, 1999.
Love Medicine and One Song / Sâkihtowin-Maskihkiy Êkwa Pêyak-Nikamowin. Victoria, B.C.: Polestar, 1997.
Native Canadiana: Songs from the Urban Rez. Victoria, B.C.: Polestar, 1996.

Leslie Marmon Silko

Storyteller. New York: Arcade, 1981.

Mary TallMountain

The Light on the Tent Wall: A Bridging. Los Angeles: American Indian Studies Center, University of California, 1990.

Luci Tapahonso

Blue Horses Rush In. Tucson: University of Arizona Press, 1997.
A Breeze Swept Through. Albuquerque, N.Mex.: West End Press, 1987.
One More Shiprock Night. San Antonio: Tejas Art Press, 1981.
Sáanii Dahataał, The Women Are Singing: Poems and Stories. Tucson: University of Arizona Press, 1993.
Seasonal Woman. Santa Fe, N.Mex.: Tooth of Time Books, 1982.

Gail Tremblay

Indian Singing. Rev. ed. Corvallis, Oreg.: Calyx Books, 1998.

Gerald Vizenor

Born in the Wind. Privately printed, 1960.
Empty Swings. Minneapolis: Nodin, 1967.
Matsushima: Pine Islands. Minneapolis: Nodin, 1984.
The Old Park Sleepers. Minneapolis: Obercraft, 1961.
Raising the Moon Vines. Minneapolis: Callimachus, 1964.
Seventeen Chirps: Haiku in English. Minneapolis: Nodin, 1964.
South of the Painted Stone. Minneapolis: Obercraft, 1963.
Two Wings in the Butterfly. Privately printed, 1962.

James Welch

Riding the Earthboy 40. Rev. ed. New York: Harper and Row, 1976.

Roberta Hill Whiteman

Philadelphia Flowers. Duluth, Minn.: Holy Cow! Press, 1996.
Star Quilt. Minneapolis: Holy Cow! Press, 1984.

Elizabeth Woody

Luminaries of the Humble. Tucson: University of Arizona Press, 1994.
Seven Hands, Seven Hearts. Portland, Oreg.: Eighth Mountain Press, 1994.

Ray A. Young Bear

Black Eagle Child: The Facepaint Narratives. Iowa City: University of Iowa Press, 1992.
The Invisible Musician. Duluth, Minn.: Holy Cow! Press, 1990.
Winter of the Salamander: The Keeper of Importance. New York: Harper and Row, 1980.

Ofelia Zepeda

Ocean Power: Poems from the Desert. Tucson: University of Arizona Press, 1995.

Literary Criticism

Ackerberg, Peggy Maddux. "Breaking Boundaries: Writing Past Gender, Genre, and Genocide in Linda Hogan." *SAIL: Studies in American Indian Literatures* 6, 3 (1994): 7–14.

Allen, Paula Gunn. *The Sacred Hoop: Recovering the Feminine in American Indian Traditions.* Boston: Beacon Press, 1986.

Ascencio, Daniel Flores. "Prisoners of Democracy." *BOMB* 66 (1999): 24–28.

Barron, Patrick. "Maurice Kenny's *Tekonwatonti, Molly Brant:* Poetic Memory and History." *MELUS* 25, 3–4 (2000): 31–64.

Bataille, Gretchen M. "Luci Tapahonso: A Navaho Voice in the Midwest." *In Native American Women in Literature and Culture,* edited by Susan Castillo and Victor M. P. Da Rosa, 69–76. Porto, Portugal: Fernando Pessoa University Press, 1997.

——. "Ray Young Bear: Tribal History and Personal Vision." *SAIL: Studies in American Indian Literatures* 5, 2 (1993): 17–20.

Berner, Robert L. "Lance Henson: Poet of the People." *World Literature Today* 64, 3 (1990): 418–421.

Blaeser, Kimberly. " 'Interior Dancers': Transformations of Vizenor's Poetic Vision." *SAIL: Studies in American Indian Literatures* 9, 1 (1997): 3–15.

——. "Like 'Reeds through the Ribs of a Basket': Native Women Weaving Stories." In *Other Sisterhoods: Literary Theory and U.S. Women of Color,* edited by Sandra Kumamoto Stanley, 265–276. Urbana, Ill.: University of Illinois Press, 1998.

——. "The Multiple Traditions of Gerald Vizenor's Haiku Poetry." In *New Voices in Native American Literary Criticism,* edited by Arnold Krupat, 344–369. Washington, D.C.: Smithsonian Institution Press, 1993.

——. "Native Literatures: Seeking a Critical Center." In *Looking at the Words of Our People: First Nations Analysis of Literature,* edited by Jeannette Armstrong, 56. Penticton, B.C.: Theytus Books, 1993.

Bleck, Melani. "Linda Hogan's Tribal Imperative: Collapsing Space through 'Living' Tribal Traditions and Nature." *SAIL: Studies in American Indian Literatures* 11, 4 (1999): 23–45.

Brill de Ramírez, Susan Berry. "Alk'idáá' jiní . . . Luci Tapahonso, Irvin Morris, and Della Frank: Interweaving Navajo and English in Their Poems and Stories." *Cimarron Review* 121 (1997): 135–153.

——. *Contemporary American Indian Literatures and the Oral Tradition.* Tucson: University of Arizona Press, 1999.

——. "Discovering the Order and Structure of Things: A Conversive Approach to Contemporary Navajo Poetry." *SAIL: Studies in American Indian Literatures* 7, 3 (1995): 51–70.

Bruchac, Joseph. "Many Tongues: Native American Poetry Today." *North Dakota Quarterly* 55, 4 (1987): 239–244.

Bryson, J. Scott. "Finding the Way Back: Place and Space in the Ecological Poetry of Joy Harjo." *MELUS* 27, 3 (2002): 169–196.

Castillo, Susan Perez. "The Construction of Gender and Ethnicity in the Poetry of Leslie Silko and Louise Erdrich." In *ICLA '91 Tokyo: The Force of Vision, II: Visions in History; Visions of the Other,* edited by Earl Miner, 637–645. Tokyo: International Comparative Literature Association, 1995.

Clarke, Joni Adamson. "Toward an Ecology of Justice: Transformative Ecological Theory and Practice." In *Reading the Earth: New Directions in the Study of Literature and Environment,* edited by Michael P. Branch, Rochelle Johnson, Daniel Patterson, and Scott Slovic, 9–17. Moscow, Idaho: University of Idaho Press, 1998.

Cliff, Michelle. "Poetry Is a Way of Reaching Out to What Is Reaching for You." *American Poetry Review* 24, 4 (1995): 29–35.

Etter, Carrie. "Dialectic to Dialogic: Negotiating Bicultural Heritage in Sherman Alexie's Sonnets." In *Telling the Stories: Essays on American Indian Literatures and Cultures,* edited by Elizabeth Hoffman Nelson, 143–151. New York: Peter Lang, 2001.

Fast, Robin Riley. "Borderland Voices in Contemporary Native American Poetry." *Contemporary Literature* 36, 3 (1995): 508–536.

——. *The Heart as a Drum: Continuance and Resistance in American Indian Poetry.* Ann Arbor: University of Michigan Press, 1999.

——. "'It Is Ours to Know': Simon J. Ortiz's from Sand Creek." *SAIL: Studies in American Indian Literatures* 12, 3 (2000): 52–63.

——. "Who Speaks, Who Listens? Questions of Community, Audience, and Language in Poems by Chrystos and Wendy Rose." In *Other Sisterhoods: Literary Theory and U.S. Women of Color,* edited by Sandra Kumamoto Stanley, 139–170. Urbana, Ill.: University of Illinois Press, 1998.

Gillan, Jennifer. "Sherman Alexie's Poetry." *American Literature* 68 (1996): 91–110.

Goodman, Jenny. "Politics and the Personal Lyric in the Poetry of Joy Harjo and C. D. Wright." *MELUS* 19, 2 (1994): 35–56.

Gould, Janice. "American Indian Women's Poetry: Strategies of Rage and Hope." *Signs: Journal of Women in Culture and Society* 20 (1995): 797–817.

——. "Disobedience (in Language) in Texts by Lesbian Native Americans." *ARIEL: A Review of International English Literature* 25, 1 (1994): 32–44.

Hafen, P. Jane. "Rock and Roll, Redskins, and Blues in Sherman Alexie's Work." *SAIL: Studies in American Indian Literatures* 9, 4 (1997): 71–78.

——. "Sacramental Language: Ritual in the Poetry of Louise Erdrich." *Great Plains Quarterly* 16 (1996): 147–155.

Hegarty, Emily. "Genocide and Extinction in Linda Hogan's Ecopoetry." In *Ecopoetry: A Critical Introduction,* edited by J. Scott Bryson and John Elder, 162–175. Salt Lake City, Utah: University of Utah Press, 2002.

Hogan, Linda. Review of *Sáanii Dahataał,* by Luci Tapahonso. *Parabola* 18 (1993): 96.

Holmes, Kristine. " 'This Woman Can Cross Any Line': Feminist Tricksters in the Works of Nora Naranjo-Morse and Joy Harjo." *SAIL: Studies in American Indian Literatures* 1 (1995): 45–63.

Hughes, Sheila Hassell. "Falls of Desire / Leaps of Faith: Religious Syncretism in Louise Erdrich's and Joy Harjo's 'Mixed-Blood' Poetry." *Religion and Literature* 33, 2 (2001): 59–83.

Irmscher, Christoph. "Anthropological Roles: The Self and Its Others in T. S. Eliot, William Carlos Williams, and Wendy Rose." *Soundings* 75, 4 (1992): 587–603.

Jahner, Elaine. "Knowing All the Way Down to Fire." In *Feminist Measures: Soundings in Poetry and Theory,* edited by Lynn Keller and Cristanne Miller, 163–183. Ann Arbor: University of Michigan Press, 1994.

Landrey, David. "Maurice Kenny: Remembering Molly." *Talisman: A Journal of Contemporary Poetry and Poetics* 11 (1993): 293–295.

Lang, Nancy. " 'Twin Gods Bending Over': Joy Harjo and Poetic Memory." *MELUS* 18, 3 (1993): 41–49.

Lincoln, Kenneth. *Sing with the Heart of a Bear: Fusions of American and Native Poetry 1890–1999.* Berkeley and Los Angeles: University of California Press, 2000.

Ludlow, Jeannie. "Working (In) the In-Between: Poetry, Criticism, Interrogation, and Interruption." *SAIL: Studies in American Indian Literature* 6 (1994): 24–42.

Maddox, Lucy. "Native American Poetry." In *The Columbia History of American Poetry,* edited by Jay Parini and Brett C. Millier, 728–749. New York: Columbia University Press, 1998.

McAdams, Janet. "Castings for a (New) New World: The Poetry of Joy Harjo." In *Women Poets of the Americas: Toward a Pan-American Gathering,* edited by Jacqueline Vaught Brogan and Cordelia Chavez Candelaria, 210–232. Notre Dame, Ind.: University of Notre Dame Press, 1999.

——. "We, I, 'Voice,' and 'Voices': Reading Contemporary Native American Poetry." *SAIL: Studies in American Indian Literatures* 7, 3 (1995): 7–16.

Monroe, Jonathan. "Untranslatable Communities, Productive Translation, and Public Transport: Rosmarie Waldrop's *A Key into the Language of America* and Joy Harjo's *The Woman Who Fell from the Sky*." In *We Who Love to Be Astonished: Experimental Women's Writing and Performance Poetics,* edited by Laura Hinton, Cynthia Hogue, and Rachel Blau DuPlessis, 90–102. Tuscaloosa: University of Alabama Press, 2002.

Moore, David L. "Myth, History, and Identity in Silko and Young Bear." In *New Voices in Native American Literary Criticism,* edited by Arnold Krupat, 370–395. Washington, D.C.: Smithsonian Institution Press, 1993.

Newton, John. "Sherman Alexie's Autoethnography." *Contemporary Literature* 42, 2 (2001): 413–428.

Oandasan, William. "Simon Ortiz: The Poet and His Landscape." *SAIL: Studies in American Indian Literatures* 11 (1987): 26–37.

Parker, Robert Dale. "To Be There, No Authority to Anything: Ontological Desire and Cultural and Poetic Authority in the Poetry of Ray A. Young Bear." *Arizona Quarterly* 50, 4 (1994): 89–115.

Peek, Charles A. "'This Profound Intuition of the Eternal': Translation and Cultural Meaning." *Platte Valley Review* 23, 2 (1995): 62–76.

Rader, Dean. "Arriving Amid a Herd of Horses: Luci Tapahonso's *Blue Horses Rush In*." *SAIL: Studies in American Indian Literatures* 10, 3 (1998): 88–94.

——. "I Don't Speak Navajo: Esther G. Belin's *In the Belly of My Beauty*." *SAIL: Studies in American Indian Literatures* 12 (2000): 14–34.

——. "Simon Ortiz and Luci Tapahonso: Symbol, Allegory, Language, Poetry." *Southwestern American Literature* 22 (1997): 75–92.

——. "Word as Weapon: Visual Culture and Contemporary American Indian Poetry." *MELUS* 27, 3 (2002): 147–168.

Revard, Carter. "Herbs of Healing: American Values in American Indian Literature." In *Family Matters and Tribal Affairs.* Tucson: University of Arizona Press, 1999.

Ruppert, James. "The Uses of Oral Tradition in Six Contemporary Native American Poets." *American Indian Culture and Research Journal* 4, 4 (1980): 87–110.

Saucerman, James R. "Wendy Rose: Searching through Shards, Creating Life." *Wicazo SA Review* 5, 2 (1989): 26–29.

Scarry, John. "Representing Real Worlds: The Evolving Poetry of Joy Harjo." *World Literature Today* 66, 2 (1992): 286–291.

Schein, Marie-Madeleine. "Simon J. Ortiz." In *Updating the Literary West.* Fort Worth: Texas Christian University Press, 1997.

Smith, Patricia Clark. "Coyote Ortiz: Canis latrans latrans in the Poetry of Simon Ortiz." In *Studies in American Indian Literature,* edited by Paula Gunn Allen, 192–210. New York: Modern Language Association of America, 1983.

Smith, Patricia Clark, and Paula Gunn Allen. "Earthly Relations, Carnal Knowledge: Southwestern American Indian Women Writers and Landscape." In *The Desert Is No Lady: Southwestern Landscapes in Women's Writing and Art,* edited by Vera Norwood and Janice Monk, 174–196. New Haven, Conn.: Yale University Press, 1987.

Stone, Albert E. *Black Eagle Child: The Facepaint Narratives.* Iowa City: University of Iowa Press, 1992.

Tongson-McCall, Karen. "The Nether World of Neither World: Hybridization in the Literature of Wendy Rose." *American Indian Culture and Research Journal* 20 (1996): 1–40.

Varró, Gabriella. "Reconciliation of Native Heritage and the Modern: Two Native American Women 'Word Warriors'." *B.A.S.: British and American Studies / Revista de Studii Britanice si Americane* (1997): 139–147.

Wiget, Andrew. "Blue Stones, Bones, and Troubled Silver: The Poetic Craft of Wendy Rose." *SAIL: Studies in American Indian Literatures* 5, 2 (1993): 29–33.

———. "Nightriding with Noni Daylight: The Many Horse Songs of Joy Harjo." In *Native American Literatures*, edited by Laura Coltelli, 185–196. Pisa: SEU, 1989.

———. "Sending a Voice: The Emergence of Contemporary Native American Poetry." *College English* 46, 6 (1984): 598–609.

Wilson, Norma. *The Nature of Native American Poetry*. Albuquerque: University of New Mexico Press, 2000.

Womack, Craig S. *Red on Red: Native American Literary Separatism*. Minneapolis: University of Minnesota Press, 1999.

Anthologies and Readers

Beck, Peggy, Anna Lee Walters, and Nia Francisco, eds. *The Sacred: Ways of Knowledge, Sources of Life*. Flagstaff, Ariz.: Northland, 1990.

Brant, Beth, ed. *A Gathering of Spirit: A Collection by North American Women*. Ithaca, N.Y.: Firebrand Books, 1988.

Bruchac, Joseph. *Survival This Way: Interviews with American Indian Poets*. Tucson: University of Arizona Press, 1987.

Coltelli, Laura. *Winged Words: American Indian Writers Speak*. Lincoln: University of Nebraska Press, 1990.

Evers, Larry, and Ofelia Zepeda, eds. *Home Places: Contemporary Native American Writing from Sun Tracks*. Tucson: University of Arizona Press, 1995.

Harjo, Joy, and Gloria Bird, eds. *Reinventing the Enemy's Language: Contemporary Native Women's Writings of North America*. New York: Norton, 1997.

Hobson, Geary, ed. *The Remembered Earth: An Anthology of Contemporary Native American Literature*. Albuquerque: University of New Mexico Press, 1990.

Niatum, Duane, ed. *Harper's Anthology of 20th Century Native American Poetry*. San Francisco: HarperCollins, 1988.

Ortiz, Simon, ed. *Speaking for the Generations: Native Writers on Writing*. Tucson: University of Arizona Press, 1998.

Purdy, John L., and James Ruppert. *Nothing but the Truth: An Anthology of Native American Literature*. Upper Saddle River, N.J.: Prentice-Hall, 2001.

Tremblay, Gail. *Indian Singing in 20th Century America*. Corvallis, Oreg.: Calyx Books, 1990.

Vizenor, Gerald. *Native American Literature: A Brief Introduction and Anthology*. New York: HarperCollins, 1995.

Wiget, Andrew, ed. *Dictionary of Native American Literature*. New York: Garland, 1994.

Zepeda, Ofelia, ed. *Mat Hekid o Ju, 'O'odham Na'Cegitodag / When it Rains, Papago and Pima Poetry*. Tucson: University of Arizona Press, 1982.

Source Acknowledgments

"Map," from *The Book of Medicines*, by Linda Hogan, © 1993. Reprinted by permission of Coffee House Press, Minneapolis.

"Version of Moon" and "Anonymous," from *Luminaries of the Humble*, by Elizabeth Woody, © 1994. Reprinted by permission of the University of Arizona Press.

"Daydreaming Primal Space: Cherokee Aesthetics as Habits of Being," from *Selu: Seeking the Corn-Mother's Wisdom*, by Marilou Awiakta, © 1993. Reprinted by permission of Fulcrum Publishing, Golden, Colorado.

"To take shape," "I Offer You a Gift," "Trail Warning," "Mother Nature Sends a Pink Slip," "Selu and Kanati: A Marriage," "On Being a Female Phoenix," "Dawn Birth," and "Song of the Swinging Bridge," from *Selu: Seeking the Corn-Mother's Wisdom*, by Marilou Awiakta, © 1993. Reprinted by permission of the author and Fulcrum Publishing, Golden, Colorado.

"Ain't Seen You Since: Dissent among Female Relatives in American Indian Poetry," by Patricia Clark Smith, from *Studies in American Indian Literature*, edited by Paula Gunn Allen, © 1983. Reprinted by permission of the Modern Language Association of America, New York.

"Crow Law," from *The Book of Medicines*, by Linda Hogan, © 1993. Reprinted by permission of Coffee House Press, Minneapolis.

"Answering the Deer: Genocide and Continuance in the Poetry of American Indian Women," from *The Sacred Hoop*, by Paula Gunn Allen, © 1986, 1992. Reprinted by permission of Beacon Press, Boston.

"Overture" from *The Blind Lion*, by Paula Gunn Allen, published by Thorp Springs Press, 1974; and "Locus," "Elegy for My Son," "On the Street: Monument," from *Life Is a Fatal Disease*, by Paula Gunn Allen, published by West End Press, 1995. Reprinted by permission of the author.

"Herbs of Healing," from *Family Matters, Tribal Affairs*, by Carter Revard, © 1998. Reprinted by permission of The University of Arizona Press.

"Never Again Would Birds' Song Be the Same," from *The Poetry of Robert Frost*, edited by Edward Connery Lathem. Copyright 1942 by Robert Frost, © 1970 by Lesley Frost Ballantine, copyright © 1969 by Henry Holt & Co., Inc. Reprinted by permission of Henry Holt & Co., Inc.

"Jacklight," from *Jacklight*, by Louise Erdrich, © 1984. Reprinted by permission of Henry Holt & Co., Inc.

"I Expected My Skin and My Blood to Ripen," by Wendy Rose, © 1985, from *New and Old Voices of Wah'Kon-Tah: Contemporary Poetry of Native Americans*, edited by Robert K. Dodge and Joseph B. McCullough, International Publishers, New York. Reprinted in *Bone Dance*, by Wendy Rose, published by the University of Arizona Press, Tucson, 1994. Reprinted by permission.

"Speaking," from *A Good Journey*, by Simon Ortiz, © 1977, Turtle Island, Berkeley, California. Reprinted in *Woven Stone*, by Simon Ortiz, published by the University of Arizona Press, Tucson, 1992. Reprinted by permission.

"Coyote Tells Why He Sings," from *Winning the Dust Bowl*, © Carter Revard, published by the University of Arizona Press, Tucson, 2001. Reprinted by permission.

"the last song," from *The Last Song*, by Joy Harjo, published by Puerto del Sol, 1975. Reprinted by permission of the author.

"Song/Poetry and Language—Expression and Perception," by Simon Ortiz, from *Symposium of the Whole*, published by the University of California Press, 1993. Reprinted by permission of the author.

Contributors

One of the foremost Native writers, **Paula Gunn Allen** describes herself as a "multicultural event," citing her Pueblo / Sioux / Lebanese / Scottish American ancestry. Paula has taught and lectured widely around the country, serving as director of the Native American studies program at San Francisco State University and a professor of Native American studies / ethnic studies at UCLA. A recipient of many fellowship grants, Paula also won the Susan Koppelman Award from the Popular and American Culture Associations, and the American Book Award from the Before Columbus Foundation for *Spider Woman's Granddaughters: Traditional Tales and Contemporary Writing by Native American Women* (1989). Her 1983 *Studies in American Indian Literature: Critical Essays and Course Designs*, and her book *The Sacred Hoop: Recovering the Feminine in American Indian Traditions*, published in 1986, are largely responsible for changing how Native American literature is read, taught, and written about.

Born and raised in New Jersey, **Eric Gary Anderson** is an associate professor of English at Oklahoma State University, where he teaches American and American Indian literatures. He is the author of *American Indian Literature and the Southwest: Contexts and Dispositions* (1999) and various book chapters and articles on topics such as Old Man Coyote, *Powwow Highway*, Linda Hogan's novels *Mean Spirit* and *Power*, and Toni Morrison's novel *Paradise*. His current project concerns criminal narratives of the American South.

Marilou Awiakta grew up on a reservation—for atoms, not Indians. During her childhood, Oak Ridge, Tennessee, was the atomic frontier, a place where tomorrow began. As a poet, storyteller, and essayist, Awiakta uniquely weaves her Cherokee / Appalachian heritage with science. Anthologies that have featured her work include *Reinventing the Enemy's Language*, *Returning the Gift*, *Literature and the Environment*, *The Reader's Companion to U.S. Women's History*, and *The Oxford Companion to Women's Writing in the United States*. Awiakta is author of *Abiding Appalachia: Where Mountain and Atom Meet* (1978), *Rising Fawn and the Fire Mystery* (1983), and the critically acclaimed *Selu: Seeking the Corn-Mother's Wisdom* (1993). She is also a recipient of the Distinguished Tennessee Writer Award (1989) and the award for Outstanding Contribution to Appalachian Literature (1991). Awiakta's reading of *Selu* earned a Grammy nomination in 1996, and the book was given the distinction of becoming a Quality Paperback Book Club selection in 1994.

Susan Berry Brill de Ramírez teaches undergraduate and graduate courses in literary criticism and theory and undergraduate courses in American Indian literatures, American literature, freshman composition, and Western civilization at Bradley University. She earned her Ph.D. in English at the University of Mexico in 1991. Her research interests straddle the diverse fields of American Indian literatures and literary criticism and theory. Her first book, *Wittgenstein and Critical Theory: Beyond Postmodern Criticisms and Toward Descriptive Investigations* (1995), introduces the value of Wittgensteinian philosophy for the practice of reading and interpreting literature. Her book *Contemporary American Indian Literatures & the Oral Tradition* was published in 1999 by the University of Arizona Press.

Qwo-Li Driskill is a Cherokee Two-Spirit/Queer, also of African, Irish, Lenape, Lumbee, and Osage *ascent*. Qwo-Li's work has appeared in numerous publications, including the journals *Many Mountains Moving* and the *Evergreen Chronicles* and the anthology *Revolutionary Voices* (2000). A poet, educator, and activist, Qwo-Li is the founder and director of Knitbone Productions: A First Nations Ensemble, which uses writing, theater, and story as tools for healing and decolonization, and is currently editing *Planting the Tree: Mixedqueers on Race, Gender, Identity, and Desire.* Qwo-Li lives in the Duwamish Nation, currently called Seattle. His first volume of poetry is forthcoming.

Janice Gould's tribal affiliation is Koyangk'auwi Maidu. She grew up in Berkeley, California, and attended UC Berkeley where she received degrees in linguistics (B.A.) and English (M.A.). She earned her Ph.D. in English at the University of New Mexico, writing about Muscogee poet Joy Harjo for her dissertation. She has published two books of poetry, *Beneath My Heart* (1990) and *Earthquake Weather* (1996), as well as a chapbook/artbook, *Alphabet.* Her work has seen publication in various journals and anthologies, including *American Poetry Review* and *Blue Mesa Review.* She has been awarded fellowships from the National Endowment for the Arts and from the Astraea Foundation. She lives in Portland, Oregon, and currently holds the Hallie Ford Chair in Creative Writing at Willamette University.

Elaine A. Jahner was for many years a professor of English and Native American studies at Dartmouth College. She was the editor of *Lakota Myth* (1983) and the coeditor of *Lakota Belief and Ritual* (1980). She published numerous articles on Native American literature and on cross-cultural literary criticism. Her forthcoming book, *Spaces of the Mind: Narrative and Community,* explores both oral and written narratives in relation to specific Native American and immigrant communities. Sadly, the day before this book went into final production, we learned of Elaine Jahner's passing. Her thoughtful contributions to Lakota studies in particular, and Native literature in general, will be greatly missed.

Daniel Heath Justice is an enrolled tribal citizen of the Cherokee Nation, a multigenerational hillbilly from the Colorado Rockies, and assistant professor of Aboriginal literatures at the University of Toronto. His work is centered in Cherokee history and literary traditions and also attends to cross-national Indigenous studies, Native intellectual/political sovereignties and treaty rights, and North American literatures of resistance.

Janet McAdams is the Robert P. Hubbard Professor of Poetry at Kenyon College. Her poetry collection *The Island of Lost Luggage* (2000) received the Diane Decorah Award from the Native Writers Circle of the Americas and an American Book Award from the

Before Columbus Foundation. Her articles on Native poetry have appeared in *Women Poets of the Americas* (1999), *SAIL: Studies in American Indian Literatures*, and the *Women's Review of Books*.

Robert M. Nelson is a professor of English at the University of Richmond. Since 1987 most of his teaching and research has been in the field of American Indian literatures, and until recently he was coeditor of the journal *SAIL: Studies in American Indian Literatures*. His book *Place and Vision: The Function of Landscape in Native American Fiction* was published in 1993.

Simon J. Ortiz is a poet, writer, sometimes storyteller from Acoma Pueblo, and currently a professor at the University of Toronto. His published works include *Woven Stone, After and Before the Lightning, From Sand Creek, Speaking for the Generations, Men on the Moon*, and *Out There Somewhere*.

Dean Rader is an assistant professor at the University of San Francisco, where he works in the English Department and the M.F.A. program in creative writing. He has published essays, reviews, poems, and translations in both national and international books and journals. He is on the editorial board of *SAIL: Studies in American Indian Literatures*, and his book *The World Is a Text*, coauthored with Jonathan Silverman, was published in 2002 by Prentice Hall. He is at work on a book on American Indian art, literature, and film. He is a native of the now-Republican stronghold of Oklahoma.

Carter Revard was born in Oklahoma and raised on the Osage reservation. After earning his undergraduate degree from the University of Tulsa, he went to England as a Rhodes scholar to study at Oxford University, where he received his master's degree. Revard received his doctorate in English in 1959 at Yale. He recently retired from Washington University in St. Louis, where he taught American Indian and medieval literature. He has published a number of books, most recently *An Eagle Nation* (1993), *Family Matters, Tribal Affairs* (1998), and *Winning the Dust Bowl* (2001), all from the University of Arizona Press.

Patricia Clark Smith has been teaching creative writing/poetry, American literature, and world literature at the University of New Mexico since she received her Ph.D. at Yale in 1970. Smith's latest book of poetry is *Changing Your Story*, published in 1991. She is also coeditor, along with Paul Davis, Gary Harrison, David Johnson, and John Crawford, of *Western Literature in a World Context* (1995). Currently, she is at work on a new book of poems called *Snowfield* and a young adult novel, *The Road to Whitetail*, about a fourteen-year-old Chiricahua Apache girl leaving an Indian boarding school in 1915.

Index